PROGRAM BUDGETING
AND THE
PERFORMANCE MOVEMENT

PROGRAM BUDGETING
AND THE
PERFORMANCE MOVEMENT

The Elusive Quest for
Efficiency in Government

WILLIAM F. WEST

georgetown university press
washington, d.c.

Georgetown University Press, Washington, D.C.
www.press.georgetown.edu

Library of Congress Cataloging-in-Publication Data

West, William F.
 Program budgeting and the performance movement : the elusive
quest for efficiency in government / William F. West.
    p. cm. — (Public management and change series)
 Includes index.
 ISBN 978-1-58901-777-1 (pbk. : alk. paper)
 1. Total quality management in government—United States.
 2. Program budgeting—United States. 3. Managerial accounting—
United States. I. Title.
 JK468.T67W47 2011
 352.4'8—dc22

                            2011003840

∞ This book is printed on acid-free paper meeting the requirements
of the American National Standard for Permanence in Paper for
Printed Library Materials.

15 14 13 12 11   9 8 7 6 5 4 3 2
First printing

Printed in the United States of America

For the children

CONTENTS

ILLUSTRATIONS

ACKNOWLEDGMENTS

This study relies heavily on interviews and e-mail exchanges with public servants from the National Oceanic and Atmospheric Administration (NOAA), the US Department of Defense, the US Department of Homeland Security, the National Aeronautics and Space Administration, the Office of Management and Budget, and other organizations. I cannot name them here for reasons of confidentiality, just as I am not able to provide specific attribution for many of the quotations and other observations used in the text. I am nonetheless grateful to the busy people who indulged my questions and in some cases commented on things that I had written. Some would endorse my conclusions and some would not, but they were all intelligent, thoughtful, and more than generous with their time.

I would also like to thank Arnie Vedlitz and the Institute for Science, Technology, and Public Policy at the Bush School of Government and Public Service of Texas A&M University for supporting portions of this research under a grant from NOAA. In addition, the Sara Lindsey Chair has provided critical funding without which it would have been difficult to complete this research, and the Bush School has been a very supportive environment for scholarship.

Several people provided direct assistance and advice with this project. Eric Lindquist and Katrina Mosher collaborated with me on an earlier study of planning, programming, budgeting at NOAA that was published in *Public Administration Review*. Kallie Gallagher collected data and Sarah Jackson helped with editing and formatting the manuscript. Both were extremely capable and conscientious research assistants. In addition, a number of professional colleagues offered valuable feedback on various parts of this work. They include Clinton Brass, Brian Cook, Bob Durant, George Frederickson, Vance Gordon, Jeryl Mumpower, Harvey Tucker, and Wendy Wagner. Beryl Radin was particularly helpful for her support and suggestions throughout, and both she and Don Jacobs of Georgetown University Press were patient in waiting for me to finish this project and were otherwise a pleasure to work with.

I am also grateful to Sara Lindsey, whose endowed chair has facilitated my research, and to Sam Kirkpatrick for his professional support. Joe Cooper had nothing to do with this project but has always been a standard of excellence. Most of all, I would like to thank my wife, Pat, and my children for putting up with me.

ABBREVIATIONS

DHS   US Department of Homeland Security

DoD   US Department of Defense

GAO   US Government Accountability Office; before 2004, US General Accounting Office

GPRA   Government Performance and Results Act

MFR   managing for results

NASA   US National Aeronautics and Space Administration

NOAA   US National Oceanic and Atmospheric Administration

NPM   New Public Management

NWS   US National Weather Service

OAR   Office of Oceanic and Atmospheric Research, NOAA

OMB   Office of Management and Budget

PA&E   Office of Program Analysis and Evaluation, DoD

PART   Program Assessment Rating Tool

PPB   planning, programming, budgeting

PPBES   planning, programming, budgeting execution systems

PPBS   planning, programming, budgeting systems

Chapter 1

Introduction: Lessons Not Learned

Public executives at all levels of government and in all kinds of organizations have increasingly been expected to articulate their objectives and to measure the effectiveness of what they do. Supported by public perceptions of governmental excess and inefficiency, such requirements have been promoted by advocates of planning and performance assessment in consulting firms, universities, legislatures, and even the bureaucracy itself. What is often called managing for results (MFR) or performance-based management is, in turn, part of a broader set of prescriptions that are loosely tied together by the assumption that public administration should be more like business administration.

Formal systems of performance-based management have had disappointing results in America, despite their continued popularity. Although advocates of MFR have often attributed this to factors that can be overcome with sufficient time and commitment, others have questioned its premises. One set of issues has to do with the validity of performance measures in many contexts. How accurately can they describe the linkages between agency activities and the "outcomes" that public organizations have been created to achieve? Do they sometimes have the potential to redefine objectives in ways that are unintended or undesirable?

To the extent that performance can be measured, a second and related set of issues has to do with the use of such information in promoting efficiency. What is it realistic to expect government officials to accomplish with planning and performance assessment given the organizational, technical, legal, and political realities that define the environment of public administration in the United States? Can MFR coordinate the allocation of resources within and among organizations that have diverse purposes and fragmented constituencies? This book is concerned with both types of issues but especially the latter. As such, it complements other analyses of the performance movement in this series (Radin 2006; Frederickson and Frederickson 2006; Moynihan 2008).

Much of this book focuses on a specific technique designed to rationalize organizational performance. Program budgeting (PPB), is a device from the 1960s that is often dismissed as an unsuccessful exercise in managerialism. It never completely disappeared, however, and it has enjoyed a modest resurgence in the federal bureaucracy. Its recent implementation has encountered the same obstacles that led to its widespread abandonment three decades ago.

Beyond its current application and historical significance, program budgeting is relevant as an effort to achieve the most important goals of the performance movement. In this regard, the following analysis helps to explain the limited substantive impact of requirements for planning and performance assessment, such as those imposed by the Government Performance and Results Act (GPRA) and by the Performance Assessment Rating Tool (PART) used by the Office of Management and Budget (OMB) during the George W. Bush administration. It also provides a context for revisiting alternatives to the value of businesslike efficiency that have been largely overlooked in the public administration literature in recent years.

Background

Planning, programming, budgeting systems (PPB) were introduced to the US Department of Defense (DoD) by Robert McNamara when he became secretary in 1961. As a former business professor and corporate executive, McNamara was drawn to PPB because it promised to yield a substantially more efficient allocation of resources and responsibilities among the various factors (weapons systems, operational units, facilities, etc.) that contributed to national defense. It was a way to rationalize the execution of DoD's mission without having to rationalize its organizational structure. PPB sought to accomplish this through an elaborate process that linked planning with budgeting by objectively evaluating and comparing the activities of organizational units in terms of the purposes they served. Accordingly, it was also a tool whereby McNamara hoped to centralize his control over services that had traditionally enjoyed a good deal of autonomy.

PPB was appealing as an alternative to traditional DoD budgeting practice, which allegedly focused decision makers' attention on organizational expenditures in isolation from their goals and which resulted in incremental (rather than strategically informed) adjustments to previous years' amounts. Influenced by its compelling logic and its apparent success at DoD, President Lyndon Johnson extended PPB to the entire federal government in 1965. It had a minimal impact on the civilian bureaucracy, however, and was terminated there after little more than five years.

Scholars offered competing explanations for the failure of PPB. Advocates of the technique attributed its demise to bureaucratic inertia and to the lack of expertise and other resources required for its successful implementation. Yet others claimed that the goals PPB sought to accomplish were fundamentally at odds with a decision-making environment characterized by complexity, uncertainty, a lack of consensus about means–ends relationships, and fragmented institutional authority. Critics such as Aaron Wildavsky (1969) and Martin Landau (1969) argued that program budgeting was unrealistic for the same reasons that comprehensive planning and analysis were unrealistic more generally.

PPB survived only at DoD during the next thirty years. Recently, however, it has reemerged in three civilian agencies—the National Oceanic and Atmospheric Administration (NOAA), the National Aeronautics and Space Administration (NASA), and the Department of Homeland Security (DHS). Much as it was at DoD under McNamara, it has been introduced in these organizations as a tool for integrative management across programs and units that contribute to similar objectives but that have historically operated with considerable independence. NOAA, NASA, and DHS face challenges of coordination that are hardly unique in this respect but that are arguably severe as a matter of degree.

The early and more recent histories of PPB suggest a number of questions. Given the obstacles it encountered in other agencies, why did PPB survive at DoD? Did it ever promote the management objectives that it was intended to serve in that organization? If so, has it continued to promote these goals? And given its ineffectiveness in the 1960s, why has it reemerged in a handful of civilian agencies? Has it been any more successful this time around than in its first life? How does more recent experience speak to the competing explanations that were offered for its abandonment forty years ago?

The current use of program budgeting remains limited, notwithstanding the magnitude of the defense budget and the importance of the other agencies that have recently adopted it. Yet PPB can also be viewed as an extension of the current performance movement that has had such a significant impact on the theory and practice of public administration in the United States and abroad. Most MFR systems thus assume that planning and the objective assessment of programmatic outcomes can be tied together to coordinate across organizational boundaries through a cyclical and iterative management process. Planning furnishes the criteria for assessment through the articulation of ends and means, just as assessment may subsequently lead to a refinement of plans. MFR further assumes that the information so generated will produce more rational spending decisions through comparisons of government activities based on their relative contributions to government objectives.

These assumptions underlie the most important manifestation of MFR at the federal level in the United States (Frederickson and Frederickson 2006). GPRA requires agencies to describe their missions and subordinate goals and activities through strategic planning. This hierarchical structure of ends and means then becomes the basis for the measurement and comparison of outcomes. Like most other performance management requirements, however, GPRA says little about *how* planning, assessment, and budgeting can be integrated to promote greater efficiency. The framers of this act assumed that these linkages would be established but left the details to be worked out later within individual agencies and on a government-wide basis by OMB. The broader relevance of PPB lies in the fact that some technique incorporating its essential elements is required if the performance movement is to promote this coordinative goal in any systematic way. In fact, each of the agencies that has resurrected program budgeting has justified it as an effort to comply with GPRA's intent.

The following chapters suggest that the most important goals of MFR cannot be realized for the same reasons that PPB cannot substantially rationalize government performance. Although these reasons include the organizational resistance and resource constraints that defenders of PPB and MFR typically cite in explaining the limited effects of such techniques, they also include more fundamental obstacles that are grounded in the realities of bounded rationality and bureaucratic politics. Indeed, the former constraints are typically difficult to disassociate from the latter. The following chapters also suggest that efforts at synoptic planning can be undesirable in ways that have received too little attention in recent years.

Organization of the Book and Principal Findings

Chapter 2 presents a historical overview of PPB that begins with a brief discussion of its two primary antecedents. One, which dates to the Progressive Era, was the idea that government expenditures could be organized in terms of functions or purposes as an aid to management. The other, which dates to the post–World War II era, was the development of analytical techniques that could be used to compare the marginal benefits of those expenditures. Chapter 2 then describes the adoption of PPB by DoD in the early 1960s, as well as its subsequent rise and fall in the civilian bureaucracy during the latter half of that decade. Although there are few detailed, contemporaneous descriptions of the implementation of program budgeting outside DoD, there are many impressionistic accounts of the problems it encountered, both generally and within particular agencies (Novick 1969; Haveman and Margolis 1970; Lyden and Miller 1972).

PPB is sometimes portrayed as a management fad that was discarded and that is no longer worthy of scholarly attention beyond the postmortems that were offered for its demise (Schick 1973). Yet program budgeting survived in an organization whose budget constitutes roughly half of all federal discretionary spending. Not surprisingly, then, although academics have given relatively little attention to the subject since the early 1970s (but see Jones and McCaffery 2008), there is no shortage of applied research by government entities and think tanks assessing the implementation of PPB at DoD (e.g., Bowsher 1983; BENS 2000; Kutz and Warren 2002; Kutz and Rhodes 2004; JDCST 2004). Relying on some of this work and on interviews with several current and former DoD officials, chapter 3 provides a broad overview of the evolution of PPB in the four decades that have passed since Robert McNamara resigned as secretary of defense.

The history of program budgeting at DoD is an interesting study in organizational change that could easily be the subject of a separate book. Although crosscutting assessments of DoD activities had a significant influence on defense policy in the 1960s, it is less clear whether this was the result of PPB per se or of a relatively informal organizational arrangement that empowered a small and loyal group of headquarters staff to advise the secretary of defense on selected issues. In either case, the PPB process at DoD has evolved in two ways that have severely undermined its usefulness as management tool. One way is its decentralization. Whereas the implementation of PPB gave the Office of the Secretary of Defense the initiative to shape policy under McNamara, centralized analysis assumed an increasingly reactive role in the 1970s that has continued to the present. The other development is the bureaucratization of the process. Though PPB has always been complex, DoD's current system has come to involve so many actors and steps and to require the development of so much information that it has moved well beyond the limits of human cognition. The upshot of these developments is the reinforcement of bounded rationality in the form of "base-plus incrementalism." Ironically, in this regard, DoD's planning and budgeting are routinely subjected to the same criticisms today that led to the implementation of PPB during the Kennedy administration (BENS 2000; JDCST 2004).

Chapters 4 and 5 present a case study of the adoption and subsequent implementation of PPB at the National Oceanic and Atmospheric Administration. NOAA is composed of organizations that were drawn together from throughout the federal government for the purpose of integrating related functions, and it was still perceived as facing important problems of coordination thirty years after its creation. In response, the retired navy admiral who was appointed NOAA administrator in 2001 instituted PPB to achieve better coordination across and within the agency's five major line components (Moore 2004). The innovative version of program budgeting developed by Conrad Lautenbacher modified the military's system by requiring line managers to assume a much greater role in planning and analysis. It did this through a matrix structure involving functionally oriented teams whose membership cut across formal organizational boundaries (NOAA 2008). Although the choice of PPB undoubtedly reflected Lautenbacher's own professional background, it also sought to address criticisms that had been levied against NOAA by its political principals and by other constituents. In addition, it was designed to comply with the general demands for planning and assessment imposed by GPRA and by performance management requirements that had recently been instituted during the George W. Bush administration.

NOAA's management system had mixed results. The development of a program structure led to a more comprehensive understanding of NOAA's goals and of how different parts of the agency furthered those objectives. The introduction of "matrix management" also improved communications and led to greater shared awareness across organizational components. Yet the system also required a good deal of time and effort from managers with other responsibilities, and its effect on the allocation of resources was confined primarily to the distribution of additional funds on a very selective basis. In these latter respects, virtually all the obstacles that impeded the implementation of program budgeting at NOAA might have been anticipated from accounts of its failure in 1960s. The agency replaced PPB with a less ambitious system of planning and budgeting in 2010.

The appendix to this book provides less detailed overviews of the adoption and implementation of program budgeting by two other federal agencies, DHS and NASA. DHS is required to use PPB by its enabling legislation, but it has nonetheless struggled to put a viable system in place. This has been due to a lack of resources, resistance from component agencies, and inadequate support from political officials in both the legislative and executive branches. Program budgeting has had an easier time at NASA because it has enjoyed the support of senior leadership and because its formal introduction was the culmination of a series of incremental changes. As in the case of NOAA, however, its substantive effects have been marginal.

The analysis here speaks to the competing explanations that were offered for PPB's earlier demise. Again, its defenders stressed the bureaucracy's lack of expertise and commitment, combined with the inherent conservatism of large organizations (e.g., Novick 1969). Agency executives allegedly did not understand or appreciate program budgeting, and bureaucrats and elected officials lacked the will to make hard decisions that would disrupt established programs and clientele relationships. In fact, it may be a truism that strong leadership support is a necessary condition for PPB to have a significant impact as a management tool. As with the introduction of any demanding organizational change, moreover, the implementation of PPB is bound to be difficult without the dedication of substantial new resources. Some or all of these factors have come into play in each of the three agencies that have recently adopted program budgeting.

In addition, however, the following chapters provide ample support for the arguments of Wildavsky (1969) and others that PPB is subject to more fundamental limitations as a practical theory. The most important of these are grounded in constraints associated with bounded rationality and with the decentralized and pluralistic political environment of public administration in the United States (Downs and Larkey 1986). Success is always contingent on one's expectations, of course, and policy analysis can influence decisions on a selective basis (again, assuming that leaders are receptive to it). A salutary result of PPB in the 1960s may have been that it hastened the institutionalization of policy analysis in the federal bureaucracy (Schick 1973; Radin 2000a). At the same time, there is little reason to believe that formal processes of strategic planning and the objective assessment of agency outputs can be used to rationalize what government does in a comprehensive or even a systematic way. The reasons for this include

- the difficulty of measuring the outputs and (especially) the outcomes of many government programs;
- problems of accountability and control that attend efforts to manage across formal organizational boundaries and lines of authority;
- the reinforcement of existing organizations, programs, and patterns of resource allocation by constituent groups and (relatedly) by the fragmentation of institutional authority between and within the legislative and executive branches;
- conceptual problems that attend efforts to arrange government activities in terms of hierarchically ordered means–ends linkages; and
- limits on human intellectual capacity that render efforts at comprehensive planning and analysis infeasible.

Ironically, in this last respect, the evolution of PPB at DoD suggests that formal systems of planning and assessment that seek to be comprehensive and that are synchronized with the annual budget cycle may well undermine the kind of selective analysis that can be beneficial. The requirement that so much be done in so little time focuses attention on small issues and stifles creativity.

Although PPB's return engagement in the civilian bureaucracy has been limited to date, what it seeks to accomplish is consistent with the aims of the performance movement that has had pervasive effects on government in America and abroad. As is discussed in chapter 6, program budgeting is an extension of objectives that are contained in many state-level reforms and in the most important effort to promote MFR at the federal level in the United States. GPRA thus requires agencies to

- engage in strategic planning for the purpose of articulating their objectives and identifying the activities that contribute to these goals;
- measure the effectiveness of these activities in terms of their contributions to the goals they serve; and
- use this performance information for the purpose of allocating resources more efficiently.

It is instructive in this last instance that the Government Accountability Office (GAO 2004) and others have been highly critical of the failure by agencies and OMB to make more extensive use of performance data for comparative purposes. Again, although GPRA does not specify how planning should be linked to budgeting, a process that incorporates the essential elements of PPB is arguably the only way to accomplish this.

The significance of the resurrection of program budgeting thus lies partly in what it says about the goals and effects of planning and performance-based management. The findings here lend perspective to the conclusions of other studies that performance information collected pursuant to GPRA and similar requirements has had a very limited substantive impact. Although such data may have other useful management applications, including the promotion of accountability and the identification of problems associated with individual programs (Moynihan 2008), the appeal of MFR is considerably diminished to the extent that it does not affect the allocation of resources across programs and organizations. This should be an important consideration in weighing the benefits of formal systems of planning and assessment against their administrative costs. Such requirements inevitably demand substantial effort and divert resources that could otherwise be expended on the accomplishment of programmatic objectives.

The broader significance of this study also lies in what it says about the doctrinal foundations of administrative reform. What explains the continued popularity of systems of strategic planning and performance assessment in light of the difficulties that such reforms have encountered? In chapter 7 I discuss the resurrection of PPB and the persistence of requirements such as GPRA that are attributable to their political appeal, to the convictions of MFR advocates who are unwilling to confront inconvenient realities, and to policymakers' ignorance of history and public administration research. In a related but more general sense, the performance movement reflects assumptions about bureaucracy and its proper role in government that date back more than a century. Based on the ideal that public administration should be an apolitical, technical process, the traditional model of the early 1900s sought to ensure that agencies were objective and efficient in carrying out their mandates. Accordingly, it held that public organizations should emulate the management practices of the private sector. In addition to their intrinsic appeal, these assumptions helped to reconcile a growing administrative state with the constitutional principles of separation of powers and representative democracy.

Notwithstanding the traditional model's attractiveness, scholars of the 1940s and 1950s concluded that its premises were unrealistic for reasons that were identical to explanations that would be offered for the failure of PPB a few years later. Among its problems were the infeasibility of comprehensive planning and analysis, and the impossibility of separating administration from politics. Pluralist critics argued that the latter constraint was especially important in a governmental system characterized by broad delegations of authority and by the fragmentation of institutional power. Yet although few scholars have since taken exception with these critical assessments of traditional theory, traditional values have never gone out of style. Indeed, they have arguably risen to the fore during the past quarter century in a reform movement that has intellectual roots in public-choice economics and neoconservative political ideology. If the assumptions of the New Public Management (NPM) are contradictory in key respects, its central thrust is to make government more efficient through the adoption of sound "business" practices. One way it seeks to accomplish this is by requiring agencies to assess what they do in terms of an objective bottom line and to manage their operations accordingly.

The long and disappointing history of such efforts suggests little reason for optimism that academic research will have a significant bearing on institutional design. This is especially apt to be the case when research yields conclusions that are at odds with popular biases. Yet, even if we seem destined to keep reformulating the same prescriptions, the following chapters highlight the limitations of the managerialism represented by the NPM and by generic performance management requirements such as GPRA. The idealized conception of efficiency that underlies these approaches is not a realistic or perhaps even a theoretically desirable model for management in the public sector.

The following chapters speak instead to an alternative and admittedly less coherent view of public administration as an art that is practiced in an uncertain, technically complex, and politically fragmented environment. This perspective was popular among students of public administration in the middle decades of the twentieth century (Gaus 1947; Appleby 1949; Long 1949; Sayre 1951) but is largely out of favor today. It begins with the premise that public administration and private administration are fundamentally different. Efficiency is hardly an irrelevant goal for the former, but it is bounded and too context-specific to be achieved through formal and comprehensive management systems. Nor is instrumental rationality a complete guide for decision making at high levels within the bureaucracy. To a considerable extent, it will always be trumped by the constitutional values that supersede efficiency in the American political system.

Chapter 2

A Brief History of Planning, Programming, Budgeting Systems

Planning, programming, budgeting (PPB) systems were first adopted by the Department of Defense (DoD) in 1961.[1] The essential purpose of PPB was to link DoD planning and budgeting functions that until then had been performed by different entities and with little coordination. As a means of centralized policymaking, it was also envisioned as a management tool that would help Secretary of Defense Robert McNamara control and rationalize the activities of services that had traditionally operated as autonomous departments.

Lyndon Johnson extended PPB to the entire federal government in 1965. It had little impact, however, and it was formally abandoned in 1971. Its use at the federal level was subsequently confined to DoD for the next three decades. The failure of PPB to take root in the civilian bureaucracy was variously attributed to the amount of work it required, to organizational inertia, to inadequate resources, to resistance by entrenched political interests, and to the limitations of its assumption that the relationships between organizational means and ends could be clearly specified and measured. In a related but more theoretical vein, some framed its failure in terms of the obstacles that confront comprehensive planning and analysis in complex and politically contentious decision-making environments.

PPB is relevant today if for no other reason than its survival at DoD, one of the world's largest and most powerful organizations. In addition, its resurrection at the National Oceanic and Atmospheric Administration and two other civilian agencies speaks to current fashion in the theory and practice of public administration, as well as to intellectual perspectives that date back one hundred years or more. As a prelude to the discussion of these issues in subsequent chapters, it is useful to examine the character of PPB and its growth and demise in the 1960s.

The Logic of Program Budgeting

Charles Hitch, who is often referred to as the father of PPB, describes the system of program budgeting that he created and instituted at DoD as consisting of two complementary functions:

1. programming—to provide a link between military planning and annual budgeting; and
2. systems analysis (or cost-effectiveness analysis)—to assist in making some of the hard choices on what goes into the program. (Hitch 1996, 258)

Although the implementation of PPB involves complex organizational processes, most current practitioners of the technique at DoD and elsewhere readily endorse this simple characterization of its basic elements.

As implied by the first goal, the relationship among planning, programming, and budgeting is sequential (but iterative). In fact, the conceptual transitions from planning to programming and from programming to budgeting are not clear-cut but rather involve differences in functional emphasis (Novick 1969). Planning thus is obviously informed by assumptions about programmatic capabilities, just as the definition of programs is informed by goals established through planning. Similarly, analysis in the programming process is motivated by the realization that budgeting is constrained by finite resources.

As also implied, programming is at the heart of PPB and is what distinguishes it from other approaches to budgeting and decision making more generally. Its essence is to think about activities and spending in terms of their contributions to organizational goals. To accomplish this, a *program structure* defines an agency's (or the government's) major purposes and arrays its activities in terms of those objectives (rather than under the agency's formal organizational units). By extracting functions from their organizational homes for analytical purposes, program budgeting is designed to allow decision makers to compare different activities and units that serve common goals. A classic illustration from DoD is the use of PPB to assess the marginal contributions of strategic bombers, land-based missiles, and submarine-based missiles to nuclear deterrence—notwithstanding their locations in different components of the department.

As articulated by two of its other architects at DoD, the theoretical advantages of PPB are embedded in several principles or "fundamental ideas" that distinguish it from traditional approaches to budgeting, management, and policymaking (Enthoven and Smith 1970, 485–90):

- Decision making should be "based on explicit criteria of the national interest as opposed to decision making based on compromise among various institutional and parochial interests." Such criteria are to be "publicly defensible," having been developed "openly and thoroughly" through debate "by all interested parties."
- Once established, such criteria should provide a basis for "an explicit consideration of alternatives at the top decision level."
- The consideration of needs and costs should occur simultaneously.
- A plan should be developed "which projects into the future the foreseeable implications of current decisions."
- There should be "active use of an analytical staff at the top policymaking levels and the regular use of analysis as an aid to judgment."
- Such analysis should be "open and explicit."

Although the mechanics of PPB vary among organizations and have evolved at DoD, these objectives provide as accurate a summary of its theoretical rationale today as they did in the 1960s (Enthoven and Smith 2005). As discussed below, the degree to which they describe its actual practice may be less clear-cut.

Intellectual and Practical Antecedents

Like most significant ideas, program budgeting did not emerge from thin air. Scholars and government reformers of the Progressive Era were well aware of the possibility that budgets could be structured as instruments for management and planning. This was most explicit in proposals that budget documents should be developed around purposes or functions as either a substitute for or a supplement to the focus on expenditures for "inputs" such as personnel and equipment (Schick 1966; Smithies 1969).[2]

Still, the dominant emphasis during the early twentieth century was on the control orientation of budgeting as an assurance against corruption. This orientation was reflected in the transition from lump-sum expenditures for agencies that were approved by legislatures on a piecemeal basis (often by different committees) to jurisdiction-wide line-item budgets prepared by chief executives. The specification of funding amounts for particular items thus provided a basis for auditing to ensure that money was spent for legitimate purposes. Preceded by similar developments in some states, the Budgeting and Accounting Act of 1921 was an important source of such reforms at the federal level.

As a matter of institutional evolution, therefore, Schick and others cite the performance-budgeting movement that began in the mid-1930s and that intensified during the next fifteen years as an immediate precursor to the rise of PPB (Schick 1966; Smithies 1969). Heightened emphasis on functional output measures as a way for managers to assess organizational performance may have been sanctioned by the success of earlier budget reforms in achieving an acceptable measure of accountability. In any case, the performance orientation was rendered more appealing by the dramatic expansion of government programs and agencies that occurred during and after the New Deal, and by the management challenges that accompanied this development. The focus on budgeting for management was reflected in the growth of the Bureau of the Budget (now the Office of Management and Budget) and in that organization's increased preference for staff who were trained in public administration as opposed to accounting (Schick 1966).

The Budget and Accounting Procedures Act of 1950 was a particularly noteworthy antecedent of PPB. Consistent with recommendations offered by the second Hoover Commission in 1949, this statute effectively required the president to submit a separate federal performance budget (in conjunction with a line-item budget) that was intended to shift attention from government inputs to the functional linkages between costs and accomplishments. As the Government Accountability Office (GAO) notes, this statute

> required the President to present in his budget submission to the Congress the "functions and activities" of the government, ultimately institutionalized as a new budget presentation: "obligations and activities." . . . These presentations were intended to describe the major programs, projects, or activities associated with each federal budget request. . . . Workload and unit cost information began to appear in the President's budget, associated with the "obligations and activities" presentations, providing a means of publicly reporting the outputs of federal spending. (GAO 1997b, 5)

Performance budgeting was, in turn, supplemented by the planning orientation of PPB. Although the terms "performance budgeting" and "program budgeting" are sometimes used interchangeably (and imprecisely in both cases), Schick (1966) argues that the latter encompasses but goes beyond the former in two respects described above. One is its projection of resource needs and costs into the future, together with its consideration of how current commitments relate to those projections. The other is the emphasis it places on the identification of objectives and the comparison of activities across organizations in terms of their marginal contributions to those goals. With characteristic insight, Schick argues that whereas performance budgeting focuses on discrete functions in relative isolation from one another and takes organizational goals as givens, PPB is as much a tool for *making* policy as for managing policy implementation. Some might contend that its purpose is to substitute rational analysis for the political process as a way of allocating scarce values.

The efficiency promised by PPB obviously places a high premium on analysis. In this regard, another important antecedent of program budgeting was the development of tools that might be loosely placed under the heading of systems analysis. Although this term is also used in various ways, it generally refers to a family of techniques that stress the clarification of ends and then the comprehensive (systemswide) assessment of the effects of alternative means of achieving those objectives. The development of systems analysis might be viewed as the critical ingredient in the transition from the concept of a performance budget to program budgeting.

Particularly germane to DoD's adoption of PPB was the War Department's use of operations research during World War II to optimize the employment of people and equipment to achieve military objectives. Its applications, which were developed largely by academics who had been recruited for the war effort, included such things as strategies to protect troop and supply convoys from enemy submarines and to conduct bombing campaigns with maximum destructive effect and minimum loss of allied aircraft. Its use continued after the war as a technique for evaluating alternatives in various areas of defense policy. The intuitive appeal and apparent success of operations research helped to legitimize the prominent role that civilian analysts (from both inside and outside of government) would come to play at DoD, both generally and in the implementation of PPB.

Welfare economics, which had first been developed in the 1930s, provided a related but more generic foundation for PPB that could be applied across the entire spectrum of government activities. The criterion of economic efficiency (or Pareto Optimality), as modified by the introduction of hypothetical side payments (or the Kaldor-Hicks Principle), offered a general theory for allocating government-controlled resources, whether in the form of rights and duties established through regulation or the distribution of loans, grants, subsidies, projects, and the like. The equation of the public interest with economic efficiency has always been controversial on philosophical and moral grounds, and it has never proved to be a realistic substitute for the political process. Nevertheless, cost/benefit and cost-effectiveness analysis were (and are) appealing as bases for measuring the direct and indirect effects of proposed activities and for making trade-offs among alternatives at the margins. By the 1950s, they were being applied as a partial basis for decision making in a number of policy areas. As broadly defined, the latter technique was the basis for programming analysis under PPB at DoD (Hitch 1996).

Adoption by the Department of Defense

Program budgeting was introduced to government at DoD at the outset of the Kennedy administration. As such, it was intended to centralize control of the services in the

Office of the Secretary of Defense and to address issues of planning and coordination that had become increasingly salient in a Cold War environment characterized by high levels of defense spending and a looming Soviet threat. Even some of its critics conceded that it had significant success in promoting these goals.

The Problem

PPB is one of several notable decision-making techniques developed by the RAND Corporation, a prestigious, technically oriented think tank that has long played an advisory role in national security policymaking. RAND was established through an army air force contract with Douglas Aircraft in 1946 to provide advice on issues of research and development, and it became an independent nonprofit organization dedicated to objective and rigorous policy analysis two years later. Although RAND's focus has since expanded to include a variety of domestic policy issues (e.g., health care), its original purpose was to bring to peacetime defense planning the kind of intellectual rigor that had informed operations research during World War II (Hoffman 1970).[3]

Several interrelated postwar developments in the environment of defense policy had arguably created a heightened need for better analysis. One was the rapid ascension of the Soviet Union as both a nuclear and conventional threat to the United States and its allies in Europe and elsewhere. Another was America's emergence as a military superpower that was spending billions of dollars on increasingly numerous and sophisticated weapons systems. The stakes associated with peacetime military planning had become much higher, both financially and in terms of national security. Economists at RAND designed program budgeting as an antidote to a perceived lack of rationality in thinking about the increasingly complex interrelationships among means and ends that accompanied these developments (Hitch and McKean 1960; Hitch 1965).

RAND also designed program budgeting as an antidote to the problems of fragmentation and parochialism that beset DoD. DoD was created by the National Security Act of 1947 to coordinate policy and operations across the services (earlier, the army and navy had been separate departments, and the air force had been an increasingly independent component of the former),[4] and the formal powers of the secretary of defense were subsequently strengthened through a series of legislative and presidential initiatives in the late 1940s and 1950s (Novick 1969).[5] Despite these reforms, critics at RAND and elsewhere felt that the army, navy, and air force of the late 1950s still operated as largely autonomous entities. As one might expect, the military services tended to promote their own institutional missions and interests, with insufficient attention to how their activities supported one another.[6] For instance, the allocation of resources to the air force was not well coordinated with the army's need for tactical air support. Nor did the services (or often units within services) effectively seek to address issues of redundancy in the pursuit of defense objectives. As mentioned, for example, this was reflected in the failure to make analytical comparisons of the contributions of bombers, intercontinental ballistic missiles, and submarine-based missiles to nuclear deterrence. Similarly, little effort was made to optimize the balance between the army and marines as conventional forces.

The peacetime management problems that confronted DoD in the 1950s were thought to be structural (as well as cultural). Although the Pentagon engaged in centralized planning, the process was divorced from budgeting, both institutionally and conceptually. Whereas needs-based planning was conducted by military officers under the Joint Chiefs of Staff, budgeting was the responsibility of DoD civilians in the Office of the Comptroller (who was designated as a civilian by statutory law). This bifurcation of the two functions allegedly undermined the effectiveness of each. One of its implications was that planning by the Joint Chiefs of Staff and by individual services did not give adequate consideration to constraints on resources. Rather than make the hard choices among competing activities that had to be made in the budgetary process, projections of needs for manpower and matériel were "wish lists" that were mutually acceptable but that far exceeded the funding that was available (Hitch 1965; Enthoven and Smith 2005).

Budgeting was in turn largely a matter of allocating fixed shares of the pie that had been established through precedent rather than through an analysis of where money could be spent most effectively. As General Maxwell Taylor asserted in 1959, the disjuncture that existed between budgeting and planning rendered the military incapable of adapting to an ever-changing defense environment: "The maintenance of the rigid percentage distribution by service of the budgets since 1953 is clear proof of the absence of flexibility in our military preparations. This frozen pattern could only be justified if the world had stood still since 1953 and I doubt that anyone would say that it has" (Taylor 1959, 129).

To the extent that there was conflict within the budgetary process, it tended to involve competing claims on *additional* resources that were resolved through compromise among institutional actors. The secretary of defense acted more as a mediator in this process than as a strong executive who set policy. His inability to play a more proactive managerial role was attributable in part to the fact that the DoD budget was prepared in a line-item format that militated against thinking about expenditures in more instrumental terms. Because budgeting was done on a year-to-year basis, moreover, it gave insufficient attention to the long-term implications of current spending decisions. The failure to integrate planning and budgeting was especially problematic with regard to capital outlays for weapons systems. Indeed, the military services had a perverse incentive to make commitments to new systems whose initial developmental costs were relatively low in comparison with their eventual costs of production, maintenance, and support (Enthoven and Smith 2005).

A quotation from Charles Hitch (1965, 24) summarizes the problems that he and other defense analysts felt limited DoD's effectiveness in the 1950s:

> Each service tended to exercise its own priorities, favoring its own unique missions to the detriment of joint missions, striving to lay the groundwork for an increased share of the budget in future years by concentrating on alluring new weapons systems, and protecting the over-all size of its own forces even at the cost or readiness. These decisions were made by patriotic generals and admirals, and by dedicated civilian leaders as well, who were convinced that they were acting in the best interest of the Nation as well as of their own service—but the end result was not balanced effective military forces.

Concerns about the quality of military policymaking were not confined to think tanks such as RAND. By the late 1950s, deficiencies in defense planning, coordination, and budgeting had become evident to many government elites as well. President Eisenhower was acutely aware of the need for better coordination within DoD and undertook several initiatives to strengthen the secretary's managerial prerogatives. Some key members of Congress were of the same mind (Hitch 1965; Enthoven and Smith 2005). For example, a 1960 report by the Symington Commission recommended the abolition of military departments as a way of ensuring more direct subordination of the service chiefs to the secretary. Much of the criticism of DoD's fragmentation focused specifically on the budgetary process and the documents that supported it. As chairman of the Senate Preparedness Investigating Subcommittee, for example, Lyndon Johnson complained in 1959 that

> "despite all the glowing statements and promises concerning unification in the Department of Defense, the testimony before this and other committees clearly shows that the 1960 budget was never considered, nor were decisions made, on a functional basis for the Department of Defense as a whole but rather decisions were made on a service-by-service basis in relation to individual expenditure targets" (Enthoven and Smith 2005, 12).

The Critical Role of Robert McNamara

Some have argued that DoD's adoption of PPB (or a technique that incorporated its essential precepts) was inevitable given the importance and the evolving character and fiscal environment of defense policymaking. Be that as it may, DoD's incorporation of program budgeting on a comprehensive basis awaited the appointment of a secretary of defense who was receptive to its goals and techniques by virtue of his intellect, his background, his policy agenda, and his management style. Robert McNamara, trained in economics and business, and a management professor at Harvard in the early 1940s, had been a practitioner of military operations research during his wartime service in the Office of Statistical Control and on the staff of Air Corps General Curtis LeMay. After World War II, he became a successful executive at Ford Motor Company, where he introduced new planning and management control systems to improve that organization's efficiency. Among those techniques was an approach to budgeting that was similar in concept to PPB (Jones and McCaffery 2008).

McNamara was by all accounts a brilliant technocrat who stressed objectivity and rigorous analysis for the purpose of making government more businesslike—a trait that evoked admiration as well as bitter criticism. Not only did he endorse PPB as his primary strategy for accomplishing this end, he fully understood the details of its implementation. In fact, he was sufficiently well versed in systems analysis that he could offer guidance to his staff about such things as the framing of issues and the appropriate (and inappropriate) use of quantitative data and statistical techniques (Enthoven and Smith 2005).

A second element of McNamara's management style was its proactive nature. As he characterized his philosophy:

> In many aspects the role of a public manager is similar to that of a private manager. In each case he may follow one of two alternative courses. He can act either as a judge or as a leader. As the former he waits until subordinates bring him problems for solution, or alternatives for choice. In the latter case, he immerses himself in his operation, leads and stimulates an examination of the objectives, the problems and alternatives. In my own case, and especially in regard to the Department of Defense, the responsible choice seemed clear. (McNamara 1968, 87–88)

This orientation was clearly at odds with precedent at DoD. Whether by personal inclination or out of perceived necessity (or frustration), McNamara's predecessors had defined the role of secretary primarily as a referee among the competing services rather than as a policymaker intent on defining institutional purposes and selecting the means to achieve them (Enthoven and Smith 2005).

Here, too, PPB was well adapted to the goals that McNamara wanted to advance. The problem in his mind was not an absence of legal authority to centralize management and policymaking. The powers of the secretary of defense, which had been somewhat ill defined at the creation of DoD, had been consolidated incrementally through a series of statutes and presidential actions beginning with the National Security Act of 1947. The problem instead was that the secretary lacked the organizational tools to exercise his authority. Program budgeting afforded a systematic mechanism for top-down planning and the allocation of resources whereby he could counteract the centrifugal forces of separate services and organizations within the services. Similarly, McNamara placed a high premium on the creation of an independent staff to exploit this mechanism. The policy analysts responsible for implementing PPB would be responsive to him alone, and not to the various institutional interests that competed for the loyalty of officials in the services and other DoD headquarters units (McNamara 1968; Enthoven and Smith 2005).

Key Elements of the PPB System at DoD

McNamara chose his comptroller at DoD specifically for the purpose of establishing PPB. Charles Hitch, who was RAND's chief economist at the time of his appointment as assistant secretary of defense for finance, had been one of the leaders in developing and advocating program budgeting. In fact, he had just completed a book in 1960 arguing for the application of systems analysis to defense policymaking. In addition to his obvious familiarity with the concepts and methods of PPB, he had connections to talented civilian analysts who would be instrumental in designing and implementing the new system. An especially important figure was Alain Enthoven, another RAND economist, who became head of the newly created Office of Systems Analysis under Hitch.

PPB at DoD had several important features. The most fundamental was a program structure—a hierarchical ordering of the department's objectives and the means to achieve them. By 1965, DoD's major programs consisted of Strategic Retaliatory Forces, Continental Defense Forces, General Purpose Forces, Airlift and Sealift, Reserve and Guard, Research and Development, General Support, Retired Pay, and Military Assistance. These provided the basis for a linear model in which about a thousand "program elements" were grouped according to the principal objectives they served. As an illustration, Strategic Retaliatory Forces included the following weapons systems, along with the equipment, personnel, and supplies that supported them (Novick 1969, 93):

- *Aircraft*: B/EB-47, RB-47, B-52, AGM-28A/B, GAM-87, B-58, KC-97, KC-135, RC-135.
- *Land-based missiles*: Atlas, Titan, Minuteman.
- *Sea-based missiles*: Polaris System, Regulus System.

As another example, General Purpose Forces consisted of program elements that were "designed to fight in limited or less than total nuclear wars." These elements included air force fighter squadrons, army divisions, and navy combat ships and aircraft, among others (Hitch 1968, 38).

DoD's program structure offered a framework for thinking about how the resources that were allocated to its different activities contributed to its core missions. This concept lay at the heart of the future years defense plan, whose purpose was to

- array resources in major force programs, as well as by service and by budget category;
- provide a map from appropriations categories to output categories; and
- facilitate analyses of capabilities by assembling complements and substitutes into mutually exclusive, collectively exhaustive sets (Gordon, McNicol, and Jack 2008).

Means–ends analysis and planning under PPB was intended to be continuous in its assessment of changing defense needs and the capabilities to address them. These were defined holistically by the United States' own capabilities as well as by the motives and capabilities of its enemies and allies. In theory, this assessment was also an iterative process in the sense that efficiencies in some program areas could trigger the reallocation of resources to other areas where similar efficiencies were not possible. If basic objectives retained constant weights (in terms of their respective contributions to national security), for example, a reconfiguration of program elements that led to greater efficiencies from strategic retaliatory forces might permit less total spending in that area and more spending on research and development or on conventional capabilities. As mentioned, in fact, reallocating resources to the latter was a Kennedy administration goal that added to the appeal of PPB. In theory, the realization of greater efficiencies within the area of defense more generally might also free up resources that could be redistributed to other national objectives (e.g., health or education) or that could be returned to taxpayers.

As implied by the word "future," a related feature of the new management system was the establishment of mechanisms for ensuring that "annual budgets [would] follow plans instead of leading them" (Hitch 1996, 259). This goal was also reflected in the preparation of a five-year budget document that displayed expenditures in terms of program structure (as opposed to separate organizations and line items). On the basis of current as well as projected needs, the purpose of the Five-Year Force Structure and Financial Program was to ensure that the planning and the comparison of alternative means would take into account the full costs and benefits of program elements.

Although a critical goal of PPB was to centralize control over DoD policy in the Office of the Secretary, it did not seek to stifle input from stakeholders within the organization. As Hitch (1965, 30–31) notes:

We envisioned [military planning and requirements determination] as a continuing year-round operation involving participation by all appropriate elements of the Defense Department in their appropriate areas of responsibility. We anticipated that the Joint Chiefs of Staff organization and the planners in the military departments would play a particularly important role. . . . What we were looking for here were not just requirement studies in the traditional sense, but military-economic studies which compared alternative ways of accomplishing national security objectives and which tried to determine the one that contributes the most for a given cost or that achieves a given objective for the least cost.

One should not infer from this statement that all the participants in DoD's process were dispassionate. In practice, PPB was (and is) a competitive system in which advocates of alternative program elements sought to justify larger shares of resources for their own activities. Yet in contrast to the assertion of bureaucratic interests, per se, which had allegedly driven budget negotiations in the past, competition under the new system was to be based on rational analysis. This occurred in part through program change proposals (PCPs), which allowed services to request modifications of five-year programs that had been approved. As David Novick (1969, 99) notes, "The submission of a PCP by a service usually comes as the culmination of a major study. Such a study is practically essential in view of the requirement that the proposal include estimates of cost and effectiveness over a long term, and consider alternatives and trade-offs. . . . The PCP system enhances the service's ability to present the Secretary of Defense with carefully worked out program proposals and pertinent data to support them."

Whereas PCPs were initiatives from the military services, the draft presidential memorandum (DPM) was a mechanism through which the secretary could set the policymaking agenda. This was a white paper for the president that analyzed needs and resources for a particular defense program. Initially prepared by the Office of Systems Analysis with an explicit rationale for its policy recommendations, it would be reviewed and amended by the secretary and only then sent to the Joint Chiefs of Staff and the individual services for their comments. The secretary would use this feedback to formulate a final version for submission to the president (Gordon, McNicol, and Jack 2008).

DPMs were taken seriously within DoD precisely because they were prepared for the White House. Moreover, they gave McNamara the initiative to shape DoD policy. Rather than reacting to and mediating institutional conflicts over resources, as had been the role of previous secretaries, DPMs allowed him and his staff to identify the key issues, define the premises that would guide debate, and control the final decisions (at least within DoD). According to Enthoven and Smith (who helped lead this process as key members of the Office of Systems Analysis), DPMs were the most effective mechanism to bring systems analysis and the secretary's perspectives to bear during the McNamara years. Their use expanded from two programs in 1961 (strategic nuclear forces and general purpose forces) to sixteen in 1968 (Enthoven and Smith 2005, 54).

Early Effects

It is unclear whether the early effects of program budgeting at DoD were attributable to the formal system it created or simply to the empowerment of a group of bright analysts. In either case, the practitioners of program budgeting in DoD could claim a number of early successes. Perhaps the most fundamental of these was the abandonment of "massive retaliation" as the overriding basis for national security policy. This doctrine had originally been based on the assumption of US nuclear dominance coupled with the belief that the Soviet Union and its Eastern Bloc satellites would inevitably overwhelm NATO forces in a conventional European war. Critics argued that both of these empirical premises were suspect, and that among the doctrine's unfortunate implications was America's failure to develop its own conventional capabilities. In fact, John Kennedy had expressed concern about this imbalanced defense posture while still a senator. Given the extreme disincentive to use nuclear force, he felt that it placed America at a strategic disadvantage that the Soviet Union (or China) could exploit incrementally through acts of limited aggression around the world. (This fear underlay the "domino theory" that provided a rationale for the United States' involvement in Vietnam.) Although PPB did not identify this issue, DoD systems analysts under McNamara developed rigorous justifications for augmenting conventional US capabilities for "flexible response" (Enthoven and Smith 2005).

Perhaps the most frequently cited success of PPB was its influence on decisions to reallocate resources among various program elements that contributed to strategic nuclear deterrence. As Enthoven and Smith (2005, 170) describe the lack of rationality in budgeting for nuclear weapons systems that existed before 1961: "The Defense Department was spending billions on the early Minuteman, Polaris, and B-52 programs; it was also spending billions on the Atlas, Titan, Snark, Thor, Jupiter, Regulus, B-47, B-58, B-70, nuclear-powered airplane, Houng Dog, Skybolt, and Nike-Zeus programs. And there was no coherent plan for deciding how much of which system we should retain or buy."

The failure to think about these systems comprehensively was precisely the kind of problem that PPB was designed to address. Based on considerations of cost-effectiveness, for example, analysts found that the United States placed too much emphasis on strategic bombers and not enough emphasis on those intercontinental ballistic missiles that were least vulnerable to an enemy first strike in a nuclear war. Polaris submarines were judged to be an especially effective contributor to nuclear deterrence for this and for other reasons.

Advocates of PPB argued that planners in the services had been disinclined to engage in objective comparative analysis because of institutional self-interest and because of the natural (and perhaps desirable) tendency of organizations to elevate the importance of their own missions. The reluctance of the air force to accept cutbacks in its bomber wings was allegedly justified by its argument that it could inflict unacceptable damages on the Soviet Union if only 20 percent of its planes survived a first strike (Enthoven and Smith 2005). More interesting, perhaps, was the navy's reluctance to expand the Polaris program at the expense of the more traditional conventional activities (e.g., destroyers, aircraft carriers) that competed for its (relatively fixed) share of the defense budget (Hitch 1968).

DoD systems analysts from the 1960s could offer other illustrations of efficiencies that had resulted from PPB. These included the termination of expensive and relatively ineffective weapons systems of both a nuclear and a conventional nature. Among the beneficial casualties were the B-70 bomber, the Skybolt missile-delivery system, and the F-111 fighter. The successes claimed for PPB also included the development of new military tactics and the provision of the equipment and organizations needed to implement them. An example here is the concept of airmobile warfare, which came to play a prominent role in the army's prosecution of the war in Vietnam.

A common denominator in these and other cases was the use of instrumental analysis to overcome the vested organizational interests and doctrinal orthodoxies that had dominated peacetime planning in the military. Advocates of PPB were quick to point out that analysis was a creative process in which methodology and design should be fitted to the problem at hand. Although some of their conclusions were based on sophisticated quantitative techniques, in many cases they were based primarily on common sense as informed by objectivity and a clear and appropriately inclusive framing of the relevant issues (Hitch 1965; Enthoven and Smith 2005).

Rise and Fall in the Civilian Bureaucracy

The logic of program budgeting was attractive to many as a way to rationalize domestic as well as military policy. Impressed by its apparent success at DoD, President Johnson extended PPB to all federal agencies in the mid-1960s. This initiative failed to live up to expectations, however, and PPB's use soon receded to its original home in DoD.

The Extension of PPB throughout Government

Some had advocated the application of program budgeting throughout government years before it was adopted by DoD (e.g., Novick 1954). To an even greater degree than in defense, domestic programs had been created willy-nilly with little thought to how they fit together (Wilson 1975). As in defense, moreover, organizational loyalties and clientele relationships stood in the way of coordination. A concern that had been frequently voiced at least since the New Deal (President's Committee on Administrative Management 1937), the problem of fragmentation in the federal government was exacerbated by the proliferation of Great Society programs in the 1960s. Although most advocates of PPB at think tanks and universities recognized the technical and political challenges it faced, many still felt that it could be used to confront issues of governmental redundancy and conflict across a wide range of policy areas (Novick 1969). Some members of Congress also found the extension of PPB to be appealing. As chair of the Subcommittee on Economy in Government of the Joint Economic Committee (and as a noted critic of waste in government), Senator William Proxmire (D-WI) argued that the kind of analysis produced by PPB should inform decisions by the congressional appropriations committees. Among other things, he felt that it would provide a needed counterpoise to the parochial interests represented by authorization committees:

> Given the institutional constraints which inhibit change in this situation, is there anything that can be done to improve the congressional budgetmaking process? In my judgment, there are a number of important steps which can be taken. Many of them entail the bringing to bear of additional PPB-type information on the appropriations process. Congressmen and Senators who are concerned with national priorities and efficiency in government must have the information and data necessary to raise and debate the right basic questions about program effectiveness and worth. (Proxmire 1970, 417)

The White House shared these sentiments. Undoubtedly influenced by his singular regard for McNamara, and motivated by his desire to promote the effectiveness of his own Great Society, Lyndon Johnson issued a memorandum in August 1965 extending PPB to the entire federal bureaucracy. In so doing, Johnson hoped to promote planning and efficient resource allocation throughout the government. As he described the rationale for PPB, it would

- Identify our national goals with precision and on a continuing basis.
- Choose among those goals the ones that are most urgent.
- Search for alternative means of achieving those goals most efficiently at the least cost.

- Inform ourselves not merely on next year's costs but on the second, third, and subsequent years' costs of programs.
- Measure the performance of our programs to ensure a dollar's worth of services for each dollar spent (Downs and Larkey 1986, 155).

The Bureau of the Budget (BOB) was given responsibility to ensure that agencies complied with the president's directive. BOB's guidelines for implementing PPB, which were issued in October 1965, consisted of requirements that sought to incorporate the primary features of program budgeting as it was being applied at DoD (Marvin and Rouse 1970). Accordingly, agencies were to develop

- *Program structures* that reflected their major, functional objectives. Consistent with the essential premise of program budgeting, it was anticipated that these would cut across formal organizational boundaries within each of the major domestic agencies where PPB was required (but not across the entire government).
- *Five-year program and financial plans* that identified what program elements were supposed to accomplish, how much they would cost, and when those costs and benefits would occur. The BOB guidelines stressed that these plans should use quantitative output measures whenever possible.
- *Program memoranda* to justify each of their programs. Similar in purpose to DoD's draft presidential memoranda, these were intended as analyses of how agency activities contributed to program goals and of how program goals served the interests of the American people. Program memoranda were designed to afford policymakers a clear understanding of the rationale behind agency goals and the means chosen to achieve those goals (Bureau of the Budget 1970).
- *Special analytic studies* that would justify the decisions reflected in the program memoranda. These might address issues that were relevant to the current budget year or longer-range planning issues (Seidman 1970).

BOB's guidelines were general in nature and gave agencies discretion to implement program budgeting in accordance with their own needs and constraints. In fact, agencies "created a wide variety of systems" that could be differentiated along a number of dimensions that varied more or less independently from one another (Marvin and Rouse 1970, 447). Among others, these included levels of staffing and expertise, the degree to which the process was centralized at the departmental level, the manner in which analysis was used by executives, and the degree to which program structures either coincided with or cut across organizational boundaries (Marvin and Rouse 1970).

Failure and Abandonment

Although many people had high expectations for PPB, even some of its creators had been skeptical about its feasibility outside DoD. None other than Charles Hitch (1969, 260) noted that

> on August 25, 1965, as I was packing my bags for Berkeley [to become president of the University of California system], President Johnson decreed that PPBS [planning, programming, budgeting systems], which had achieved

such "astounding success" in the Department of Defense, was to be adopted and applied in every other department and agency of the federal government. I thought at the time that this was foolish—almost certain to lead to confusion, and likely to end up discrediting the management techniques it was trying to promote.

As Hitch added, "both happened." Although attempts to implement PPB varied in their diligence across organizations, many agencies did not undertake serious efforts to comply with its requirements (Schick 1973). Moreover, the effects of PPB were disappointing even in those agencies that were most committed to its success. One of these was the Department of Health, Education, and Welfare (HEW). Reflecting on her three-year effort to establish a viable system of program budgeting at HEW, Alice Rivlin (1970, 511, 516) noted that, although PPB served some useful purposes, perhaps its most important effect was the "discovery of how little is known, either about the status of the nation's health, education, and welfare or about what to do to change things. . . . Anyone who thought that PPBS was a magic formula to make the allocation of federal resources easy had better think again." Based on a comprehensive study of the implementation of PPB four years after its introduction to the civilian bureaucracy, Keith Marvin and Andrew Rouse observed that "the fact that many structure and output definition problems remain unresolved creates an impression that PPB has been unsuccessful. In retrospect, it is clear that the expectations of federal agencies exceeded their ability to satisfy" (1970, 447). Consequently, PPB was formally abandoned by the Office of Management and Budget (renamed from BOB in 1970) in 1971.

Explanations

The literature from the 1960s and 1970s offers a number of explanations for the demise of program budgeting. Even its advocates conceded that it faced important technical challenges in many contexts. One was the difficulty of measuring costs and benefits. In the case of inputs, although budget figures were readily available, determining what expenditures supported what goals was not always straightforward. In the case of outputs, the effects of many government programs were difficult to quantify. What is the value of a human life or a more scenic environment, for example? Although economists had developed a variety of techniques for assigning "shadow prices" to socalled soft values (and although these techniques have become increasingly sophisticated in the intervening decades), efforts at objective measurement of program effects remained highly speculative in many areas of domestic policy (Margolis 1970).

A more fundamental challenge had to do with the assumption of PPB that government objectives and the means to accomplish them could be ordered in a hierarchical fashion. There was no basis for the kind of linear analysis that lay at the heart of PPB in the absence of a priori assumptions about the purposes of activities, yet those assumptions often proved to be arbitrary. This was because many agency activities served multiple objectives under any conceivable program structure. What were the ultimate national goals served by public education or interstate highways, for example? Although one response to this dilemma was to say that X percent of an activity contributed to goal A and that Y percent contributed to goal B, these determinations were often perceived to be arbitrary as well (Freeman 1970).

A related obstacle had to do with the relationship between program budgeting and the structure of the federal bureaucracy. Although one could formulate a reasonable program structure for transportation policy, for example, most program goals were supported by multiple organizations. Hence there was no authority to promote the kind of rational coordination that PPB sought to achieve. Comparing the United States with other developed nations, John Meyer (1969, 147) noted that

> transport development in the United States is a function of many agencies, bureaus, and departments and, in particular, there is no one bureau, depart-ment, or ministry of transportation. . . . Without a central ministry for direct-ing the transportation activities of the national government, the application of program-budgeting techniques is, of course, complicated. Also compli-cated is the problem of accurately estimating government transport expendi-tures, particularly as they relate to different functional objective.

Other studies found that similar problems of organizational fragmentation inhibited PPB in health, natural resources, foreign affairs, and other policy areas.

An ironic implication of these studies was that, although PPB was devised and advocated as a way to rationalize organizational activities without having to rationalize organizational structure, its success depended on the application of hierarchical author-ity. This condition existed at DoD (at least within the constraints of a political system characterized by the fragmentation of institutional power and bureaucratic-clientele relationships), where the results of program budgeting could inform managerial deci-sions by the secretary. Although the Executive Office of the President might conceivably have sought to play such a centralizing role with regard to domestic policy, there was lit-tle inclination to do so within the White House or the Bureau of the Budget.

As a practical matter, of course, any meaningful attempt at government-wide program budgeting within the executive branch would have required a great deal of effort and expertise. This was true at the agency level as well. Common to all expla-nations for the failure of PPB was an acknowledgment of its complexity and the ana-lytical resources it required, coupled with the observation that agencies simply lacked the personnel needed to carry it out effectively. Writing from their respective vantage points in GAO and the Office of Management and Budget, Marvin and Rouse (1970, 447) note that, although there were about 1,600 full-time PPB employees across the civilian bureaucracy by the late 1960s, neither their numbers nor their capabilities were adequate for the task at hand:

> The across-the-board introduction of PPB in the civil agencies had . . . important consequences which tended to defeat what was expected of PPB. One was that hundreds of analysts were needed, of which there were almost none, either in the government outside Defense, or the private sector. The result was to spread then existing talent and to literally reclassify as "policy analysts" large numbers of men without the requisite training. Result: ana-lytic studies were extremely variable in quality; almost non-existent in some agencies.

This same theme was expressed in Rivlin's (1970, 511–12) insider account of HEW (again, one of the agencies that took PPB most seriously):

> Analytical effort in HEW has been hampered by two main factors—lack of staff and lack of information. Studies . . . take many man-months of effort.

The present staff of analysts under the assistant secretary for planning and evaluation can handle only a small number of studies each year, and must choose the three or four issues which seem to be of importance in upcoming budgetary or legislative decisions, perhaps leaving aside issues of more basic long-run importance.

Whether any feasible dedication of resources would have been adequate to staff PPB is obviously a matter of speculation. Be this as it may, policy analysts were in far shorter supply in the 1960s than they are today. Moreover, PPB could not be successfully implemented by *any* analysts. As in the area of defense, it required people who combined the requisite technical skills with a contextual knowledge of agency-specific issues and policymaking environments. Although these obstacles would have been formidable under the best of circumstances, staffing for PPB was further undermined by the escalation of the Vietnam War and the constraints this imposed on the funding of domestic activities.

Bureaucratic resistance to change was another common explanation for the failure of PPB (Schick 1973). The effects of organizational inertia, always an impediment to change, were reinforced by the complexity of PPB and by the lack of additional resources needed to carry it out. As Allen Schick notes in a widely cited account, "Budgeting is the routinization of public choice by means of standardized procedures, timetables, classifications, and rules. PPB failed because it did not penetrate the vital routines of putting together and justifying a budget" (Schick 1973, 146).

Resistance to PPB was not grounded solely in the inconvenience of adopting new routines; it was fueled perhaps to an even greater extent by vested interests. These included the agency officials and the constituent groups that respectively administered and benefited from established programs. They also included the politicians who represented those constituents. Another irony of PPB was that, although it was theoretically appealing because resources were finite, it proved to be especially difficult in precisely those areas where fiscal constraints were most severe. In this respect as well, the impact of program budgeting may have been undermined by the diversion of funds to Vietnam.

Some analysts also cited agencies' failure to involve Congress as an explanation for the failure of PPB. Noting that "any effort to link plans and budgets . . . must explicitly involve both branches of our government," a report by GAO (1997b, 7) went on to observe that

> PPB . . . faltered in large part because [it] intentionally attempted to develop performance plans and measures in isolation from congressional oversight and resource allocation processes. Since goals, objectives, and activities were not jointly discussed and agreed upon, there was no consensus on what performance should be, how to measure it, or how to integrate performance information with resource decisions.

Even if the bureaucracy had made better efforts to include the legislature, observers pointed out that Congress was less than an ideal partner in efforts at rational planning and resource allocation. The fragmentation of power via the committee system was deemed an especially important impediment to PPB. Departments and even many agencies were subject to oversight and legislative control by multiple committees and subcommittees that were allegedly organized to serve parochial interests and that attracted their members accordingly (Marvin and Rouse 1970; Hoffman 1970). For example, the agriculture committees and appropriation subcommittees were composed primarily of legislators who represented agricultural states and congressional districts, just as the interior committees drew legislators from the western states (Proxmire 1970). Whatever recommendations it might produce within the bureaucracy, PPB was rendered sterile to the extent that narrow political concerns trumped objective analysis in the legislative process.

Strong executive support was critical to the success of program budgeting given the organizational and political challenges it faced. Its presence or absence was manifested in the willingness (or lack thereof) to design effective systems, to devote adequate resources to the implementation of those systems, and to take the results of analysis seriously in making and then defending policy decisions. Marvin and Rouse (1970, 454) found that, although leadership commitment to PPB varied a great deal across agencies, it was lacking in many cases. This was a primary explanation for their finding that only three of the sixteen agencies they examined in 1968 had made "progress toward the use of analysis and planning in decisionmaking." In addition to competing demands on resources and the political exigencies they faced, many federal executives simply did not understand PPB or otherwise failed to appreciate its benefits as an aid to decision making. As Schick (1973, 78) notes, "The main problem was that, unlike McNamara, whose initiative enabled him to forge his own PPB system, civilian agency heads were ordered to graft an alien . . . system onto their regular budgetary processes."

The lack of leadership support at the agency level could be attributed in part to a lack of support from the Executive Office of the President. Despite his initial enthusiasm, President Johnson made little subsequent effort to ensure the success of PPB (Marvin and Rouse 1970). Nor did BOB offer the necessary guidance and support. This was true even with regard to fundamental questions such as whether PPB was intended primarily to be an internal agency management tool or a source of information that BOB would use in the budgetary process (Marvin and Rouse 1970). Writing from his vantage point at HEW, for example, David Seidman (1970, 317) observed that BOB was inconsistent concerning the purpose of the program memorandum:

> The current view of the Program Memorandum as the decision document which addresses a highly *selective* list of issues and discusses nothing beyond those issues is a relatively recent development. Until 1968, the PMs were regarded as more comprehensive documents requiring some discussion of every program. During 1968, conflicting directives came from the Bureau of the Budget concerning the Program Memorandum—the PPB staff required selectivity and the budgeting examining staff required comprehensiveness. These conflicting requests have not as yet been resolved.

What many construed as BOB's ambivalence was reflected in the small size of its staff devoted to PPB.

The Pluralist Critique

The challenges confronting program budgeting had received considerable attention from both its advocates and its critics by the time it was formally abandoned. The two groups could be distinguished more by whether they thought PPB could or should be saved in the civilian bureaucracy than by their characterizations of the problems it faced there. Among those critics who thought it was destined to fail, Aaron Wildavsky (1969, 1974) offered what were perhaps the most influential indictments of the process. Wildavsky's contribution was not so much to add to the list of impediments as it was to place them in broader perspective—both empirically and normatively. In so doing, he stressed two concepts that were central to theories of policymaking and administration in American government.

One was *bounded rationality*. First articulated by Herbert Simon (an academic who had helped to develop operations research during World War II), this was posed as a more realistic alternative to *comprehensive rationality* as a strategy for decision making. The latter was a sequential process in which goals were clearly defined and then all feasible alternatives were thoroughly evaluated in terms of their direct and indirect costs and benefits. Even if such an approach was possible in theory, Simon and others argued that its benefits would not outweigh its analytical costs in a complex environment. In the real world, therefore, decision makers "satisficed" in various ways. That is, they relied on strategies of limited search and analysis designed to find solutions that were acceptable as opposed to optimal (Simon 1947).

The other conceptual indictment of PPB was that the criterion of instrumental rationality (whether comprehensive or bounded) simply did not apply to much decision making in the public sector. This was because clear, a priori goals often did not exist as a basis for policy choice. Different people had different values or interests (or at least assigned different weights to competing values). Even the relationship between ends and means was often ambiguous. For example, one legislator might support a NASA contract because of its contribution to the space effort, whereas another one might support it because it brought money to her district. Inherent to the policymaking process in all democracies, these realities were amplified by the fragmentation of institutional power in American government. Although it did not dismiss a consideration of policy effects, therefore, political decision making was often as much the product of "partisan mutual adjustment" (various mechanisms for compromise and logrolling) as of rational analysis. The test of a good decision under these conditions was often simply that people could agree on it (if for different reasons) (Lindblom 1959).

Wildavsky's (1969, 195) critique of program budgeting incorporated both these ideas. As he noted with respect to the difficulties of comprehensive analysis,

> It would have been sufficient to say that the wholesale introduction of PPBS presented insuperable difficulties of calculation. All the obstacles . . . may be summed up in a single statement: *No one knows how to do program budgeting.* Another way of putting it may be to say that many know what program budgeting should be like in general, but no one knows what it should be in any particular case.

And as he noted with respect to the political naïveté of PPB,

> Once the political process becomes a focus of attention, it is evident that the principal participants may not be clear about their goals. What we call goals or objectives may, in large part, be operationally determined by the policies we can agree upon. The mixtures of values found in complex policies may have to be taken in packages, so that policies may determine goals as much as general objectives determine policies. In a political situation, then, the need

for support assumes central importance. Not simply the economic, but the *political* costs and benefits turn out to be crucial. (Wildavsky 1974, 191–92).

Indeed, the thesis of Wildavsky's most influential work, *The Politics of the Budgetary Process* (1974), was expressed in the epigram "Budgeting is politics with dollar signs attached."

Wildavsky's critique of PPB may have targeted the assumptions of its more zealous advocates as opposed to the more nuanced and practical views expressed by people such as Hitch and Enthoven. In any case, he contrasted the ideal world of planning and objective analysis that the theory of program budgeting seemed to promise with the realities of budgeting and policymaking as he saw them. The latter were defined by institutional norms and roles that simplified and lent predictability to the process and facilitated compromise. For example, agencies were expected to be advocates for their budgets, and the appropriations committees in Congress (especially the House) were expected to be guardians of the purse (Wildavsky 1974).

Although it was deemphasized in his later work, the concept of incrementalism was especially important in Wildavsky's writing during the 1960s and 1970s. Similar to Lindblom's (1959) concept of "limited successive comparisons," this was the idea that decision making on expenditures in most areas proceeded from a base established the previous year. Adjustments to this base tended to be relatively small, with any large changes in the allocation of resources taking place gradually over time. Incrementalism was a form of bounded rationality that circumvented the impossible task "redoing things from scratch" based on comprehensive analysis. Given the extreme uncertainty that characterized decision making in complex environments (and given that small errors could have large effects on analytical outcomes), incrementalism also limited the consequences of mistakes. From a political perspective, moreover, it facilitated the accommodation of competing interests by keeping conflict within acceptable bounds.

Wildavsky's critique had as much to do with the normative premises of PPB as with its feasibility. Like other pluralists of the era, he was suspicious of centralized planning in the public interest as a threat to constitutional values. On most issues, at least, the public interest was no more discernible through objective analysis than it was a manifestation of simple majorities or overarching moral imperatives. Rather, it consisted of a *process* that reflected the interplay of group interests and of the various centers of power within government that served as "access points" for those groups. Indeed, the fragmentation of the bureaucracy, which PPB was designed to counter, was a further manifestation of Madisonian democracy. Although Wildavsky felt that analysis could play a salutary role in policymaking, it was not a substitute for politics.

Conclusion

Program budgeting was born of the marriage between the Progressive Era concept of a functional budget and techniques from systems analysis and economics that were developed in the 1930s and 1940s. By evaluating activities in terms of the objectives they serve, it is a tool for management and policymaking that promises to rationalize the allocation of resources and responsibilities across organizational boundaries. As such, its appeal is easy to understand: It is a plausible solution to the inefficiencies associated with the ad hoc creation of programs and agencies in American government.

Instituted at DoD in 1961, PPB was extended to the entire federal government in 1965. It had little impact, however, and was soon abandoned outside DoD. Although scholars offered surprisingly few detailed studies of its implementation, there was no shortage of explanations for its failure. Some observers attributed its demise primarily to bureaucratic inertia and to the lack of needed expertise and resources. Others attributed its failure to more fundamental incompatibilities between comprehensive planning and analysis, on the one hand, and an administrative environment that was defined by bounded rationality and by the fragmentation of interests and institutional authority, on the other.

Yet appealing reforms in public administration seldom disappear permanently, even when they seem to have been thoroughly discredited. Rather, they are relabeled and recycled. This is attributable in part, at least, to our ambivalence regarding the essential character of administration. PPB remains relevant in this regard as an extension of the current emphasis on businesslike efficiency in government. Before examining this issue, however, it is useful to consider the evolution and effects of PPB in the one federal agency where it survived after the early 1970s. As it has been implemented by DoD in recent decades, PPB has diverged in important ways from the principles that were articulated by its architects in the 1960s.

Notes

1. Program budgeting is also often referred to as PPBS—for "planning, programming, budgeting systems." DoD changed the name to planning, programming, budgeting, and execution systems (or PPBES) in 2003 to reflect some (relatively minor) changes that were made in the process under Donald Rumsfeld. In this book, for the sake of simplicity, program budgeting is usually referred to as PPB— for "planning, programming, budgeting."

2. E.g., the New York Bureau of Municipal Research "published a 'sample memorandum' that contained 125 pages of functional accounts and data for the New York City Health Department" in 1907, and the Taft Commission of 1912 eschewed "object-of-expenditure appropriations" in favor of a model budget that "included several functional classifications" (Schick 1966, 16, 21).

3. Today, roughly half of RAND's portfolio consists of issues that are not directly related to national security in the traditional sense. This is reflected in the composition of the faculty that teach in its graduate school of policy analysis. Nevertheless, RAND is still regarded as the leading think tank in defense policy and still works closely with DoD on defense issues.

4. Public Law No. 235, 80th Cong. 61 Stat. 496, 50 U.S.C. chap. 115.

5. In 1949, for example, amendments to the National Security Act strengthened the secretary of defense by increasing the size of his staff and appointing a permanent chairman of the Joint Chiefs of Staff to provide him with advice independent of the individual services.

6. To expect otherwise would arguably have been to dismiss the importance of the services' pride in their missions.

Chapter 3

The Survival and Evolution of Program Budgeting at the Department of Defense

Although little has been written about program budgeting since the early 1970s, it is of more than historical interest for several reasons. Its resurrection in several civilian agencies might be viewed as a natural extension of the performance movement. As will be discussed in subsequent chapters, its viability as a means of planning and coordination speaks to the underlying goals and assumptions of requirements such as the Government Performance and Results Act in ways that have been largely overlooked in recent years. Advocates of performance management typically endorse it as a means of coordination, yet they seldom reveal how coordination is to be accomplished.

Program budgeting is also of interest because its first life never completely came to an end; weak versions have survived in some state and local jurisdictions. Typically these include a program structure and a multiyear budget without incorporating efforts at rigorous, crosscutting analysis. Institutional vestiges of planning, programming, budgeting (PPB) have persisted in a few federal agencies as well. For example, the Office of Systems Analysis (OSA) that was created by the Department of Health, Education, and Welfare to satisfy the requirements of PPB in the 1960s has evolved into the Office of Planning and Development in today's Department of Health and Human Services.

Most germane to the present concerns is the survival of PPB in the Department of Defense (DoD). This is significant if for no other reason than that defense is so important to the nation and that it constitutes such a large share of federal discretionary spending. Given that the reintroduction of PPB to some civilian agencies has occurred primarily at the initiative of people with DoD backgrounds, moreover, its evolution at DoD is directly relevant to its implementation outside that agency.

An obvious question to ask here is why program budgeting survived at DoD and nowhere else. Considering the difficulties it faced in the civilian bureaucracy, it is also appropriate to ask whether PPB was effective at DoD. And insofar as it was effective, has it continued to yield the kinds of results that it produced in its early years? Although the following discussion does not attempt to answer these questions in a thorough or definitive way, one observation seems clear: The current role of headquarters analysts in coordinating policy and resources across DoD's internal boundaries is less vital than it was in the 1960s.

Program budgeting at DoD always had less impact as a formal system than as a venue that allowed policy analysts to advise the secretary on selected issues. Whether or not it was inevitable, the attenuation of this advisory role was precipitated by Robert McNamara's departure. Without his counteractive influence as an executive who understood and supported it, the use of incisive analysis as a management tool fell victim to the organizational inertia and the bureaucratic and political fragmentation that it had been instituted to overcome. These forces are reflected in the institutional character of PPB itself. Although its basic logic and structural elements have changed relatively little, the decision-making process has become much more decentralized and complex.

Why PPB Survived at DoD

Several explanations have been offered for the fact that PPB survived in DoD. One is the availability of people with the knowledge to make the system work. As discussed, the civilian bureaucracy was required to implement PPB in short order and with little in the way of additional resources. Policy analysts were in limited supply at the time, and little thought had been given to how PPB might be applied in most domestic settings (Schick 1973; Wildavsky 1974). In contrast, DoD was able to draw on bright people from the RAND Corporation and elsewhere who had been thinking for years about how functional analysis might address questions of efficiency in national defense. Indeed, some of the issues that these analysts confronted under the authority of PPB had already received considerable attention before the system was introduced at DoD (Novick 1969). As Wildavsky (1969, 191) notes: "The first requisite of program budgeting in defense was a small group of talented people who had spent years developing insights into the special problems of defense strategy and logistics. The second requisite was a common terminology, an accepted collection of analytical approaches, and the beginnings of theoretical statements to guide policy analysis."

Aside from the human resources that DoD could allocate to its implementation, the adoption of PPB was facilitated by the growth of defense spending in the 1960s. This stood in contrast to the resource constraints of many domestic agencies, where competition among programs or program elements was rendered a zero-sum game by the competing fiscal demands of the Vietnam War (Schick 1973). The fact that cost-effectiveness comparisons at DoD were often used as a basis for allocating increments rather than for making budget cuts made PPB more palatable within the organization and among the legislators and other constituents who had stakes in particular units and programs. Notwithstanding its theoretical appeal as a technique for getting more out of the same or less, the impact of crosscutting analysis in DoD and elsewhere has usually been confined to the distribution of additional resources.

DoD's mission was also arguably well suited to PPB. Not only did many domestic activities serve multiple objectives under any conceivable program structure; their contributions to those goals were frequently difficult to measure. Although these problems also existed to some extent in defense policy (e.g., some military bases and other kinds of infrastructure contributed to multiple goals), DoD had a relatively coherent mission that lent itself to the kind of hierarchical ordering that PPB required (Wildavsky 1969; Downs and Larkey 1986). And although actual performance measures were obviously not available for many program elements in defense (thankfully, "outcome measures" for nuclear weapons systems were not available), modeling and other techniques existed that allowed analysts to make educated predictions about the capabilities of weapons systems, combat units, and support structures under various scenarios. Here again, the fact that people had been thinking about these issues for years eased the introduction of program budgeting to DoD (Wildavsky 1969).

In addition, national security policy was implemented primarily by one organization. Although PPB was instituted as a means of consolidating control over the services, the centralization of legal authority in the Office of the Secretary of Defense was also an important precondition for the system to work as intended. This stood in contrast to the neighboring domain of foreign affairs (Schilling 1968) and many areas of domestic policy, where contributions to government's functional objectives were spread across multiple organizations (Meyer 1969). The presidency was the only institution with the authority to attempt to integrate policy in these areas under a PPB system, and the Executive Office of the President lacked the resources and inclination to do so. For example, the Bureau of the Budget (later the Office of Management and Budget) never made a serious effort to standardize PPB, much less use it as a basis for systematic crosscutting analysis (Marvin and Rouse 1970; Schick 1973).

Assuming that hierarchical authority exists to coordinate across organizational boundaries, leaders must also be willing to use that authority in support of PPB. They must be willing to devote adequate resources to its implementation, and they must use the information it generates in making decisions. As Thomas Schilling observed in 1968:

> Systems analysis and other modern techniques of evaluation require a consumer, some responsible person or body that wants an orderly technique for bringing judgment to bear on a decision. PPBS [planning, programming, budgeting systems] works best for an aggressive master; and where there is no master, or where the master wants the machinery to produce his decisions without his own participation, the value of PPBS is likely to be modest and, depending on the people, may even be negative. (Schilling 1968, 27)

Although this support was frequently missing in civilian agencies, where program budgeting was often thrust upon political executives with little knowledge of or appreciation for the process (Wildavsky 1969; Marvin and Rouse 1970; Schick 1973), Robert McNamara was the ideal patron for PPB in DoD. A technocrat to the core by most accounts, he was thoroughly familiar with the process and strongly supportive of his analytical staff (Hitch 1965; Enthoven and Smith 2005).

PPB has far outlasted McNamara, and some of his successors have been much less enthusiastic about it than he was. This helps to explain important changes that have vitiated its managerial role. Given the resistance that naturally accompanies the introduction of new routines (and that initially greeted program budgeting at DoD), however, McNamara's tenure as the longest-serving secretary of defense before or since (1961–68) may have been critical in allowing PPB to take root within DoD. By the same token, the bureaucratic inertia that McNamara had to overcome in the 1960s may have protected program budgeting once it became established in the culture of DoD. Even if PPB is not particularly effective today, for example, adopting a new set of budgeting routines in such a large and complex organization could be more expensive and disruptive than it is worth in agency resources and morale (Jones and McCaffery 2008).

There are other possible explanations as well. The military may be less inclined to resist new requirements because acceptance of authority is such an important element of its culture. Or as Jones and McCaffery (2005) argue, perhaps defense budgeting is simply too important to approach through less systematic means. That is, perhaps the analytical costs of PPB are justified in DoD but not elsewhere because of the size and critical importance of its budget. Some of the foregoing factors are interrelated, of course, and most if not all may help to explain the survival of PPB at DoD.

Evaluating the Effects of Program Budgeting at DoD

To say that PPB has survived at DoD for almost fifty years is not to imply that it has been an unqualified success. Two observations are important here. Although it had some significant effects, program budgeting was never applied across DoD in a comprehensive way. Its impact had much less to do with the formal system it imposed than with the empowerment of a small group of analysts at DoD headquarters. Moreover, the impact of analysis as an aid to management reached its zenith in the 1960s. Many assessments of DoD planning and budgeting in the intervening decades and up until the present stress precisely the problems that PPB was designed to address.

Assessing Its Early Role

Whether program budgeting was "successful" under McNamara depends on one's assumptions about its goals. Although some analysts have argued that the same useful analysis could have been undertaken without the elaborate and resource-intensive structure of PPB (Wildavsky 1969), there is no doubt that it led to a clearer definition of objectives and that it facilitated or at least validated the assessment and comparison of means to those ends on a selective basis. Systems analysis at DoD headquarters reportedly produced more than a hundred draft presidential memorandums (DPMs) analyzing particular programs for the secretary of defense during the 1960s (Enthoven and Smith 2005; Gordon, McNicol, and Jack 2008). These in turn led to the reallocation of resources in some important areas related to both nuclear and conventional preparedness. Without considering the substantive merits of these decisions, accounts by practitioners such as Hitch (1965) and Enthoven and Smith (2005) offer strong arguments that their efforts produced significant efficiencies in the allocation of resources.

At the same time, there is no doubt that PPB fell short of the more ambitious objective, implicit in its design and voiced by some of its more enthusiastic advocates, that it would rationalize DoD's activities across organizational boundaries in a more comprehensive way. This observation is underscored by those who were in the best position to observe the effects of PPB in the McNamara years. Although the architects of program budgeting at DoD obviously believed in the technique and were quick to point out its benefits, their assessments were often refreshingly balanced and objective. Consider the following reflections by Alain Enthoven and K. Wayne Smith, who were respectively the head and special assistant to the head of DoD's OSA between 1961 and 1968. After discussing the theoretical advantages of program budgeting and describing some of its accomplishments, they added that it was a work in progress that had yet to overcome a number of important challenges:

> PPB as it now exists [in DoD] is a good foundation on which to build, but it is by no means complete. Indeed, one of the more desirable aspects of the system is that it has helped to identify additional areas where improvements are needed. Four such problem areas are: (1) the quality and usefulness of analyses; (2) the lack of good cost estimates and test data on new equipment; (3) the lack of an adequate theory of requirements in many areas; and (4)inadequate economic discipline in the services. . . .
>
> While some of the study effort on defense programs has been excellent, much has been relatively poor. Ideally, the large-scale study effort within the services, the Joint Staff, and the major study contract organizations should

provide a base of knowledge which can be drawn on when specific program decisions are being considered. Yet while hundreds or possibly thousands of studies are turned out each year, few of them are of any real value for decisions at the Secretary of Defense level. For example, the number of major studies of total US requirements for tactical air forces by the services and contract study organizations over the last five years must number in the dozens. Many involved large study groups and complex computer models. All came up with conclusions and recommendations. None shed much light on the subject. In fact, what few confident conclusions can be drawn on the subject have come from the development of much simpler analyses and measures, mostly by the Office of the Secretary of Defense staff. (Enthoven and Smith 1970, 492–93)

That informative comparisons of programs and program elements were done only on a selective basis and by a small headquarters staff might be explained in part by the fact that many of DoD's activities did not lend themselves to the kind of linear modeling that made PPB so appealing as a way to assess logistical operations, weapons systems, and other activities that could be linked with discrete missions. Summarizing a joint DoD–GAO study on PPB conducted in 1983, Aaron Wildavsky notes that "a whole host of essential activities are difficult to accommodate within the program framework of PPBS—recruiting, medical care, housing, food, repairs, provisions, on and on. They amount to more than 30 percent of the service budgets" (Wildavsky 1988, 352).

That *good* studies were confined to selected issues under McNamara also reflected the fact that, although DoD had much more expertise at its disposal than most agencies, its capacity was nevertheless small in relation to PPB's ostensible goal of regular and comprehensive planning and analysis. There was no shortage of effort throughout DoD in response to the requirements of PPB; as Enthoven and Smith note, the system produced many studies and reports by the services (and components thereof), the Joint Chiefs of Staff, and various outside contractors. The problem was rather a shortage of high-quality, objective analysis. The professional military often lacked the requisite training, and each of the services naturally tended to produce studies that supported its own missions. Although DoD's Office of Systems Analysis employed talented analysts with DoD-wide perspectives, it was limited in size during the 1960s. This may well have reflected McNamara's preference for an advisory staff that was flexible and responsive to him alone (BENS 2000).

Subsequent Effects

Given Enthoven and Smith's characterization of PPB as a "good foundation on which to build," one might expect the problems that they observed in 1970 to have become less acute as DoD refined the system based on experience. In fact this has not occurred. Although there has been little attention to the subsequent evolution and effects of PPB in the academic literature, there have been numerous assessments of the process by Congress, think tanks, and DoD itself. The clear implication of these analyses is that DoD's planning and budgeting practices have not improved during the intervening decades. For example, an extensive report prepared for the secretary of defense by a Joint Defense Capabilities Study Team (JDCST 2004, 2-2) characterizes the current system as "broken." It concludes that "the Department of Defense may have produced the best armed forces in the world, but its [planning and budgeting] processes do not optimize the investment in joint capabilities to meet current and future security challenges" (JDCST 2004, 4-4). Another study notes that "instead of charting a path to the future, [PPBS] produces results similar to those of the past even during a period of significant strategic and technological change" (BENS 2000, 10).

Other reports prepared in the 1980s, 1990s, and 2000s offer similar assessments. Although a thorough review of these documents is beyond the scope of this chapter, their observations are strikingly consistent. Also striking and perhaps ironic is the degree to which their characterizations of DoD planning and financial management mirror the indictments that led to the institution of program budgeting. Efforts to place PPB in historical perspective thus conclude that it has substantially atrophied as a management tool since the 1960s (BENS 2000; Gordon, McNicol, and Jack 2008). Leaving the institutional determinants of this trend aside until later in the chapter, the following paragraphs summarize the principal critiques of PPB during the past three decades. Among the chronic problems identified are poor accounting practices, inadequate goals and performance measures, parochial service orientations and lack of coordination, and lack of discipline and incremental decision making.

Poor Accounting Practices

The most frequent and widely publicized criticisms of management in DoD focus on its cost-accounting and business practices. For example, a GAO study notes that "DoD faces a range of financial management and related business process challenges that are complex, long-standing, pervasive, and deeply rooted in virtually all business operations throughout the department," and that these challenges "have resulted in billions of dollars in annual wasted resources in a time of increasing fiscal constraint" (Kutz and Rhodes 2004, 6).

Other government studies arrive at similar conclusions, sometimes on the basis of detailed case studies examining financial practices across areas ranging from housing allowances to depot maintenance to force modernization (e.g., Bowsher 1983). A common theme is DoD's inability to anticipate accurately the full costs over time of weapons systems and other large expenditures for facilities and equipment. Another is its failure to account for the money that it does spend. As one study notes, "Further evidence of DOD's problems is the long-standing inability of any military service or major defense component to pass the test of an independent financial audit because of pervasive weaknesses in financial management systems, operations, and controls" (Kutz and Rhodes 2004, 3).

Studies have found that discretionary transfers of funds from one fiscal period to another and from one purpose to another as budgets are being executed pose especially important problems of transparency and control. Citing numerous examples of "reprogramming," one report to Congress notes that "funding requests are justified to Congress for specific purposes; authorizing and appropriations acts identify amounts approved for specific accounts and in some cases programs within accounts. However, each year millions of dollars are not spent for the purposes budgeted" (Bowsher 1983, vi). Twenty years later, another GAO report concluded that DoD "has not developed systems that can sufficiently track the movement of funds. For example, DOD does not have reports to show how it used much of the $47 billion appropriated from fiscal years 1999 through 2001 that it moved among or into its operation maintenance accounts" (Walker 2003, 12). Assessments have also found that DoD's data systems lack consistency and vary a great deal in quality and in the type and detail of information they provide. As one notes, "At the military units we visited, the methods [used to inventory similar types of items] . . . ranged from automated information systems, to spreadsheet applications, to paper, to dry erase board, to none" (Kutz and Warren 2002, 3).

DoD's business and accounting practices are frequently cited as an invitation to waste and corruption, especially with regard to its relations with the private sector. Particularly relevant to the present concerns is that poor accounting also limits DoD's ability to plan and allocate resources in a rational way. Without accurate information on how much things cost, that is, DoD obviously cannot assess and compare their cost-effectiveness. As another report described the problem:

> A continuing inability to capture and report the full cost of its programs represents one of the most significant impediments facing DOD. DOD does not have the systems and processes in place to capture the required cost information from hundreds of millions of transactions it processes each year. Lacking complete and accurate life-cycle cost information for weapons systems impairs DOD's and congressional decision makers' ability to make fully informed judgments on funding comparable weapon systems. (Walker 2003, 13)

Inadequate Goals and Performance Measures

Assessments of DoD's planning and budgeting processes also frequently cite deficiencies on the output side. Critics thus have faulted DoD for its failure to develop better indicators of program success. Summarizing the findings of a study that looked across the organization, GAO observes that "DOD does not generally establish budget criteria in terms of outputs, such as increased performance or capability" and that "expected achievement is rarely, if ever, the basis for budget justification" (Bowsher 1983, 90, 92). Subsequent reports by GAO and other entities have arrived at similar conclusions, sometimes expressing frustration at the lack of progress in developing performance measures.

Of course, it is impossible to measure success in the absence of a priori standards. Although the purpose of PPB is to provide such criteria through planning and the articulation of a program structure, critics also cite deficiencies there. An extensive examination of planning, resourcing, and execution commissioned by DoD itself found that "strategic objectives and joint needs" tended to be expressed in terms of "specific platforms and systems" and not in terms of "outcomes (what is to be accomplished)" (JDCST 2004, 2-1). As is discussed below, DoD's failure to develop clear and concise objectives that can serve as a basis for evaluating its activities is attributable in part to the decentralization of the planning process under PPB. The same report notes that program assessment and integration were inhibited by the fact that DoD's objectives are conveyed in numerous documents, many of which are outdated or contradictory (JDCST 2004, 2-3).

Parochial Service Orientations and Lack of Coordination

DoD's failure to develop clear means–ends linkages has also been a source of concern for Congress, which has felt obliged in some cases to perform the kind of crosscutting analysis that PPB is supposed to furnish (Robb 1996–97; BENS 2000). Referring to the elimination and redistribution of proposed funding for the F-22 fighter, for example, a former DoD official notes that "if PPBS was working as it should, it should not have fallen to the House of Representatives to ask this question or raise this issue about tactical aviation modernization" (BENS 2000, 6). The same individual added that the planning issues surrounding the F-22 were obvious and that the Office of the Secretary of Defense (OSD) should have foreseen them, "even if the Air Force, for equally obvious reasons did not" (BENS 2000, 6). As this statement implies, one would not expect the air force voluntarily to relinquish its largest procurement program given the realities of human nature and organizational behavior. As it also concludes, however, PPB did not perform its essential role of transcending service loyalties to coordinate the allocation of resources based on department-wide, functional criteria.

Charges of parochialism that is grounded in traditional service missions and priorities are, in fact, ubiquitous in critiques of DoD planning and budgeting. As the 2004 Joint Defense Capabilities Study Team (JDCST) Report characterizes the process:

> The Services dominate planning for capabilities, even when those capabilities are inherently joint and specifically support the CoComs [the major Combatant Commands that encompass all U.S. military forces in particular regions of the world]. Historically, the services have defined the needs, developed the alternatives, and selected and resourced the solutions. These actions are typically accomplished in a stovepiped fashion, with minimal consideration of cross-Service trades or multi-Service efficiencies. . . .
>
> The Services were primarily responsible for creating mission need statements within their assigned domains. Needs that were uniquely joint were slow to be identified and filled when no specific Service had responsibility. In some cases, joint needs were incongruent with the Services' strategic direction or they competed with the Service priorities and were therefore ignored (JDCST 2004, 2-4).

In much the same vein, a GAO report completed in the same year concludes that "cultural resistance to change, military service parochialism, and stovepiped operations have all contributed significantly to the failure of previous attempts to implement broad-based management reforms at DOD. The department has acknowledged that it confronts decades-old problems deeply grounded in the bureaucratic history and operating practices of a complex, multifaceted organization and that many of these practices were developed piecemeal and evolved to accommodate different organizations, each with its own policies and procedures" (Kutz and Rhodes 2004, 13).

Critics of DoD's fragmented planning processes do not hope for a millennium in which the services willingly sacrifice their interests for the greater good. Such prescriptions are viewed as unrealistic and as abandoning the natural advantages of organizational competition. Proposals for reform instead generally prescribe a more centralized process characterized by more focused needs assessment and by clearer and more timely guidance from the secretary of defense (as informed by more meaningful input from the Combatant Commands) that can serve as a basis for formulating and evaluating service proposals. Although OSD staff spend considerable time and effort evaluating program objective memorandums, this allegedly occurs at such a late stage and is so poorly focused that those recommendations are largely faits accomplis.

That said, indictments of parochialism in defense planning and budgeting also frequently identify DoD headquarters staff as part of the problem rather than as a source of more effective integration. Thus, the distinctive perspectives and interests of functional offices at the departmental level are cited as a further impediment to planning and coordination under PPB (JDCST 2004). As a report prepared for DoD in 1995 noted, the role of OSD staff has become blurred because that staff has acquired an increasingly functional orientation. In other words, many of the OSD staff offices now focus primarily on what is being done in their broad functional areas (such as logistics, personnel management, etc.) at the expense of their primary role of providing objective advice to the Secretary. This makes integration of the defense program more difficult and constrains the Department's ability to adjust and respond to new missions. (Commission on Roles and Missions of the Armed Forces 1995, 4-3).

Lack of Discipline and Incremental Decision Making

Given the above-noted characterizations of the process, it is not surprising that accounts of DoD's implementation of PPB find that it has not yielded the results that it is designed to produce. In theory, program budgeting promotes efficiency by ensuring that decision making is informed by realistic assumptions about available resources. In practice, such constraints are brought to bear so late by the OSD that they have little effect as a basis for rational planning. As the JDCST Report notes,

> the resourcing process focuses senior leadership effort on fixing problems at the end of the process rather than being involved early in the planning process. OSD programming guidance exceeds available resources and does not provide realistic priorities for joint needs. "Jointness" is forced into the program late in the process during an adversarial and time-consuming program review. The resulting program does not best meet joint needs, or provide the best value for the nation's defense investment. (JDCST 2004, iii)

Incremental decision making is the alternative to resource-constrained planning and analysis based on a priori goals (Lindblom 1959). Thus, virtually all critiques of PPB characterize DoD budgeting as a process in which spending for organizations and programs proceeds from an established base and tends to change relatively little from one year to the next. One of these studies notes that the purpose of analysis under PPB is not to compare the cost-effectiveness of activities but to justify requests for additional funding on a program-by-program basis. In so doing, "DOD has historically *measured* its performance by resource components such as the amount of money spent, people employed, or number of tasks completed" (emphasis added) (Kutz and Rhodes 2004, 18). Another study concludes that "there remains the concern that the continuing consistency of the resource percentages allocated to the services . . . suggests a chronic inability of the current PPBS process to significantly reshape the defense program across the well-defined service 'stovepipes.' If true, this suggests that PPBS has provided less strategic direction than expected" (BENS 2000, 10).

These observations are consistent with the findings of one of the few recent academic studies of PPB, which was written by two professors from the Naval War College. This is easily the most detailed description of budgeting and financial management in DoD to date. Although their intent is not to criticize or reform the system, Jones and McCaffery (2008) repeatedly emphasize its incremental character:

> In the main, the process is incremental, historical, and reactive. (p. 83)

> [General David] Jones . . . suggested that because of the decentralized and fragmented resource allocation process driven by parochial service loyalties,

there was always more program than budget to buy it; that the focus was always on service programs; that changes were always marginal when perhaps better analysis would have led to more sweeping changes; that it was impossible to focus on critical cross-service needs; and the result was that the amalgamation of service needs prevailed. (p. 144)

Participants . . . count on the products they are expected to produce not changing dramatically from one year to the next and they know that if they wait until the official guidance there will not be enough time to meet the deadlines and still produce a product that will allow them to compete advantageously for programs and funds. (p. 447)

Diminished Impact

Current descriptions of DoD planning and budgeting bear little resemblance to program budgeting in theory, and the coordinative role of PPB has atrophied substantially since the 1960s. Although it was never used to rationalize the allocation of resources in a systematic way, centralized analysis had significant effects in selected areas under McNamara (Hitch 1965; Enthoven and Smith 2005). A veteran DoD analyst was lamenting the weakening if not the disappearance of this role when he remarked that "very little is left of the truly penetrating history of PPB." He added that "PPB [as it was originally understood and implemented] may be dead."

Part of the explanation for PPB's diminished impact may be that the low-hanging fruit was picked early on. Analysts came to DoD from the RAND Corporation and elsewhere with preexisting agendas, at least some components of which had already received considerable attention. Thus, perhaps the substantive changes that PPB facilitated in the 1960s resulted in a distribution of resources that was about right (or about as good as it could be within the confines of political and managerial constraints), establishing a framework that would only require incremental adjustments in the future.

Yet although the rate of organizational change that results from the introduction of any new management system is likely to diminish over time, this cannot fully account for the weaknesses in comprehensive planning and crosscutting analysis that are widely alleged to characterize DoD budgeting today. The most obvious limitation of this explanation is that it can only be valid to the extent that DoD operates within a static task environment. In fact, the observation that the strategic and tactical parameters of national defense planning are vastly different (and much more fluid and complex) today than they were in the bipolar era when PPB was introduced often reinforces criticisms of the department's fragmented and incremental decision making.

Without arguing that the planning and budgeting processes of the 1960s would be a panacea for DoD's current challenges—and without endorsing McNamara's wisdom as a leader in a more general sense—it is apparent that PPB has evolved in ways that have made it less viable as a mechanism for adaptive planning and budgeting. As one recent study notes:

Are decisions made "based upon explicit criteria of national interest?" Satisfying this objective requires the creation and articulation of "explicit criteria." Although Secretary McNamara felt that he and his staff provided clear guidance to the services, over time specific guidance regarding specific actions, outcome expectations, and priorities has greatly diminished. The planning process produces few such explicit criteria, and when it does, . . . they are rarely met. (BENS 2000, 7)

The most important organizational developments that have undermined the effectiveness of PPB might be subsumed under two broad and interrelated changes: decentralization and increased complexity. These have been reinforced by (and to some extent have resulted from) changes in the environment of defense policymaking and budgeting. Particularly important has been the increased fragmentation and specificity of congressional involvement in the process.

Decentralization and Fragmentation

PPB was a primary means through which Robert McNamara sought to consolidate control over the services in the OSD. As Schilling notes, "Secretary McNamara surely did not use PPBS and other techniques of financial management merely to cut waste and improve efficiency or to save money. He took advantage of his central role in the defense-budgeting process to exercise what he believed to be his authority over military policy" (Schilling 1968, 29).

This goal was shared by John Kennedy, just as it had been expressed by his predecessor, Dwight Eisenhower. Yet although a stronger role for the OSD was endorsed in other quarters as well, it was opposed by many senior members of the officer corps who enjoyed the support of powerful politicians. As Gordon, McNicol, and Jack (2008) observe in a brief but insightful history, many of the early complaints about PPB by the uniformed military were directed through their allies in Congress rather than through the executive chain of command.

One source of resistance to PPB was the long-standing tradition of service autonomy and the dispersal of political power (within the legislative committee system as well as the military bureaucracy) that accompanied it. As with the attempt to apply PPB in the civilian bureaucracy, the potential for the process to reallocate resources threatened "subgovernments" in which legislators and DoD officials served and were served by private interests (e.g., defense contractors and businesses near military bases). Another source of resistance was the difficulty of adopting complex new routines, especially when their practical effect was to alter the rules of the game in such a way as to shift policymaking influence from senior officers (most of whom were ill prepared to participate in arguments based on policy analysis) to civilians with little military experience. Hostility on the latter score was reinforced by the youth and arrogance of some of the analysts who had been recruited to implement PPB. This resentment was reflected in one US representative's hyperbolic characterization of the director of systems analysis under McNamara (Alain Enthoven) as "the most dangerous man in the country" (Gordon, McNicol, and Jack 2008, 8). The tension between PPB and the perspectives of the professional military both added to and was exacerbated by a more general antipathy toward the Kennedy administration by prominent members of the officer corps.

The backlash against McNamara's management system was also manifested in Richard Nixon's 1968 campaign promise to remove the "Whiz Kids" (systems analysts) from the Pentagon and in proposed legislation to eliminate the OSA. Although these changes did not come to pass, it was a year before a replacement was appointed to head the OSA after Enthoven's departure from that post in January 1969. President Nixon's secretary of defense, Melvin Laird, also delegated a good deal of the authority that had been centralized in the OSD under McNamara's version of PPB back to the individual services. Laird had been highly skeptical about the value of systems analysis at DoD while he was a member of Congress in the 1960s, and he strongly believed in returning discretion for policymaking and budgeting to the service secretaries (Gordon, McNicol, and Jack 2008). As he said, "Many decisions should be made by the service secretaries and they should have the responsibilities for running their own programs. I have no business being involved in how many 20-millimeter guns should go on a destroyer. That is the Secretary of the Navy's business. I must let the services take a greater role" (Jones and McCaffery 2008, 143).

Subsequent secretaries of defense have varied in their enthusiasm (or lack thereof) for PPB and in their desire to coordinate defense policy more generally (e.g., the Carter administration made significant if largely ineffective efforts to revitalize the process). That said, none have come close to replicating McNamara's efforts to centralize and rationalize the allocation of resources across services through policy analysis. In fact, each of the services has been given substantial latitude to develop its own PPB system, with the result that the structures and cultures that define the process vary in significant ways (Jones and McCaffrey 2008). Although a detailed discussion of how PPB has evolved is beyond the present scope, several general and interrelated changes have contributed to its erosion as a means of centralized management: a return to fixed bases for the services, a weaker role for DoD's office of systems analysis, and inclusiveness.

A Return to Fixed Bases for the Services

PPB was designed to replace a system in which individual services began with fixed shares of the total defense budget and in which the allocation of increments or decrements was determined primarily through bargaining among institutional actors. The secretary acted more as a referee than a policy leader under this system. Although McNamara sought to remedy this through PPB, Jones and McCaffery note that the operational concept of fixed bases was reintroduced in the early 1970s and persists to this day:

> Laird [President Nixon's secretary of defense] . . . returned to the use of service programs and budget ceilings (fixed shares) and required services to program within these ceilings. The concept of ceilings or "top-line" endured for most of the next 40 years and still influences DoD budget requests today, as services are expected to balance their program and budget against the TOA [total obligational authority] they are given at various stages of the planning and budget process. (2008, 143)

A Weaker Role for DoD's Office of Systems Analysis

The major decisions that were made under the auspices of PPB in the 1960s were driven by analysts in the OSD. (According to some veteran analysts at DoD, Enthoven enjoyed such a close relationship with McNamara that he spent two to three hours per day with the secretary during the programming phase of PPB.) The most important products of the analyses conducted at the departmental level were the DPMs that articulated the secretary's policy and budgeting advice (and the rationale for it) to the president within selected program areas. These provided clear criteria for planning and resource allocation, the impact of which was underscored by the fact that they were prepared for the commander in chief (Enthoven and Smith 2005). Although DPMs were vetted with the services, this occurred at a relatively late stage of the process, after OSD staff had developed detailed and well-supported recommendations. Appeals by the services reportedly did not fare well with McNamara (Gordon, McNicol, and Jack 2008).

DPMs were eliminated in the 1970s and replaced by program objective memorandums (POMs) that were prepared by the individual services. POMs remain the most important documents among many produced by program budgeting at DoD. This development has been accompanied by a dramatic expansion in the size and competence of the services' analytical staffs. Moreover, service chiefs have assumed much stronger control over their subordinates' involvement in PPB. Systems analysts in DoD headquarters often communicated directly with service analysts and midlevel managers under McNamara, and the recommendations contained in DPMs often came as a surprise to service secretaries and senior officers as a result (Gordon, McNicol, and Jack 2008). Since the 1970s, the services have exercised much more effective control over the flow of information.

Some observers have suggested that the decentralization of programming responsibility has led to a greater acceptance of or even an appreciation for PPB among the military as a means of justifying programs and program elements. Certainly, it has enhanced the careers of officers who have mastered the skills needed to participate effectively in the process (Jones and McCaffery 2008; Gordon, McNicol, and Jack 2008). Not surprisingly, the uniformed military has nurtured the development of planning and budgeting expertise among its own as a counter to the influence of civilian analysts in defense policymaking. Obviously, however, the analysis conducted for POMs is largely for the purpose of institutional advocacy as opposed to the objective comparison of activities across institutions. PPB is a competitive system, albeit for marginal increments in most cases.

POMs are reviewed and consolidated at the departmental level, of course, and systems analysts in the OSD are central to that process. Yet the power to offer initial proposals is critical in decision making, and the substitution of POMs for DPMs represents an abdication of the initiative that the latter gave to the OSD. The role of OSD staff thus has changed from a proactive to a reactive one that focuses on relatively small details as opposed to broad policy issues. Although the internal dynamics of DoD decision making are not readily accessible, moreover, circumstantial evidence suggests that system analysts at the departmental level have lost a good deal of the influence that they had under McNamara. It may be instructive that, in their 717-page treatise, Jones and McCaffery (2008) give little attention to the current organization, culture, and activities of the Office of Program Analysis and Evaluation (formerly OSA). This, despite the fact that the authors go into considerable detail in describing the roles of other actors in the process.

The post-McNamara decline in the influence of systems analysis might also be inferred from the position of that office within DoD's hierarchy. Upon his departure from DoD in 1965, Charles Hitch was responsible for moving Alain Enthoven out of the Office of the Comptroller (which Hitch headed) and for simultaneously elevating him from a director to an assistant secretary whose immediate superior was the secretary of defense. Among the reasons for this was Hitch's (prescient) desire to protect the OSA in the event that a future comptroller or secretary might be less sympathetic to its mission. During the 1970s, however, the head of OSA—which was renamed the Office of Policy Analysis and Evaluation (PA&E) in 1973—was demoted and elevated four times. The last change was the reduction of PA&E to its current status as a directorate in 1981 (Gordon, McNichol, and Jack 2008).

Inclusiveness

Notwithstanding its goal of centralization, openness (within DoD) and opportunities for stakeholder participation were guiding principles of the system of program budgeting established at DoD in the 1960s. DPMs were submitted to the Joint Chiefs of Staff (JCS) and to the services for their review and feedback, for example, and Program Change Proposals allowed components of DoD to suggest and justify alterations in five-year plans for consideration by the other services and the secretary. As a matter of degree, however, PPB has become considerably more fragmented in terms of the institutional actors that play significant roles in the process. The challenges that this has posed for planning and coordination have been reinforced by DoD's failure to provide early guidance to focus their input.

The increasingly pluralistic and decentralized character of PPB is attributable in part to the competitive nature of budgeting and the resultant need to include all relevant organizational interests in the decision-making process. As Jones and McCaffery (2008, 191) note: "The PPBS process expanded continually since the 1960s to include more participants in program and budget decision making because resource competition is the crux of the political process. As such, more and more players were successful in finding roles that permitted them to compete for a piece of the budget action."

This dynamic has both resulted from and been reinforced by the increased differentiation of DoD itself. As has happened throughout the federal bureaucracy, staff offices and advisory bodies have been added in response to the demands of an increasingly complex policymaking environment. Among the key developments have been

- The establishment of the Defense Systems Acquisitions Review Committee in 1969 and the supporting Cost Analysis Improvement Group in 1972 to help control cost overruns on weapons systems that had become increasingly problematic during the 1960s (despite the long-range planning orientation of PPB, which was designed to counteract such problems) (Gordon, McNichol, and Jack 2008).
- The addition or strengthening of headquarters positions with specific functional responsibilities. These have included the director of research and engineering, assistant secretaries for intelligence and telecommunications (combined in 1983), the assistant secretary for manpower and reserve affairs, and the assistant secretary for health affairs. As Gordon, McNichol, and Jack (2008, 14) note, "Increasingly, these offices assumed, at least in part, the role of spokesmen to the secretary for their communities. The responsibility for analysis and the manpower to do it were transferred from PA&E to the new elements. In most cases, the analytic capability atrophied quickly, its products not being serviceable for advocacy."
- The creation of separate systems and sets of actors for formulating and reviewing DoD's operations and acquisitions budgets. As a result, consolidated review and coordination of these two components of defense spending occur only at a high level and at a relatively late stage in the process. This bifurcation of functions violates the PPB principle that all of the resources that contribute to a given objective should be considered as an integrated whole.

The Goldwater-Nichols Department of Defense Reorganization Act of 1986 introduced other structural changes that added to the list of stakeholders that play significant roles in the implementation of PPB. Among the provisions of this sweeping and complex legislation were requirements that strengthened the advisory authority and resources of the JCS. Goldwater-Nichols specifically "identified important phases in the PPBS process where the JCS would set requirements and review the plans of other players" (Jones and McCaffery 2008, 145). At the same time, the legislation created a new operational command structure that bypassed the JCS. Unified commanders in chief (now called Combatant Commands), who were responsible for integrated military operations in particular regions of the world, thus reported directly to the secretary of defense and were not dependent on the heads of the individual services for the resources needed to accomplish their missions. Perforce, they assumed roles in PPB. These included the review of POMs as well as the prerogative to submit their own program change proposals (which in turn would be reviewed by the other participants in the process).

A complete discussion of the various actors with significant roles in PPB would be much longer. The more general point is that, although it exists for understandable reasons, a system of participatory management that attempts to give expression to the competing perspectives and interests that exist within such a massive organization is antithetical to the hierarchical ordering of goals that is the essence of program budgeting. One paper illustrates this tension with a quotation from a DoD press release describing deliberations on the Theater Ballistic Missile Defense Program:

> On 26 October, the Joint Requirements Oversight Council (JROC) reviewed ongoing Office of the Secretary of Defense (OSD), Joint theater Air Missile Defense Organization (JTAMDO), and Ballistic Missile Defense Organization (BMDO) alternative analysis efforts to the BMDO Program Objective Memorandum (POM). OSD Program Analysis and Evaluation (PA&E) presented an information briefing on the ongoing Theater Ballistic Missile Defense (TBMD) Family of Systems analysis in support of the Program Review Group (PRG) process. OSD, JTAMDO, and BMDO are examining the acquisition, architecture, and procurement issues of the PMDO POM. The emerging results are being briefed to the Services during the weekly PRG issue team meetings (BENS 2000, 9).

The study goes on to note that "this statement certainly suggests the possibility of too many players, with too many perspectives, and too many differing assumptions. If the intent of such efforts is to develop alternatives for the secretary of defense, such an effort is more likely to confuse than to clarify his understanding of the real issues involved and options available" (BENS 2000, 9).

In theory, PPB uses broad stakeholder participation as a basis for planning and coordination. Its purpose is to help ensure that no relevant considerations are overlooked. In practice, efforts to transform disparate perspectives into coherent objectives at the departmental level are difficult and time consuming. They are further limited by the fact that they occur late in the process, when there is little time left to resolve differences and after the positions of participants have hardened as the result of sunk costs in supporting analysis and intra-service conflict resolution. (Again, presidential decision memoranda that provided an initial set of evaluative criteria for participation under McNamara were replaced by a less centralized system that ceded the planning initiative to the services.) Centralized coordination is also limited by the need to resolve specific (but related) issues on a piecemeal basis. There is no guarantee that the serial results of bargaining and compromise will be informed by cohesive objectives.

Increased Bureaucratization and Complexity

A closely related change in PPB has been a tremendous expansion in the number of staff involved in its implementation. As a seasoned manager who undoubtedly understood the tendency of large organizations to become rigid and unresponsive, McNamara preferred a small and agile group of analysts that could adapt to changing circumstances and that would be dedicated only to his interests. This helps to explain the earlier observation that there were many fewer systems analysts and budgeters in DoD headquarters during the 1960s than there are today. As PA&E has grown and has become more bureaucratized, it has naturally developed its own institutional interests and perspectives that are distinct from those of the secretary of defense. Even greater growth has occurred in the analytical staffs of the individual services and of the various other entities (described above) that have been given significant roles in PPB (BENS 2000; Gordon, McNicol, and Jack 2008).

As the number of offices and individuals involved in PPB has expanded, the process has become more formal and more complex as a way to accommodate their input. The current bureaucratization of PPB is evident from a perusal of the various flow charts that the services and DoD have produced to describe the process and provide guidance for its implementation. One of many possible illustrations is a foldout diagram contained in a handbook for senior leaders produced by the US Army War College (1999, 9–29), "Events of the Biennial PPBS/PPBES Cycle," which is organized by a timeline across the top and by levels in the decision-making hierarchy of the army and DoD on the vertical axis. The diagram contains ninety boxes, circles, ovals, and other geometrical shapes, the great majority of which represent separate documents that must be generated at various stages of the process. These are interconnected by sixty-six lines and arrows, most of which represent a requirement for one set of actors to respond to something that another set of actors has produced. Beneath the figure is a glossary of the fifty-one acronyms that are contained within the diagram.

Other documents could be cited that are similar in their complexity but that vary in their specifics. As mentioned, each of the services has had the discretion to develop its own, somewhat distinctive system of PPB, and even within services one can find documents that describe the process in different ways. As one more illustration, figure 3.1 was included in a presentation given by a senior analyst at DoD headquarters. The fact that it is much less detailed than the Army War College diagram cited above allows for its reproduction here.

Diagrams and standard operating procedures from the 1960s are not available that allow for a comparison of the mechanics of PPB then and now. Yet although program budgeting was certainly criticized in its early years for the amount of reporting and other kinds of red tape it required, veteran analysts from DoD are confident that the actual decision-making process has become much more complex and convoluted over the intervening decades. One individual notes that—whatever the appearance of PPB on paper—Charles Hitch and Alain Enthoven were elegant thinkers who "despised complexity." Like the decentralization of PPB, the bureaucratization of the process has detracted from its incisiveness as a management tool. As the BENS report summarizes the problem: "Rather than conduct detailed planning when needed, DoD's planning tends to be rather vague but rigidly regular. Rather than focusing on major issues, DoD staff tends to tackle a wide array of issues that are minor and that could be left with little impact to . . . the individual services" (BENS 2000, 14).

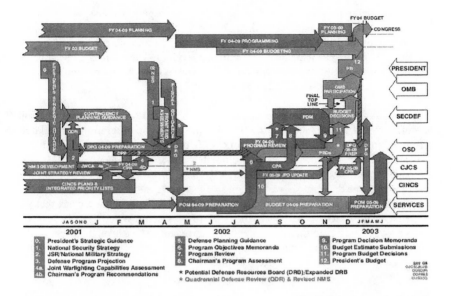

Figure 3.1. The Defense PPB System
Source: Office of Program Analysis and Evaluation (Office of the Secretary of Defense).

The proliferation of staff, documents, and clearances in PPB reflects the natural tendency for bureaucracy to expand and to develop increasingly detailed and formalized rules governing almost any activity (e.g., Downs 1967). These developments are also obviously intertwined with the increasingly decentralized and inclusive character of the process. In addition to noting the return of planning initiative to the services after McNamara's departure, a thoughtful DoD analyst stressed the introduction of additional "assistant secretaries with their own missions and bases of congressional support" as a factor that contributed to the bureaucratization of PPB. To the extent that complexity had been generated by the individual services, moreover, the same individual felt that it reflected the desire to protect their base resources by insulating decision making from effective review. As such, it was a strategically designed instrument of incremental budgeting (especially given the limited time frame for completing the PPB process). Offering a more charitable interpretation of the motives behind incrementalism, another official felt that the increased bureaucratization of PPB was intended to prevent the mistakes that might result from more synoptic decision-making strategies. As he noted, "We seem to have developed a bureaucratic process designed not to let anything bad happen too quickly. Of course, it doesn't allow anything good to happen too quickly either" (BENS 2000, 9).

Whatever the explanations for its complexity, the current PPB process has so many interrelated stages, documents, and moving parts that even veteran participants may not be able to understand how its components fit together. As Jones and McCaffery observe:

PPBES has four distinct phases, with each phase overlapping the other phases. . . . Because the interrelationships are so complex, players in each phase attempt to stay informed on issues in their respective phases as well as issues in other phases affecting them. However, the size of DoD and the complexity of the PPBES process render this virtually impossible. It is difficult enough for the participants in one military service to keep abreast of what is happening in their own process, much less what is done in other branches of the military. (Jones and McCaffery 2008, 147–48)

Jones and McCaffery are referring to the cognitive challenges that confront military officers and civilian employees with full-time planning, programming, and budgeting responsibilities. Understanding the PPB process is an even more daunting challenge for the DoD executives who ultimately make policy decisions. With characteristic tactfulness, Secretary of Defense Donald Rumsfeld offered the following assessment of the diagram shown in figure 3.1 in a 2002 memorandum to the undersecretaries, service secretaries, and chairman of the JCS: "Attached is a chart that was used in a briefing recently to explain the [DoD] PPB system. When I saw it, I asked if it was a joke. It turns out that it is apparently not meant to be a joke. It struck me that those of us in the Senior Review Group ought to think about whether maybe it is a joke, even though it is not intended to be one."

The Role of Congress

Whatever its strengths or weaknesses, PPB only furnishes recommendations to be acted upon by DoD's political principals. It is important to add in this regard that, although Congress has often been critical of DoD's planning and financial management, the fragmentation and complexity that have limited the effectiveness of those processes within the department have been reinforced by similar developments in Congress. To some extent, in fact, the former has been an organizational adaptation to the later.

One should take care not to exaggerate the degree to which Congress has ever spoken with a common voice on defense policy (or practically any other issue). At the time PPB was instituted, however, DoD authorization and appropriation decision making was influenced to a greater extent by a group of legislative elites who were able to approach issues with a more coherent perspective (Jones and McCaffery 2008). Since the 1970s, congressional involvement has become much more diffuse. As Jones and McCaffery (2008, 81) note:

In the 1950s, the defense budget was composed and reviewed in approximately 6 committees. By the mid-1960s, the number had expanded to 10 (Wildavsky 1988). Since then, there has been a proliferation of committees involved in defense policymaking and budgeting. Now, defense policy and budget hearings are held in approximately 28 different committees and subcommittees. This includes the full appropriations committees and five subcommittees (military construction, defense, energy, and water, HUD (Department of Housing and Urban Development), and the independent agencies, and commerce, justice, and state), the Budget Committees and the committees on armed services, commerce, energy, government affairs, select intelligence, small business, and veterans affairs of their analogs in each chamber.

The proliferation of legislative actors involved in defense policymaking and budgeting has resulted in part from institutional changes that have weakened (but hardly eliminated) the power of seniority and that have strengthened subcommittees at the expense of committee chairs. This development has no doubt been intertwined with a more general expansion in the number and diversity of constituent groups that have a perceived stake in various aspects of defense policy.

Congressional input also became much more specific during the same time frame. As Robert Art (1985) suggests, increased legislative attention to the details of defense policy and spending may reflect a general skepticism about executive power that took root during the Nixon administration. Not only has Congress had reservations about the substance of presidential initiatives in many areas; it also became increasingly concerned with the need to guard its own policymaking prerogatives against executive encroachment (West and Cooper 1989). Increased detail has also been a natural by-product of more fragmented legislative involvement, as different actors have sought to ensure that their interests are not overlooked.

The increased fragmentation of legislative input and the increased specificity of legislative output have been antithetical to the kind of broad analysis and planning that PPB seeks to furnish. As Art (1985, 228) notes:

> Financial and programmatic oversight deal, respectively, with the efficiency with which funds are being spent and with how effectively *particular programs* [my italics] are being managed. Policy oversight deals with the larger questions of whether particular programs are needed, how they serve the specific missions the Pentagon has delineated, and with whether those missions and the strategies they in turn serve are sensible. Both financial and programmatic oversight focus on the individual building blocks of the defense budget; policy oversight, on how all the blocks fit together. In my judgment, the congressional treatment of defense has suffered from so great a preoccupation with next year's budget that it has tended to crowd out consideration of the more basic questions and the longer term perspective.

Although Congress was never a good customer for PPB, it is certainly not a good one now. Moreover, its increased unwillingness to defer to the executive undermines the likelihood that even a viable PPB process could ultimately have much of a substantive effect on defense policy and spending.

Summary and Discussion

In light of the problems it encountered elsewhere, why has program budgeting survived at DoD for almost fifty years? One explanation may be that DoD's cohesive mission is compatible with the hierarchical logic of PPB. The multiyear planning orientation of PPB may also be especially appealing at DoD because of the extreme expense and long-term commitments associated with weapons systems and other investments (Jones and McCaffery 2005). Alternatively, perhaps PPB's survival is attributable to the fact that organizational arrangements tend to persist once they become established (Kaufman 1976). Program budgeting has become part of DoD's culture and has generated its own set of institutional stakeholders, some of whom believe strongly in its virtues. Interestingly, however, those who become adept in its use often view it not as a technique for getting more out of less but as a way to justify expenditures. There is a belief within the military that PPB can be credited for DoD's budgetary success over the years.

It is important to add that no one has suggested a compelling alternative to PPB that would justify the disruptions that would accompany its replacement. In fact, PPB may be the best that DoD can do. Although it is easy enough to criticize defense planning and budgeting, one should not expect anything approaching perfection in such a large and complex organization. If nothing else, PPB provides a framework of procedures, information, and role expectations that lends stability and predictability to the process. Its program structure also undoubtedly provides senior leaders with a clearer understanding of how DoD's components relate to its mission and to one another in a functional sense (Schlesinger 1997). And although PPB requires a great deal of time and effort, the resources it consumes are a minuscule portion of the defense budget.

With the caveat that success or failure is always dependent on one's choice of objectives, however, it is clear that PPB never lived up to its promise. It has never been used to rationalize the allocation of resources across organizational boundaries in more than a selective way. Despite some early successes of crosscutting analysis, moreover, assessments of DoD's planning and budgeting during the past thirty years have repeatedly stressed the very problems that program budgeting was designed to confront. These include the failure to develop operational performance measures based on clear objectives. They also include decision-making processes that emphasize parochial service orientations and that result in spending patterns characterized by "base-plus incrementalism." Whatever incisive, countervailing role that systems analysis played in the 1960s appears almost to have vanished. Ironically, moreover, the annual PPB process has gotten in the way of the kind of focused analysis and coherent planning that is possible on a selective basis.

The diminished impact of program budgeting as a management tool in DoD can be explained by the absence of consistent leadership support for its goals, coupled with the proliferation of internal and external actors (especially in Congress) that have a role in defense policymaking and budgeting. Manifested most significantly in the abandonment of DPMs and the elevation of POMs as the key foci for decision making, the decentralization of initiative has been a natural product of these factors. The decline of PPB as a management tool can also be explained by the sheer complexity of the process as it has evolved. This development has conformed with universal laws of bureaucratic behavior (Downs 1967) and no doubt has also occurred in order to accommodate more participants in the process. The result has been a system that is so convoluted, with so many stages and documents, that it is impossible for at least a moderately intelligent person to grasp how its parts fit together.

Recent Reform Proposals

The criticisms of DoD's planning and budgeting processes outlined above have led to frequent suggestions for reform. In light of Rumsfeld's reaction noted above, for example, it is not surprising that he initiated a review of the system that produced a number of recommendations for change (JDCST 2004). Although these were not intended to alter the essential logic and structure of PPB, they were designed to make the process more manageable and to restore some of the power that the secretary of defense had lost since the McNamara era.

One of Rumsfeld's initiatives was an attempt to simplify the preparation of POMs and to merge programming with budget review. This included a consolidation of the databases used for the development of POMs and for budgeting. A rationale for this change was that building POMs from the field level up each year was a labor-intensive and time-consuming process, the benefits of which did not justify the costs. Many of the data it produced varied little from year to year. By the same token, the separation of the two processes had sometimes resulted in the neglect of good programming analyses by decision makers during the budgeting phase. Because the development of POMs took so long, moreover, it left too little time in the annual cycle for the consideration of key spending issues by DoD headquarters (Jones and McCaffery 2008).

Another recommendation was to involve the OSD at an earlier stage of PPB, before decisions had become foregone conclusions. This was intended to emphasize department-wide planning and direction as a counter to the traditional service perspectives that informed the preparation of POMs. As such, it was consistent with Rumsfeld's goal of making DoD more nimble in responding to varied and often unpredictable threats in a post-bipolar national security environment (including the ability to engage more effectively in so-called asymmetric warfare). In addition, there was increased emphasis on integrating the execution phase of the budgetary process with the other phases. This included the institution of measures designed to ensure that spending decisions would be more accountable and that they would be incorporated more effectively in future planning and programming decisions. The latter changes resulted in the renaming of DoD's system from PPBS to PPBES (the army had already included "Execution" in the name of its PPB system several years earlier).

Inherent Obstacles

Although the success of Rumsfeld's reforms is yet to be determined, history offers little reason to be optimistic. Assessments of PPB such as those cited throughout this chapter are replete with expressions of disappointment over DoD's failure to address past criticisms of its weaknesses in planning, performance assessment, coordination, and accounting. A retired officer and former faculty member at the Army War College referred to this when he observed that "criticizing, reforming, re-engineering, continuously improving, and transforming the PPBS process is a perennial DC issue, . . . and has been since McNamara imposed it. It has been a career for some of my friends in think tanks."

The obstacles that stand between the theory and the reality of PPB include challenges to analysis that are specific to defense policy. Objective performance assessment is impeded by the fact that the effects of many DoD activities are difficult or impossible to measure. DoD, itself, has noted in response to congressional criticism that it cannot link spending with levels of performance because the "product" of defense is "intangible" (Bowsher 1983, xiii). In lieu of empirical analysis, DoD often relies on models to estimate the military and deterrent contributions of weapons systems, force structures, and other types of programs. The results of such efforts are highly sensitive to various assumptions, including ones about the capabilities and predispositions of actual or potential opponents. The tendency of analysts for the individual services to manipulate such assumptions to produce studies that support their own activities in relation to those of the other services is sometimes a source of amusement among their counterparts at DoD headquarters. Ironically, the expansion of analytical capabilities at the service level in the decades since PPB was instituted has contributed to the fragmentation of authority in the process by eliminating the monopoly on sophisticated expertise that the analysts in the OSD often enjoyed under McNamara.

Although DoD's mission lends itself to program budgeting because of its cohesiveness, moreover, the department's ability to plan and to articulate concrete, subordinate objectives is limited by the instability and unpredictability of the national security environment—especially in the wake of the Soviet Union's demise. This difficulty explains recent interest in "capabilities-based planning" as an alternative to "threat-based planning" (Davis 2002; JDCST 2004; Henry 2005–6). Given the fluidity of international affairs, analysts in DoD and defense think tanks have sought to separate needs for weapons systems, personnel, and other resources from specific threats (e.g., the development of nuclear missiles by Iran or North Korea; or Russian incursions into neighboring republics). The desire to facilitate such an approach to planning is central to some of the suggestions for reforming PPB offered by Rumsfeld's JDCST report, and the capabilities concept provided the foundation for much of DoD's 2006 Quadrennial Defense Review.

In important respects, however, capabilities-based planning illustrates rather than resolves the issues that confront DoD. Separating possible needs from real-world problems (either actual or projected) is a conceptually muddled undertaking. As currently defined, moreover, capabilities-based planning violates the core principle of PPB that projected force elements and other resources be placed into "mutually exclusive, collectively exhaustive categories." As one former analyst in DoD headquarters expressed the dilemma, "It is not possible to construct a useful and coherent program budget [using capabilities-based planning] because most force elements possess multiple capabilities" (Gordon n.d.). As reflected in concerns expressed by Rumsfeld's successor, Robert Gates, capabilities-based planning also has the potential to focus on hypothetical future needs at the expense of immediate resource requirements.

Efforts at comprehensive planning and coordination within DoD are also limited by the sheer size and complexity of the organization, and by long-standing centrifugal tendencies that are grounded in traditions of service autonomy and competition. The latter are externally reinforced by fragmented lines of constituency support and institutional accountability. Notwithstanding its original purpose, PPB has done little to alter these characteristics of DoD in the five decades it has existed. To the contrary, PPB, itself, has evolved in ways that have brought it into closer alignment with its organizational and external environments. The tendencies toward greater decentralization and complexity that have led to this indeed were evident almost from the outset. In a 1963 memo to Charles Hitch, for example, Alain Enthoven noted that the services were increasingly using detailed Program Change Proposals to contest headquarters initiatives. Among the undesirable results were to make the programming process more resource-intensive and unwieldy, and thus diminish its usefulness to the secretary. Enthoven's characterization of the problem is as prescient as it is insightful: "The programming process started out as a convenient, simple, flexible aggregate device, but it has moved far in the direction of becoming a detailed system for financial control. And the result now seems to be that it is combining the disadvantages of both; too detailed to be useful in the overall review of forces, not detailed enough for the real job of financial control."

Conclusion

One suspects for these reasons that tweaking the current structure of PPB is a limited strategy for revitalizing its role. It is instructive McNamara's successors as secretary of defense have often relied on relatively small task forces of internal and external experts for fresh policy advice. This is presumably because the many stakeholders, the complex organizational processes, and the tight time constraints associated with PPB (and the development of Quadrennial Defense Reviews as well) have been inimical to incisive analysis. As just one example, PPB played little role in the downsizing of DoD that followed the breakup of the Soviet Union in the late 1980s. In fact, although they were influenced by some earlier studies conducted by the OSA, major defense policy and resource allocation decisions were made outside of the formal PPB process as early as President Nixon's first term in office (Gordon, McNicol, and Jack 2008).

The focused energy of a strong leader and a small and cohesive staff thus is the most effective alternative to the fragmentation that has come to characterize DoD planning and resource allocation. Such a strategy is consistent with current management doctrine, as well as with the actual approach taken by McNamara (if not with the formal system he instituted) (BENS 2000). Notwithstanding complaints about the amount of work it required, the process in the 1960s allowed for key decisions to be made in a much more centralized and informal manner than is possible under the system as it has evolved. Indeed, it is not clear how much of the success of PPB under McNamara was attributable to the *process* as distinct from the influence of a group of bright analysts who had the ear of the secretary and the flexibility to focus on important issues (again, some of which had been identified well before PPB was put into place).

In any case, the return to such a system would have to overcome a great deal of inertia and many vested interests within and outside of DoD. Not the least of the obstacles would be a legislature that has become increasingly fragmented and increasingly reluctant to defer budgetary authority to the executive. A revitalization of the role played by analysis at DoD headquarters would require a sustained investment of energy by a forceful secretary with a good deal of political capital to spend.

Even so, centralized decision making based on the input of a small staff could only address issues of coordination on a selective basis. In this regard, there may be little more than rhetorical differences between the salutary role attributed to PPB in the 1960s by reasonable advocates such as Hitch (1965) and Enthoven and Smith (2005) and the important but limited potential for policy analysis identified by critics such as Aaron Wildavsky (1988). Herein lies the tension between the theory of PPB and the reality of planning and resource allocation in DoD. To put it as an oxymoron: To attempt comprehensive planning and analysis that considers all stakeholder input in an environment as technically and politically complex as that of DoD may only be possible through a process that is so complex itself as to be unworkable. The evolution of PPB at DoD might be understood in these terms as a return to an equilibrium that is defined by constraints on bounded rationality and bureaucratic politics.

The significance of PPB is underscored, not only by its survival at DoD, but by its recent revival in a handful of civilian agencies. As it was in the 1960s, moreover, program budgeting is today an extension of the popular idea that performance measures can be used to make government more efficient. Specifically, it seeks to use objective outputs and outcomes, not only to improve the management of individual programs, but to coordinate across programs. It may illustrate the kind of doctrinal recycling that some scholars have argued is central to the theory and practice of public administration. In a related but more practical vein, the implementation of PPB speaks to a goal of the performance movement that is frequently cited but seldom developed in operational terms. Is it any more possible now than in the 1960s to use policy analysis to coordinate across organizations? It is to these issues that we now turn.

Chapter 4

NOAA's Adoption of PPB and Matrix Management

P rogram budgeting was abandoned by the civilian bureaucracy after a brief trial in the mid and late 1960s. Thereafter, its federal use was confined to its original home until its resurrection by the National Oceanic and Atmospheric Administration (NOAA) in 2002. As supplemented by matrix management, NOAA's adoption of PPB was intended to address management challenges that had vexed the agency since its inception.

Program budgeting was imported to NOAA from the organization where it had survived. If the initiative came from former DoD officials, it also reflected the more general ascendancy of businesslike efficiency as a norm for public administration. It was a logical extension of the idea that the articulation of goals through strategic planning and the identification of performance measures could be used to rationalize the implementation of policy. As is discussed in later chapters, it was consistent in this respect with the objectives of the Government Performance and Results Act (GPRA) and with the Performance Assessment Rating Tool (PART) reviews that had been instituted by President George W. Bush. Moreover, NOAA seemed the ideal candidate for PPB in much the same way as had DoD under Robert McNamara. As an agency whose components performed similar or interrelated functions but operated independently of one another, NOAA's problems of coordination were perceived to be acute even by the standards of the federal bureaucracy.

The earlier failure of PPB in civilian agencies as well as the attenuation of its role at DoD naturally help frame the context for an examination of how well it worked at NOAA. In fact, it was replaced by a less ambitious system in 2010. Leaving these issues aside until chapter 5, the present discussion examines NOAA's adoption of PPB and matrix management. It begins with a brief overview of the agency's organizational structure and the functions it performs and then describes the management challenges that resulted in increased pressures for organizational reform. It concludes with a description of the system of PPB and matrix management that NOAA adopted.

Overview

NOAA was pieced together in an effort to integrate policy across organizations that had been spread throughout the federal government. Defined by the environmental and ecological concerns of its components, it gathers and disseminates information on weather and ocean conditions, and it conducts and supports research on climate change, marine resources, and ocean and coastal environments. Though it is often characterized as a scientific agency, it provides important services for the public and the private sector as well. It also has significant regulatory responsibilities for the protection of marine and coastal ecosystems and for the conservation of marine species for commercial and sport fishermen.

NOAA's Creation

NOAA was established within the Department of Commerce on October 3, 1970, pursuant to the approval of a reorganization proposal submitted to Congress by Richard Nixon. As expressed in the president's proposal, the new agency's purpose would be to provide "for better protection of life and property from natural hazards . . . for a better understanding of the total environment . . . [and] for exploration and development leading to the intelligent use of our marine resources" (NOAA 2005, 1).

NOAA emerged from the same reorganization plan that created the Environmental Protection Agency (EPA). As with EPA, its establishment was informed by the conventional wisdom that the consolidation of government activities along functional lines would improve the efficiency and effectiveness of programs and organizations that had grown up haphazardly. This premise—which had been ubiquitous in analyses of the federal executive by various blue ribbon commissions during the past century (Arnold 1980; National Commission on the Public Service 2003)—informed a 1969 report to Congress that was solicited under the Marine Resources and Engineering Development Act of 1966. This report was prepared by the so-called Stratton Commission, which was composed of fifteen leaders from business and government (US Commission on Marine Sciences, Engineering, and Resources 1969). The commission's report envisioned NOAA as an organization that would rationalize policy relating to "the oceans and atmospheric components of the global environment" (NOAA 2005, 2). This same prescription was included among the structural reforms recommended by Nixon's Ash Council in an effort to make government more businesslike in its operations (President's Advisory Council on Executive Reorganization 1971; NOAA 2005; US Commission on Ocean Policy 2004).

Neither the Stratton Commission nor the Ash Council had its way concerning NOAA's location within the government. The former advocated the creation of an independent agency within the executive branch. As in the case of EPA (which was so constituted), this would arguably have helped to ensure that NOAA's mission would not be compromised by conflicting programmatic objectives and competing demands on scarce resources (US Commission on Marine Sciences, Engineering, and Resources 1969). In contrast, the Ash Council proposed that NOAA be included within a new Department of Natural Resources that would replace the Department of Interior. The proposed department would have combined some of Interior's elements with the Environmental Science Services Administration from the Department of Commerce (President's Advisory Council on Executive Reorganization 1971).

The kinds of institutional and political factors that explain the rejection of these proposals are familiar (Seidman and Gilmour 1986). As is usually the case with questions of organizational structure and location, NOAA's creation was informed not only by considerations of sound administrative practice but by infighting that was grounded in claims on bureaucratic turf and in agency relationships with clientele groups and members of Congress. President Nixon's recommendation to place NOAA within the Department of Commerce was influenced by these dynamics. It was also influenced by Nixon's strained relationship with his secretary of the interior and by Commerce Secretary Maurice Stans's argument that the Environmental

Science Services Administration would account for more than two-thirds of the proposed organization's budget. As Stans subsequently stated, "We already have in the Department [of Commerce] a solid base of science and technology which will buttress the foundation of an exciting and vigorous NOAA" (NOAA 2005, 3). Nixon's placement of NOAA within a department whose primary goal was to serve business may have also been a way to assuage constituents who were leery of environmental programs and who had lobbied against the creation of an independent EPA.

NOAA was not given all the elements that its proponents wanted it to have. Most notably, although the Stratton Commission had hoped that the new agency would include the Coast Guard, that organization remained within the Department of Transportation (DOT). This may have been due in part to the fact that the Coast Guard had been transferred to DOT from the navy only three years earlier. Still, NOAA encompassed an impressive list of agencies and programs that were drawn from throughout the bureaucracy. Some of its original components were among the oldest entities in the federal government:

- The *Coast and Geodetic Survey*, which was created in the Jefferson administration, was transferred to NOAA from the Army Corps of Engineers. Among its missions was the charting of coastal waters and the conduct and support of ocean exploration through the development and application of new technologies.
- The *Weather Bureau*, which was already in the Department of Commerce, could trace its ancestry to 1817. It had existed as a civilian organization under that name (and under various cabinet departments) since 1891. Its missions included forecasting and the compilation of climatological data, and its clients ranged from the general public to the scientific community to specific industries (e.g., agriculture and aviation) that relied on accurate weather information.
- The *Bureau of Fisheries*, whose roots also extended back to the nineteenth century, had been transferred among a number of organizational homes, the most recent of which was the Department of Interior. Created to conduct research that would inform conservation efforts, it later acquired significant regulatory responsibilities for marine fisheries that were exercised by its five regional centers.
- The *Environmental Science Services Administration*, which was already in the Department of Commerce, was made up in 1970 of eleven research laboratories with specific missions relating to the oceans, the atmosphere, and the Earth. Its purpose was to expand knowledge of the environment through its own projects and by supporting the research of universities and other outside entities.

Other charter components of NOAA included the *Marine Sport Fishery Program* (Department of the Interior), the *Office of Sea Grant Programs* (National Science Foundation), the *United States Lake Survey* (army corps of engineers), the *National Data Buoy Project* (coast guard), the *National Oceanographic Data Center* (sponsored by ten agencies), the *National Oceanographic Instrumentation Center* (navy), and the *Marine Minerals Technology Center* (Department of Interior) (NOAA 2005).

In January 1971, NOAA organized its original elements into six line organizations with major programmatic responsibilities: the National Marine Fisheries Service (managed through five regional offices), the Environmental Research Laboratories (composed of ten facilities spread across the country), the National Weather Service (managed through six regional offices), the Environmental Data Center (composed of three centers responsible for oceanographic, climatic, and geophysical data), the National Ocean Survey (with Atlantic and Pacific centers and several seismology and geomagnetic stations), and the National Environmental Satellite Service. These entities were complemented by several headquarters offices responsible for various support functions (e.g., planning, administration, and technical services) and the administration of more minor programs (e.g., National Sea Grant, Marine Minerals Technology, Oceanographic Instrumentation).

Expanding Responsibilities

Although NOAA's original portfolio was the sum of existing programs and agencies, it has taken on new missions in the decades since its creation. Some programs have been established to support commercial activities, and some reflect policymakers' growing awareness of threats to ecosystems and the environment. As a former administrator noted in testimony before Congress, "In 1970, we were not aware of the extent to which we were exploiting fisheries; we were not able to forecast an El Niño or understand the role of humans in global climate change, and we were just seeing the beginning of the decline in protected marine mammals" (Baker 2004, 2). Many of NOAA's new missions have resulted from legislation, but others are initiatives that have been pursued by the agency in response to needs it has identified. Without attempting to offer a complete inventory, its additional roles include

- *Managing the nation's fisheries*: The Fisheries Service (formerly the Bureau of Fisheries) has acquired important new regulatory responsibilities under the Magnuson-Stevens Fisheries Conservation and Management Act of 1976. These were augmented by the Sustainable Fisheries Act of 1996 and by amendments to Magnuson-Stevens in 2007. In response to the depletion of fish stocks, the service has been empowered to establish annual take limits for commercial and sport fishermen in an extended zone of US waters through a system of five regional offices and advisory councils that provide policymaking representation for different stakeholders.
- *Protecting marine species and conserving coast lands and shorelines*: NOAA has been given significant new environmental and conservation responsibilities through legislation such as the Coastal Zone Management Act (1972); the Marine Mammal Protection Act (1972); the Marine Protection, Restoration, and Sanctuaries Act (1973); the Endangered Species Act (1973); and the Ocean Pollution Planning Act (1978). Additional regulatory programs not directly implemented by NOAA (e.g., the National Environmental Protection Act) have created heightened demands for NOAA research and data collection in evaluating the environmental effects of other agencies' activities.
- *Modernizing weather forecasting*: The National Weather Service has incorporated new programs to improve its capabilities for predicting weather conditions and for communicating those forecasts to stakeholders. These have included the adoption of new satellite, radar, and data-processing technologies, as well as the development of organizational networks for collecting and disseminating weather information.

■ *Conducting atmospheric and oceanic research*: Growing concerns about the environment, weather patterns, and short- and long-term climate change have led to the expansion of NOAA's scientific activities in a variety of areas. Among others, these have included efforts to gain a better understanding of ozone depletion, acid rain, El Niño, ocean pollutants, marine ecosystems, and marine energy and mineral resources. Some of these efforts have come at NOAA's initiative and some have resulted from statutory requirements such as the National Acid Precipitation Act (1980) and the Ocean Thermal Energy Conservation Act (1980) (NOAA 2005).

Current Organization

NOAA has been reorganized many times, partly to accommodate its expanding responsibilities. Currently, its headquarters consists of about a dozen offices, most of which perform staff functions that are common to federal agencies. Its operational responsibilities are divided among six major line components, which are described in the following paragraphs.

The *Office of Oceanic and Atmospheric Research* (OAR) conducts and funds research to enhance understanding of environmental phenomena in a variety of areas relating to oceans and the atmosphere. Much of the knowledge it produces supports the missions of other NOAA components such as the National Weather Service and the Fisheries Service. It consists of four program offices located in Silver Spring, Maryland,[1] and seven research laboratories (located in seven states) that are devoted to specific areas of scientific inquiry.[2]

The *National Environmental Satellite, Data and Information Service* (NESDIS) manages the nation's environmental satellites. vIts purpose is to collect and disseminate data from these and other sources. It encompasses thirteen centers and offices, spread throughout the country, that are responsible for the implementation of specific programs.

The *National Ocean Service* (NOS) conducts and facilitates research and disseminates information related to the nations' oceans and coastal areas. It also has significant regulatory responsibilities, including implementation of the Coastal Zone Management Act and the protection of national marine sanctuaries. It is composed of two staff offices and eight major programs. It is headquartered in Silver Spring, and its regional and field offices are spread throughout the United States.

The *National Weather Service* (NWS) forecasts weather conditions and disseminates that information to the public. It also conducts research for the purpose of understanding weather patterns and developing better forecast techniques. The largest of NOAA's line components, it consists of 9 headquarters offices, 6 national centers, 6 regional headquarters, 4 administrative support centers, 19 specialized centers, 13 river forecast centers, 6 regional climate centers, and 136 weather offices located in 49 states and territories.

The *National Marine Fisheries Service* (NMFS) has both regulatory and research responsibilities relating to the conservation and protection of living marine resources within the United States' 200-mile exclusive economic zone. Its regulatory functions are conducted by six regional offices, four support offices, and eight regional fisheries councils that represent various stakeholders in the policymaking process (state governments, commercial fishermen, sport fishermen, environmentalists, etc.). Its scientific research is conducted through six regional centers.

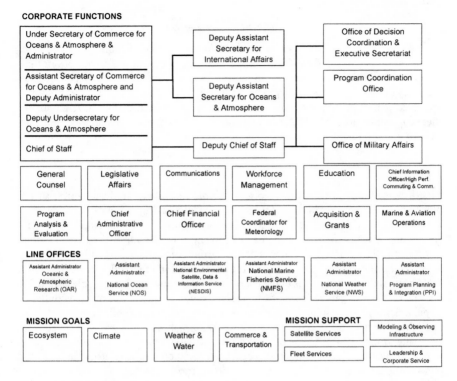

CORPORATE FUNCTIONS

Under Secretary of Commerce for Oceans & Atmosphere & Administrator	Deputy Assistant Secretary for International Affairs	Office of Decision Coordination & Executive Secretariat
Assistant Secretary of Commerce for Oceans & Atmosphere and Deputy Administrator	Deputy Assistant Secretary for Oceans & Atmosphere	Program Coordination Office
Deputy Undersecretary for Oceans & Atmosphere		
Chief of Staff	Deputy Chief of Staff	Office of Military Affairs

General Counsel	Legislative Affairs	Communications	Workforce Management	Education	Chief Information Officer/High Perf. Commuting & Comm.
Program Analysis & Evaluation	Chief Administrative Officer	Chief Financial Officer	Federal Coordinator for Meteorology	Acquisition & Grants	Marine & Aviation Operations

LINE OFFICES

Assistant Administrator Oceanic & Atmospheric Research (OAR)	Assistant Administrator National Ocean Service (NOS)	Assistant Administrator National Environmental Satellite, Data & Information Service (NESDIS)	Assistant Administrator National Marine Fisheries Service (NMFS)	Assistant Administrator National Weather Service (NWS)	Assistant Administrator Program Planning & Integration (PPI)

MISSION GOALS | **MISSION SUPPORT**

Ecosystem	Climate	Weather & Water	Commerce & Transportation	Satellite Services	Modeling & Observing Infrastructure
				Fleet Services	Leadership & Corporate Service

Figure 4.1. NOAA Organization

Source: NOAA.

And the sixth component, *NOAA Marine and Aviation Operations* (MAO), operates ships and aircraft, and manages facilities in support of NOAA's various missions. It includes a 300-member uniformed officer corps. Although it can be viewed as a support organization, many of its officers have scientific or technical training and participate in (and sometimes manage) the implementation of programs conducted by other NOAA components (figure 4.1).

In turn, NOAA's major line components are differentiated into a variety of offices, centers, laboratories, and other units. These are organized around both functional and geographical criteria. The regional focus of many of these units is obviously attributable to the fact that their tasks (e.g., weather forecasting, ecological research, resource conservation) are defined by local needs and conditions.

Each of NOAA's six line components is headed by an assistant administrator (or a director in the case of Marine and Aviation Operations) who reports to the undersecretary of commerce for oceans and atmosphere, also known as the NOAA administrator. Another assistant administrator for program planning and integration also reports directly to the NOAA administrator. The latter official's status within the agency's hierarchy reflects issues of coordination that many feel are especially critical at NOAA.

Management Challenges

NOAA's management challenges today are a continuation of the concerns that led to its creation: They reflect the difficulty of rationalizing activities and organizations that have been established incrementally in response to particular demands that have made their way onto NOAA's and the legislature's agendas. Heightened fiscal constraints and increased expectations for government efficiency and accountability have amplified these concerns. Although NOAA has reorganized often, this has had limited utility as a coordinative strategy.

Interrelated Functions

Whether—or the context in which—organizational redundancy in the pursuit of social objectives is necessarily a bad thing might be debated. Leaving this question aside until the final chapter, the lack of integration among organizations with similar or interrelated objectives is commonly cited as a problem in public administration. As indicated above, the assumption that this detracts from efficiency has provided the impetus for recommendations to restructure the executive along rational, hierarchical lines that began in the early decades of the twentieth century and that have hardly abated. In arguing for the reorganization of the federal bureaucracy into departments with functional missions, for example, the National Commission on the Public Service noted in 2003 that the piecemeal accumulation of federal programs and agencies had led to a "virtually unmanageable tangle of government activities" (US Commission on Ocean Policy 2004, 109). The most notable recent manifestation of this strategy was the creation of the Department of Homeland Security in 2002.

NOAA has a comparatively narrow and cohesive set of goals. Because of this and because of the interconnectedness of environmental and ecological issues generally, all its major components perform activities that are related to other components' missions. To offer just a few examples:

- Research conducted by the Geophysical Fluid Dynamics Lab and Pacific Marine Environmental Lab of the Office of Oceanic and Atmospheric Research is relevant to the scientific and ecological missions of the Fisheries Service and the NOS. OAR's Climate Research and Severe Storms Labs do work that is relevant to the mission of the NWS, and its Atmospheric Research Lab addresses concerns of the Satellite Service.
- Data and analysis on atmospheric and ocean conditions produced by the National Environmental Satellite, Data, and Information Service are relevant to multiple programs relating to climate and ocean conditions that are administered by the NWS, OAR, and the NOS.
- Ecological analyses by the NOS are relevant to conservation efforts by the Fisheries Service, just as NOS mapping and research in the area of geodesy complement OAR's research objectives.
- Research by the Fisheries Science Centers of the Fisheries Service ties in with the mission of the NOS to develop a better understanding of the ocean ecology and to seek solutions to natural resource issues that will "grow our nation's coastal economy while sustaining a healthy and productive environment" (NOS 2009, 1).

There is also substantial overlap *within* some of NOAA's major line components. Until a recent consolidation of its seven Boulder, Colorado, labs, for example, the mission statements of eight OAR labs indicated that they were concerned with the character and quality of the atmosphere, and at least five suggested that they were concerned with climate change. Six of OAR's labs were devoted to the study of ocean conditions (OAR 2005, 3, 4).

There are many more examples of NOAA activities that cut across the missions of multiple organizational components. Of course, what seem to be fine differences in research focus to a layperson can be important distinctions to a scientist. Suffice it to say, however, that many research programs complement other research programs, and that many also produce knowledge that is relevant to the agency's service and regulatory programs. And although redundancy may be in the eye of the beholder, there is at least a high potential for duplication of effort in its scientific endeavors.

To many, the interrelationships that exist among NOAA's activities present important challenges of coordination and planning. To an even greater extent than most bureaucracies, NOAA is a collection of programs and implementing organizations that have been created on a piecemeal basis. Most of them were established through statutory law, and many had developed their own identities and bases of constituent support before NOAA came into being. Some components, such as the NWS, have distinctive cultures and tend to view themselves as independent agencies.

Fragmentation within NOAA has been reinforced by a tradition of scientific autonomy in some parts of the organization. Research fiefdoms have been consistent with a culture, not unlike that in academia, that accords status to intellectual accomplishment and that places a high value on freedom in the pursuit of knowledge. They have also provided a way for an organization that defines itself in terms of scientific excellence to retain talented individuals who might otherwise choose to pursue their interests in universities, think tanks, and industry.

External Concerns

Problems are subjective. In the case of public organizations, they are defined largely by the perceptions of external stakeholders and of the political principals (legislators and political executives) who control agency budgets and authorizing legislation. In this regard, although NOAA's existence attests to significant support for its missions, enthusiasm for its environmental and conservation goals is hardly uniform. The agency thus has been criticized by groups, such as developers, fishermen, and energy companies, that are adversely affected by the implementation of policies such as the Marine Mammals Protection Act and the Coastal Zone Management Act. Nor is there a broad consensus about the desirability of NOAA's programs in basic research or about whether it is even appropriate as a matter of principle for the public to fund the pursuit of knowledge as an end in itself. Accordingly, NOAA has experienced increased pressure to relate its scientific activities to tangible benefits for society.

Apart from the desirability of what it does, critics have questioned whether NOAA is effective in carrying out its mandates. These concerns, which have often been voiced by proponents of the agency's ecological missions, have led to frequent reorganization proposals throughout NOAA's brief history by members of Congress, the White House, and various outside commissions. They led to eleven proposals between 1971 and 1978 to place NOAA within a new Department of Natural Resources, eight proposals between 1979 and 1999 to make NOAA an independent agency, and four proposals between 1993 and 1998 to place NOAA in a cabinet department other than Commerce (US Commission on Ocean Policy 2004, chap. 7).

Allegations of ineffectiveness have also sustained threats to NOAA's resources. This has been the case at least since the early years of the Reagan administration, when recommendations for drastic budget cuts were accompanied by proposals to outsource important functions performed by the NWS and much of the work performed by NOAA's laboratories and other research centers (Rubin 2003). In 1995, efforts by Republican legislators to streamline government resulted in significant budget cuts for the NWS as well as proposals to eliminate NOAA and redistribute its functions among various other agencies. Nor have challenges to NOAA resources been confined to those ideologically opposed to its missions. Pursuant to its National Performance Review, the Clinton administration concluded that the activities of the NOAA Corps could be performed more effectively by a civilian force. Accordingly, it proposed legislation that would have eliminated the Corps (GAO 1996).

Criticism of NOAA's performance has often been motivated by the perception that the agency is poorly organized and (in a related vein) that it lacks clearly defined and practically beneficial objectives to focus its efforts (NOAA interviews). The structure of OAR and other research units has come under especially close scrutiny in these respects. Long-standing concerns about the implementation of NOAA's scientific programs were brought to a head in a 2004 report by the House and Senate Consolidated Appropriations Committee. "In recognition of current resource limitations," the committee directed NOAA "to review the continued requirements for twelve separate laboratories" and to submit a laboratory consolidation plan. It also directed NOAA to "assess the costs and benefits of breaking OAR up into its constituent parts and distributing those parts . . . to other lines units" (Moore 2004, 2).

NOAA asked its external Science Advisory Board to address these issues. In response, the board appointed a research review team to evaluate the agency's organizational structure and management practices. The team was composed of two NOAA officials (from OAR and the NOS) and four board members with distinguished records in oceanic and atmospheric research at universities and institutes. On the basis of agency documents and extensive interviews with stakeholders (including agency officials), the team noted that NOAA had done a great deal of high-quality and socially beneficial research. At the same time, it concluded that there was a great deal of room for improvement in how the agency managed its research efforts (Moore 2004).

The review team's report emphasized the challenges posed by the fragmentation of NOAA's scientific programs. As it noted, "Given the vital importance of research to the agency, it is perhaps not surprising to learn that research has spread across NOAA; there are twenty-nine somewhat heterogeneous NOAA Laboratories and Centers and 18 Joint Institutes associated with research in NOAA. . . . such complexity can work to the disadvantage of NOAA's mission" (Moore 2004, 19). Although the team did not recommend a massive restructuring of the agency, it was critical of the lack of centralized planning, direction, and coordination. Among its principal findings were that

- NOAA's line components exercised too little control over the research of their units. The directors of individual labs and centers exercised "substantial independence" in establishing their agendas and often did not articulate clear research goals that could be used as a basis for accountability and control (Moore 2004, 22).

- Although much of NOAA's scientific research ultimately had practical benefits (some very substantial), there was little explicit effort within the agency to ensure that these efforts were driven by the needs of the public or of agency components, such as the NWS and the Fisheries Service, that directly served the public.
- Many of the management problems associated with NOAA's fragmentation could be attributed to deficiencies in communication across its units. Although research labs did sometimes share information and coordinate their efforts, this was confined to informal communications that occurred on an idiosyncratic basis. The same could be said of the relationship between researchers and officials implementing service programs.
- NOAA was ineffective in describing its activities and communicating their importance to Congress, the Office of Management and Budget (OMB), and other external actors. This was partly the result of its failure clearly to articulate its scientific objectives and how its activities related to those goals.
- Efforts to achieve better planning, communication, and integration were impeded by a culture of autonomy and insularity within research units (Moore 2004).

The central thrust of the review team's report was captured by its characterization of NOAA as a holding company as opposed to a corporation. In its cover letter forwarding the report to NOAA's administrator, the Science Advisory Board emphasized that these findings were not new.

> Many of the problems highlighted and addressed . . . had been identified in past reviews of NOAA science and operations. . . . Recurring issues are the lack of a comprehensive science plan for NOAA research over the near, medium, and long terms; the uneven and often weak integration of science activities across (and sometimes within) line offices; and the absence of structures and processes which ensure timely and efficient transition of NOAA efforts from research to operations. (Moore 2004, 9)

The review team also conceded that addressing these issues would not be easy. Although it noted that effective scientific leadership was critical for integrating NOAA's operations, it did not attempt to define that quality. "Whatever it [effective leadership] was," moreover, it would be like "herding butterflies" or "refereeing a hockey game" (Moore 2004, 9, 10).

Generic Constraints

Government-wide expectations that agencies plan and demonstrate the effectiveness of what they do have overlay with specific concerns about the management of NOAA's operations. Like other agencies, NOAA has had to comply with GPRA. To satisfy the act's requirements, it has been required to engage in strategic planning for the purpose of articulating its goals. It has also had to devise performance measures by which managers, stakeholders, and political principals can assess programs in terms of their contribution to those objectives.

The so-called performance movement has also been manifested in executive initiatives such as Bill Clinton's National Performance Review and OMB's 2001 directive that agencies evaluate and streamline their organizational structures (OMB 2001). Particularly important to the present discussion is the PART that was developed by OMB under George W. Bush. Ostensibly intended to implement (and standardize) GPRA's requirements for performance-based management, PART reviews were based on an extensive questionnaire that was administered and evaluated by the same program examiners that review agencies' budget requests.[3]

Neither GPRA nor PART established an explicit mechanism for agencies to coordinate their activities. This is a general goal of the performance movement, however, and it is implicit in GPRA's requirement that agencies (1) articulate their objectives through strategic planning and (2) assess their programs in terms of those goals in order to promote an efficient allocation of resources. NOAA's senior management has certainly interpreted GPRA to require such coordinative efforts, as have more recent legislative assessments of the act's implementation in other agencies (GAO 2004). It is also instructive that indictments of NOAA's poor integration (e.g., the Scientific Advisory Board's review team report) typically cite inadequate attention to strategic planning and performance assessment as explanations for this shortcoming.

Restructuring and Its Limitations

The reorganization that was so common in NOAA's early years has not gone out of style as a way of addressing its management challenges. In response to legislative concerns and the review team report discussed above, for example, OAR consolidated its six Boulder laboratories into a "super" Earth Systems Research Lab with centers for global monitoring, physical sciences, chemical sciences, and global systems. NOAA also conducted an internal study and instituted a number of structural reforms pursuant to the aforementioned OMB requirement that agencies consider streamlining their operations. The principal changes that resulted from these efforts were its elimination of levels of management in various parts of the organization (NOAA 2002).[4]

Yet perceptive critics of the lack of coordination within NOAA have recognized that reorganization is a limited strategy. In forwarding the review team report, for example, the Science Advisory Board stressed that "many of the changes needed in NOAA are fundamentally cultural. NOAA critics must understand that change in NOAA culture is more important than merely making changes in organizational structure" (Pietrafesa 2004, 2). The limits of restructuring as a coordinative strategy at NOAA are also defined by considerations of administrative and political feasibility. The review team was adamant in its opposition to disbanding OAR and dividing its functions among NOAA's other line divisions (Moore 2004). In fact, although NOAA has undergone many organizational changes, with responsibilities being added and reshuffled over the years, most of these have not been fundamental. The agency's basic structure at the assistant administrator level is quite similar to the one it established in 1971.

As in other bureaucracies, practical considerations limit the extent to which NOAA can rely on structural reforms in addressing issues of coordination. One is the cost of disrupting the routines and relationships that sustain ongoing operations. This consideration was evident in reactions to the relatively modest changes proposed in the review team's draft report. A coalition of thirty corporations, professional associations, and academic institutions stressed the complexity and importance of existing organizational relationships, both within NOAA and between NOAA and its stakeholders.

Accordingly, it urged the team to gather more information about the potentially disruptive implications of its recommendations for NOAA's organizational ecology:

> As we are sure the Review Team is aware, the OAR labs collaborate extensively with NOAA's joint and cooperative institutes. . . . These institutes are extremely important in the access they give NOAA researchers to collaborative work with experts external to NOAA. . . . We cannot overemphasize this point and, at the risk of repeating ourselves, again encourage the Team to visit as many of the institutes as is humanly possible in order to get the full story about the complex set of external relationships that occur through these cooperative relationships and that extend far into the scientific community. The results produce incredible value for the nation. (Ban 2004, 3)

Restructuring is also limited by statutory requirements in many cases and by the political influence of constituencies that become attached to (and that are sometimes created by) organizations, program missions, and even particular individuals. Significant organizational changes almost always redefine organizational goals and thus are fraught with conflict. In opposing the break-up of OAR, for example, the Advisory Board's review team argued that such an initiative would deemphasize NOAA's traditional scientific mission. Somewhat inconsistently, perhaps, it stressed the continuing need for research that might not have immediate practical benefits in terms of NOAA's service and regulatory functions—even at the risk that some of it might lead down blind alleys (Moore 2004).

A New Management System

In brief, the generally applicable requirements of GPRA and PART that were designed to promote efficiency in government reinforced specific demands that NOAA do a better job of assessing and integrating its activities. At the same time, the traditional strategy of restructuring had limited feasibility as a way of achieving this goal. As an alternative, therefore, NOAA sought to rationalize its activities through decision-making processes that cut across organizational boundaries. Particularly notable is the system of program budgeting and matrix management that it adopted in 2002 and retained until 2010.

NOAA's Adoption of PPBES

The rationale behind NOAA's new management system was evident in a May 2002 report that examined issues of organizational alignment, efficiency, and resource allocation within the agency. The report was prepared for Vice Admiral (Retired) Conrad Lautenbacher, who had recently been appointed NOAA administrator with the expectation that he would improve the agency's management and budgeting practices. The internal program review team (PRT) that drafted the report consisted of sixteen NOAA political appointees and career officials. Although the PRT solicited input from throughout the organization, its recommendations were closely in line with the admiral's objectives.

The PRT recommended that NOAA should eventually be reorganized "around a suite of products and services based on discrete functions." Under this plan, all of the agency's activities would be redistributed among three line divisions: Environmental

Observations; Oceans, Coasts, and Fisheries; and Weather and Climate. Although the PRT chairman favored an immediate implementation of that plan, most of the team's members felt that the costs of such a radical transformation would outweigh its benefits in the foreseeable future. Opponents included the careerists representing all the agency's major line components. Among their objections was that, rather than helping to integrate NOAA's missions, "the reorganization would exacerbate the division between atmospheric and ocean programs." In lieu of restructuring, therefore, the report advocated refocusing the agency's management processes "along thematic as opposed to organizational lines" (Lautenbacher 2002, 3, 15). As endorsed by Admiral Lautenbacher and his executive council, it repeatedly stressed the need for improved "business" and "corporate" practices.

One of the PRT's recommendations was that NOAA place greater emphasis on objective performance assessment and requirements-based management as means of promoting accountability and allocating resources. To that end, it suggested establishing an Office of Program Analysis and Evaluation (PA&E) at NOAA headquarters. This recommendation was subsequently adopted. The PRT also recommended that NOAA do a more effective job of strategic planning through the (sequential) formulation of visions, missions, goals, and guidelines. Such a process would gather input and secure buy-in from internal as well as external stakeholders. The PRT underscored this prescription by suggesting that NOAA create an Office of Program Planning and Integration (PPI) under an assistant administrator whose authority would be coequal with that of the executives who headed its major line divisions (Lautenbacher 2002). This recommendation was also adopted.

The PRT's report noted that a heightened emphasis on planning and performance assessment was consistent with the goals of GPRA and of the President's Management Agenda that had been established more recently under George W. Bush. (An OMB document describing the latter was included as an appendix to the PRT's report.) It also endorsed a more ambitious set of management objectives that can be viewed as an extension of the goals of GPRA and the President's Management Agenda. Quoting a 2000 study of NOAA's financial management practices by the National Academy of Public Administration, it noted that "strategic management, to be effective, must have a system that connects resources to results and adheres to a decision-making process that is corporate in nature." It further observed that NOAA's "planning, budget formulation, and execution processes [were] not effectively integrated" and that its "budget structure [was] not functional [i.e., not presented in terms of functional categories]" (Lautenbacher 2002, 17).[5]

These latter observations begged the question of *how* the integration of planning, performance assessment, and budgeting might take place. Without offering a detailed description of its implementation, the PRT noted that NOAA had recently adopted a system of program budgeting that would promote the corporate values that had been missing within the agency. This technique had risen to prominence in the 1960s and then had all but disappeared outside of its original home in DoD after the early 1970s. The report also endorsed matrix management as a complement to PPB that would further promote coordination across organizational boundaries. This, too, was a management technique that had been popular at one time but that had fallen out of favor.

It is not a coincidence that program budgeting was resurrected in the civilian bureaucracy by someone who came from the only federal organization where it had survived. Although he had held a variety of staff and command positions in a distinguished navy career, Admiral Lautenbacher was best known within DoD as an accomplished technocrat (or "bean counter" in the military's vernacular)—an expert in financial operations and in the application of analytical management techniques. An Annapolis graduate with a Harvard PhD in applied mathematics, he had been a leader in the use of information technology to improve command-and-control systems within the navy. He had also served as deputy chief of naval operations in charge of navy programs and budget in his final tour of duty, and he had earlier served as head of the Program Planning Branch in the Navy Program Planning Directorate.

The admiral reinforced his commitment to the military's system of financial management by appointing a number of former DoD budgeting and planning specialists to help design and implement a system of program budgeting. Among them were the women who became NOAA's chief financial officer (CFO) and head of the newly created Office of PA&E. Both hired several former DoD personnel as subordinates. Although the head of PPI was a longtime NOAA careerist, she recruited several former DoD personnel as well.

NOAA's adoption of PPB in 2002 can be explained in terms of a familiar dynamic: When successful executives move to new organizations, they often bring with them management approaches that are familiar and that served them well in the past. Yet whatever Admiral Lautenbacher's predilections, the appeal of program budgeting is easy to understand as a response to the problems of planning and coordination that were widely thought to afflict NOAA. Even many of the agency's careerists who were in management positions conceded the deficiencies of its old system. NOAA's adoption of PPB is also consistent with the general emphasis on efficiency that has characterized thinking and institutional reform in public administration during the past two decades. As with its first incarnation in the 1960s, when it evolved from performance management, program budgeting is a natural extension of the idea that the allocation of resources and responsibilities should be informed by a clear definition of goals and an assessment of organizational outputs in terms of those objectives.

An essential premise of PPB is that spending decisions should include a consideration of fiscal commitments and program benefits extending into the future. To accomplish this, annual budgets should be replaced with multiyear budgets. A related premise of PPB is that spending should be assessed in terms of its contribution to organizational objectives. To accomplish this, activities are removed from their organizational units for analytical purposes. So doing allows managers and policymakers to hold implementing officials accountable for their performance, to identify redundancies among activities, and to assess the marginal utility of spending on different activities with similar goals. Program budgeting thus stresses the objective measurement and comparison of outputs as a means of coordination and of achieving (or at least moving toward) an optimal allocation of resources.

The Program Structure

Modeled after DoD's system of the same name, NOAA's version of planning, programming, budgeting execution systems (PPBES) was based on a program structure that moved from the general to the specific. Its starting point was a strategic plan that articulated a hierarchical set of principles and objectives. For example, NOAA's updated strategic plan for fiscal years 2005–10 set forth the following vision, mission, and core values:

- *Vision:* An informed society that uses a comprehensive understanding of the role of the oceans, coasts, and atmosphere in the global ecosystem to make the best social and economic decisions.
- *Mission:* To understand and predict changes in the Earth's environment and conserve and manage coastal and marine resources to meet our nation's economic, social, and environmental needs.
- *Core values:* people, integrity, excellence, teamwork, ingenuity (NOAA 2004, 2).

The strategic plan also articulated five goals that were subordinate to its mission:

- *Weather and water:* Serve society's needs for weather and water information.
- *Climate:* Understand climate variability and change to enhance society's ability to plan and respond.
- *Ecosystem:* Protect, restore, and manage the use of coastal and ocean resources through an ecosystem approach to management.
- *Commerce and transportation:* Support the nation's commerce with information for safe, efficient, and environmentally sound transportation.
- *Mission support:* Provide critical support for NOAA's mission (NOAA 2004, 3).

Each of these goals was accompanied by expected outcomes, performance objectives, and strategies. As illustrated by the weather and water mission goal, these consisted of fairly inclusive lists of criteria:

- *Expected outcomes* (three): reduced loss of life, injury, and damage to the economy; better, quicker, and more valuable weather and water information to support improved decisions; increased customer satisfaction with weather and water information and services.
- *Performance objectives* (seven): increased lead time and accuracy for weather and water warnings and forecasts; improve predictability of the onset, duration, and impact of hazardous and severe weather and water events; increase application and accessibility of weather and water information as the foundation for creating and leveraging public (i.e., federal, state, local, tribal) private and academic partnerships; increase the development, application, and transition of advanced science and technology to operations and services; increase the coordination of weather and water information and services with integration of local, regional, and global observations systems; reduce the uncertainty associated with weather and water decision tools and assessments; enhance environmental literacy and improve understanding, value, and use of weather and water information and services.
- *Strategies* (six): improve the reliability, lead time, and effectiveness of weather and water information and services that predict changes in environmental conditions; integrate an information enterprise that incorporates all stages from research to delivery, seeks better coordination of employee skills and training, and engages customers; develop and infuse research results and new technologies more efficiently to improve products and services, streamline dissemination, and communicate vital information more effectively; work with private industry, universities, and national and international agencies to create and leverage partnerships that foster more effective information

services; build a broad-based and coordinated education and outreach program by engaging individuals in continuous learning toward a greater understanding of the impacts of weather and water on their lives; employ scientific and emerging technological capabilities to advance decision-support services and educate stakeholders (NOAA 2004, 9).

As indicated in table 4.1, each of NOAA's forty-four programs was grouped under one or another of its five goals, and each was to be evaluated in terms of its contributions to that goal's expected outcomes and performance objectives. As such, the agency's program structure was consistent with the cardinal principle of PPB that all activities and resources be divided among mutually exclusive categories.

Actors

NOAA's implementation of PPB relied heavily on its line managers. Assessments at the program level were developed by teams of officials from the units (often more than one unit) responsible for the activities or "elements" that made up those programs. Each program team was led by a manager who came from one of the participating units (e.g., a division chief, the deputy director of an office, or the head of a lab). The contributions that programs made to their respective goals were, in turn, evaluated by goal teams. These were also composed of implementing officials, and their leaders were senior line managers. For example, the last weather and water goal team leader worked in the NWS and had formerly been the deputy director of the Office of Hydrologic Development. The climate goal team leader was the head of NOAA's climate office and the ecosystem goal team lead was the chief science adviser for the Fisheries Service.

NOAA's heavy reliance on line officials was perhaps its most conspicuous departure from DoD's system of PPB, in which hundreds of uniformed personnel, civil servants, and outside consultants were dedicated exclusively to the implementation of the process. As a retired officer who had come to NOAA from DoD noted, it was only when he was assigned to the Pentagon after twenty years of service that he became aware that PPB existed. NOAA's reliance on teams of line personnel for much of the analysis in planning and programming was based in part on the perceived need for scientific expertise in program assessment. It was also based on the assumption that such an approach would encourage—indeed require—the kind of communications across organizational boundaries that NOAA's critics had found to be lacking.

Although line officials did much of the heavy lifting in PPB, the process was managed by planning and budgeting offices at NOAA headquarters. These included the Office of PPI, the Office of PA&E, and the CFO. As indicated above, PPI and PA&E were created under Admiral Lautenbacher specifically for the purpose of implementing program budgeting. They orchestrated the process and consolidated and analyzed the data that it generated. They also provided guidance and support for program and goal teams. Each had a staff whose responsibilities for planning and policy analysis were differentiated on the basis of NOAA's four strategic goals.

PPB did not automatically produce policy decisions; as with any analytical technique, its purpose was to advise the organization's leaders. Agency executives thus furnished guidance and made final decisions at critical junctures of the process. Although this could occur informally, NOAA's executive council provided an institutional mechanism for vetting the most important issues that arose at the various stages of PPB (and other policy and management issues as well). The council was chaired by the

Goal	Program	FY 2012 ID Code	Goal/Sub-Goal Lead Secondary	Program Manager
NOAA Program Structure with Program Managers				
Ecosystems			Steve Murawski (NMFS) Peg Brady (NMFS) (acting)	
	Aquaculture	AQC		Michael Rubino (NMFS)
	Coastal & Marine Resources	CMR		Tim Goodspeed (NOS)
	Coral Reef Conservation	COR		Kacky Andrews (NOS)
	Ecosystem Observations	EOP		Ned Cyr (NMFS)
	Ecosystem Research	ERP		Leon Cammen (OAR)
	Enforcement	ENF		Dale Jones (NMFS)
	Fisheries Management	FMP		Galen Tromble (NMFS)
	Habitat	HAB		Brian Pawlak (NMFS)
	Protected Species	PSP		Phil Williams (NMFS)
Climate		CL	Chet Koblinsky (OAR) Krisa Arzayus (OAR)	
	Climate Observations & Monitoring	COM		David Goodrich (OAR) (Acting)
	Climate Research & Modeling	CRM		Venkatachalam Ramaswamy (OAR)
	Climate Service Development	CSD		Margaret Davidson (NOS)
Weather & Water		WW	Ed Johnson (NWS) (acting) Monica Montague (NWS) (acting)	
	Air Quality	AQL		Jim Meagher (OAR)
	Coasts, Estuaries, & Oceans	CEO		Keeling Kuipers (NOS)
	Integrated Water Forecasting	IWF		Gary Carter (NWS)
	Local Forecasts & Warnings	LFW		Andrew Stern (NWS)
	Science, Technology, & Infusion	WWS		Marty Ralph (OAR)
	Space Weather	SWX		Tom Bogdan (NWS)
	Tsunami	TSU		Therese Pierce (NWS)
Commerce & Transportation		CT	CAPT Gerd Glang (NOS)	
	Aviation Weather	AWX		Cyndie Abelman (NWS)
	Geodesy	GEO		Doug Brown (NOS)
	Marine Transportation System	MTS		Rich Edwing (NOS)
	Marine Weather	MWX		Ming Ji (NWS)
	NOAA Emergency Response	EMR		William Conner (NOS)
	Surface Weather	SFX		Jim O'Sullivan (NWS)
Mission Support		MS		
			Tajr Hull (OMAO) Leo Carling (OMAO)	
	Fleet Services Sub-Goal			
	Aircraft Replacement	ACR		Tajr Hull (OMAO)
	Aircraft Services	ACF		Tajr Hull (OMAO) (Acting)
	Fleet Replacement	FLT		Tajr Hull (OMAO)
	Marine Operations & Maintenance	SHP		Tajr Hull (OMAO) (Acting)
			Bill Broglie (CAO) Sandra Manning (CAO)	
	Leadership & Corporate Services Sub-Goal			
	Acquisitions & Grants	ACG		Bob Stockman (AGO)
	Administrative Services	ADM		Sandra Manning (CAO)
	Facilities	FCY		John Beeman (CAO)
	Financial Services	FNC		Daniel Bess (CFO)
	Homeland Security	HLS		Christopher Moore (CIO)
	Information Technology Services	ITT		Dennis Morgan (CIO)
	Line Office Headquarters	LOH		John Potts (NOAA) (Acting)
	NOAA Headquarters	NHQ		Christos Michalopoulos (USAO)
	Workforce Management	WMO		Joseph Abbott (WFMO)
			Kenneth McDonald (NESDIS) Peter Roohr (NWS)	
	Modeling & Observing Infrastructure Sub-Goal			
	Environmental Modeling	EMP		Don Anderson (OAR)
	Integrated Ocean Observing System	IOS		Carl Gouldman (NOS)
	Technical Requirements, Planning & Integration	TRP		Pam Taylor (NESDIDS)
	Satellite Sub-Goal		Peter Wilczynski (NESDIS)	
	Commercial Space Services	CSS		Eve Douglas (NESDIS)
	Geostationary Satellite Acquisition	STG		Greg Mandt (NESDIS)
	Polar Satellite Acquisition	STP		Michael Mignogno (NESDIS)
	Satellite Services	SSV		Kathy Kelly (NESDIS)

LEGEND:
Matrix Program
Non-Matrix Program

Structure Revised: 06/05/2009
Personnel Revised: 04/06/2010

Table 4.1. NOAA Program Structure with Program Managers

Source: NOAA.

administrator, and it included the heads of all of the agency's major line components and headquarters staff offices. Issues of lesser importance (or that had not fully "ripened") were vetted through an executive panel chaired by NOAA's deputy administrator. Although the purpose of these bodies was to build an "informed consensus," final authority obviously rested with the administrator.

The Process

The implementation of PPB was a sequential but iterative process. The planning phase, which was led by PPI, was initiated three years before the beginning of the fiscal year. It was designed to assess programs in terms of their contributions to NOAA's strategic goals. It was also designed to evaluate and perhaps modify those goals based on considerations of feasibility (as revealed by assessments of program performance) and on possible changes in the agency's operating environment. The latter might include factors such as new legislative mandates, new presidential priorities, new demands from groups served or otherwise affected by agency programs, and new problems or opportunities arising from natural events or identified by scientific research. Planning was structured so as to involve participation by goal team leaders, program managers, the heads of NOAA's line and staff offices, and representatives from the various councils that NOAA had created to secure input from its external stakeholders.[6]

To achieve these ends, planning required program teams and then goal teams to prepare formal assessments of their activities in terms of the objectives articulated in NOAA's program structure. These were called Program Baseline Assessments and Goal Assessments, respectively. Planning culminated in an annual guidance memorandum (AGM) issued by the administrator. As indicated in Admiral Lautenbacher's introduction to the 2008–12 AGM, this was a general document that identified key priorities based on the more detailed analysis contained in the program baseline and goal assessments:

> By its nature, the Annual Guidance Memorandum does not and cannot refer to all significant program and managerial efforts. . . . Based on an extensive internal assessment of capacity and capability gaps that must be closed to satisfy NOAA's entire set of mission requirements, this Annual Guidance Memorandum identifies a limited number of high-level programmatic and managerial priorities that are NOAA-wide in nature (e.g., interdisciplinary, interorganizational initiatives), require significant and sustained financial or managerial resources and effort, and have a singular impact on NOAA's ability to achieve its long-term strategic goals. (Lautenbacher 2005, 1)

As an illustration, the 2008–12 AGM established general sets of priorities and strategic outcomes pertaining to five "core functions." Related to but not to be confused with the substantive goals that provided the basis for NOAA's program structure, these were observations systems, data, and models; information services, forecasts and predictions; ocean and coastal ecosystems management; environmental literacy; and breakthrough organizational performance. The priorities articulated in the AGM were identified through analyses of "key trends and requirements" and selected on the basis of potential impact, customer needs, and the ability to "leverage" contributions from outside the agency. Pursuant to an international Earth Observation Summit and subsequent directives from the Bush administration, for example, the observation systems priorities stressed the importance of cooperative efforts across US and international agencies to develop a worldwide "system of observation systems" (Lautenbacher 2005, 5).

The next stage—*programming*—was a process of identifying and evaluating hierarchical chains of ends and means that was designed to allow NOAA's leadership to allocate funds in support of the agency's missions. It began with the AGM that emerged from the planning phase and culminated in the development of a program plan (PP) and a program decision memorandum (PDM) that provided the basis for the budget. As with PPB generally, programming was the essential and distinctive feature of PPB at NOAA. It provided the framework for the analysis that linked planning and the allocation of resources.

Programming consisted of two phases. *Program review* "compared [existing] capabilities and capacities with those needed to perform current and future missions." Its purpose was to identify deficiencies as well as excesses in the resources devoted to the accomplishment of program goals. Program review in turn provided the basis for *program development*. This phase produced a "fiscally balanced" five-year plan (as articulated in the PP and PDM) based on a comparison and integration of NOAA's forty-four programs in terms of the contributions they made to the agency's goals and mission (NOAA 2008, 40).

The Office of PA&E led the programming process. It was made up of professional planners and analysts (some of whom had DoD backgrounds) who directed, evaluated, revised, and consolidated the baseline and goal assessments that were prepared by program and goal teams. To the extent that PPB employed objective analysis to compare activities and allocate resources within NOAA, this was done primarily by PA&E as it developed a PP and PDM. Among the techniques in its arsenal were requirements validation; cost, schedule, and performance analysis; performance measures and return-on-investment analysis; and analysis of execution and appropriations trends (NOAA 2008, 40).

Although PA&E was at the center of the programming phase, it relied on assistance and guidance from other agency actors. It often asked program and goal teams for additional data and clarifying information as it conducted its analyses, and it sometimes solicited similar input about the effects of agency activities directly from NOAA's line offices or from the members of external advisory councils. PA&E also relied on NOAA's CFO and the line component (e.g., the NWS) budget offices for fiscal guidance. Because PPs and PDMs were issued by the administrator, moreover, PA&E necessarily communicated extensively with the executive council and executive panel as it prepared these documents.

The *budgeting* phase of PPB, which was managed by NOAA's CFO, translated the program decision memorandum into an actual budget that reflected program needs in light of agency goals and priorities. Budgeting was also constrained by guidelines and priorities furnished by the Department of Commerce and OMB. During this phase, the Budget Formulation Division in the CFO's office was at the center of a process that involved extensive communications with NOAA line and staff officials, as well as with officials from Commerce and OMB.

Finally, the *execution* phase of PPB involved the actual administration of programs and the disbursement of funds during the fiscal year. It required oversight of spending by NOAA's line managers to ensure accountability and effectiveness, and it sometimes included the reapportionment of resources based on an assessment of performance or changing needs. Among its formal requirements were the development and implementation of annual operating plans that assigned work requirements and that provided for the preparation of monthly, quarterly, and annual performance reports; the comparison of desired and actual performance levels; and the implementation of needed changes to plans based on performance. Execution culminated with the preparation of an Annual Business Report (NOAA 2008, 29).

Matrix Management

Although it was designed to promote top-down planning and functional integration, NOAA's implementation of PPB also required extensive input from its line units in assessing program effectiveness and resource needs. Given that some programs combined activities by different components, the agency sought to promote coordination across organizational boundaries through what it calls "matrix management." This was not a separate system but rather an adaptation of PPB to NOAA's particular needs.

A matrix organization is defined by crosscutting lines of accountability. In one version, individuals who belong to *functional divisions* (engineering, policy analysis, law, accounting, etc.) are assigned to *teams* to work on specific projects. Teams can be temporary and tailored to the task at hand under this variant, with their members being reassigned to new projects once their work is complete. As in the case of NOAA, another version of the matrix concept involves teams that represent and coordinate the work of permanent units with similar or interdependent responsibilities. In either case, the team approach is designed to facilitate the kind of communication and coordination across specialties or divisions that is needed to solve complex problems and that is arguably impeded by the differentiation of organizations along traditional lines.[7]

The matrix concept was popular in the management literature and among business consultants in the 1970s and 1980s, and it had a significant impact on private-sector organizations during that period. It also influenced some public bureaucracies. For example, the Consumer Products Safety Commission adopted matrix management in 1977 in recognition of the idiosyncratic character of regulatory problems and of the fact that the development of sound policies often required expertise from different fields (Simon 1983; Johnson 1990). As with program budgeting, however, interest in matrix management had largely disappeared at the time of its adoption by NOAA. This was reportedly because its implementation required an excessive amount of work and because of the confusion created by crosscutting lines of accountability (Ford and Randolph 1992).

Like program budgeting, moreover, matrix management reemerged at NOAA as a way of coordinating and rationalizing activities across the agency's internal boundaries. Although the agency first applied the concept on a limited basis in the 1990s, it was formalized and elaborated under Admiral Lautenbacher. Given their experiences, it is tempting to speculate that Lautenbacher and others who were transplanted from the military viewed the matrix concept (as well as the involvement of line personnel more generally) as a modification of PPB that would help to alleviate the fragmentation that had come to characterize program budgeting in the Department of Defense. Policymaking initiatives in DoD's system of PPB had become increasingly decentralized and fragmented since the early 1970s.

NOAA's current matrix teams were not ad hoc and temporary; rather, they were superimposed on existing missions to coordinate the activities of different organizational units that contributed to similar objectives. The agency thus designated as "matrix programs" combinations of activities contributing to twenty-six functions that involved contributions from more than one of its five line offices (out of a total of forty-four programs) (NOAA 2004). As one illustration, its Habitat Restoration Matrix Structure included officials from the National Marine Fisheries Service, the NOS, and the Office of Oceanic and Atmospheric Research.

For each of its matrix programs, NOAA designated a program manager, a program coordinator who advised the manager, and several key individuals from the contributing line units. Each team member was accountable to two people. Key individuals reported to the matrix program manager as well as to their line office supervisors. The matrix program manager reported to his or her goal team leader, to his or her line supervisor, and to the assistant administrator who ran the Office of PPI (NOAA 2008).

In addition to these primary actors, a senior management team consisting of high-level officials from each of the relevant line offices was supposed to provide overall policy guidance for matrix participants. Its role was analogous to that of a board of directors in this respect. Although NOAA encouraged its officials to deal with conflicts at the lowest possible level, senior management teams also operated as appeals boards for resolving issues of coordination between line offices that could not be worked out among key individuals and the program managers. Beyond this, conflicts further escalated to the deputy assistant administrators who headed the line offices and then to the executive council that advised the administrator of NOAA. Matrix programs could also create thematic working groups on an ad hoc basis to provide planning and policy advice to the senior management team (NOAA 2008).

One should emphasize that NOAA's matrix structure was an extension of or supplement to PPB. That is, matrix teams *were* the program teams for PPB in the areas where they existed. One should also add that most of NOAA's eighteen remaining programs involved contributions by multiple units within one of its line components. As such, they often effectively operated as matrix teams as well.

Conclusion

To say that organizations are created to get things done is not to say that the structure of public bureaucracies always embodies a rational integration of means and ends. The piecemeal accumulation of programs and units to carry them out is antithetical to comprehensive planning and organizational design. In addition, the goals of public agencies are usually not hierarchical and discrete but conflicting and overlapping. Structural choices, themselves, may be influenced as much by the struggle among contending stakeholders as by considerations of efficient or effective policy implementation (Seidman and Gilmour 1986; Moe 1989).

NOAA appears to be an extreme example of the gap that typically exists between the reality of public organization and the Weberian ideal of neatly differentiated functions. The agency was cobbled together in an effort to coordinate policy in an interrelated set of areas, but its creation in 1970 did not eliminate the problems it was designed to address. It merely placed them under one roof. The potential for redundancy and conflict among NOAA's constituent parts became even more problematic as it acquired new responsibilities for scientific research and environmental protection. These management issues became increasingly salient as its political principals questioned the agency's efficiency.

Organizational restructuring had proved to be of limited value in addressing NOAA's issues of coordination. Although its adoption of PPB and matrix management derived from the experiences of the admiral who became NOAA administrator in 2002, therefore, this reform was also an attempt to achieve the integration that had eluded the agency since its inception. It was also notable as an effort to promote the objectives of the performance movement. Although advocates of strategic planning and performance-based management are seldom explicit as to how such coordination might be achieved, their most important purpose is arguably to rationalize the allocation of resources across organizational boundaries.

It remains to be asked how well PPBES and matrix management worked. The management system introduced by Admiral Lautenbacher had a significant effect in promoting communication and shared awareness across organizational boundaries. Yet as reflected in its recent disappearance at NOAA, PPB imposed substantial organizational costs and had relatively little effect on the allocation of resources. The various problems it faced were identical to those that had led to the failure of PPB forty years earlier. It is to these issues that the discussion now turns.

Notes

1. The Climate Program Office, the National Sea Grant Program, the Undersea Research Program, and the Office of Ocean Exploration.
2. The Air Resources Lab (Silver Spring, MD), the Atlantic Oceanographic and Meteorological Lab (Miami), the Earth System Research Lab (Boulder, CO), the Geophysical Fluid Dynamics Lab (Princeton, NJ), the Great Lakes Environmental Research Lab (Ann Arbor, MI), the National Severe Storms Lab (Norman, OK), and the Pacific Marine Environmental Lab (Seattle).
3. PART reviews focused on a sample of agency programs each year on a rotating basis. Although OMB portrayed the PART as an effort to comply with GPRA, there was a good deal of disagreement as to how faithfully it did so (Radin 2006).
4. The consolidation of NOAA's Boulder labs is anomalous in this regard because it had the practical effect of creating an additional level of hierarchy within the organization.
5. It added that "the need to improve corporate decision making—i.e., to effectively integrate strategic planning, budgeting, and performance evaluation—is not unique to NOAA. The President's Management Agenda recognized similar problems across the federal government" (Lautenbacher 2002, 17).
6. Some NOAA insiders have suggested that the actual role of these external actors in the planning process has been negligible.
7. The use of teams is also consistent with the premise of human relations theory that organizations should encourage their members to exercise creativity and initiative. Matrix organizations are thus posed as an alternative to traditional, "mechanistic" organizations whose hierarchy, rigid division of labor, and heavy reliance on standard operating procedures arguably stifle these qualities.

Chapter 5

Evaluating NOAA's Management Initiatives

As has been discussed in previous chapters, program budgeting seeks to promote instrumental rationality in the management of bureaucracy. It does this by requiring agencies to plan and evaluate what they do in terms of means–ends linkages. This is designed to allow decision makers to identify redundancies and conflicts within their organizations, to compare the relative effectiveness of activities, and to prioritize the allocation of resources in light of such comparisons. These goals were clearly articulated in NOAA's justification for its adoption of PPB:

> PPBES [planning, programming, budgeting execution systems] focuses on annual objectives for using all available NOAA resources to achieve the best return on investment in pursuit of fulfilling NOAA's strategic goals. PPBES allows for careful planning, the prioritization of resources across competing requirements, fact-based assessments of best program options, objective evaluations of performance, and a strict focus on accountability. And PPBES serves as a program, project, and milestone system to orient and influence all NOAA activity levels and requirements. (NOAA 2008, 1)

NOAA seemed to be an especially attractive candidate for program budgeting. The fact that its organizational components performed similar and interrelated functions while operating with a good deal of autonomy had resulted in substantial criticism of the agency by the early 2000s. Accordingly, NOAA's version of PPB relied heavily on collaborative planning and assessment by teams of line personnel representing activities and programs that contributed to similar goals. More than half the teams were responsible for "matrix programs" that combined activities from two or more of the agency's five major line components: the National Weather Service; the National Environmental Satellite, Data, and Information Service; the National Ocean Service; the National Marine Fisheries Service; and the Office of Oceanic and Atmospheric Research.

This chapter focuses on the effects of PPB and matrix management at NOAA. One might have modest expectations for NOAA's reforms in light of the obstacles that program budgeting encountered when it was extended from the Department of Defense (DoD) to the entire federal government in the 1960s. These allegedly included organizational inertia, inadequate expertise and staff resources, opposition from entrenched bureaucratic/political constituencies, the conceptual difficulty of organizing functions around discrete goals, and the inherent limitations of comprehensive rational analysis. Even Charles Hitch—the father of PPB and the primary agent for its introduction to DoD—had counseled against its use in the civilian bureaucracy for most if not all these reasons (Hitch 1996).

Yet perhaps the impediments to program budgeting have become less formidable in the intervening decades. Policy analysis, which lies at the heart of the process, is no longer a foreign activity as it was to much of the bureaucracy in the 1960s (Meltsner 1976; McGarity 1991; Radin 2000a). The pursuit of objective, performance-based management, which provides a second and related foundation for PPB, has also enjoyed a surge in popularity since the 1980s. It, too, has been institutionalized throughout the government by statutory requirements and executive orders (Radin 2006; Moynihan 2008). Some technique that incorporates the essential elements of PPB is arguably the only way fully to realize the goals of the performance movement.

Beyond these general developments, NOAA seems to be an especially hospitable environment for program budgeting. Like DoD (and unlike agencies with more diverse sets of mandates), the relative cohesiveness of its mission should facilitate the hierarchical integration of means and ends that is the conceptual framework for PPB. Most of NOAA's research, service, and regulatory activities thus center on the collection and application of environmental and ecological knowledge. As in DoD under Robert McNamara, moreover, PPB was introduced by NOAA's leadership. Most agency heads in the 1960s had little understanding of or appreciation for program budgeting (Haveman and Margolis 1970; Lyden and Miller 1972). In contrast, Admiral Lautenbacher had been an accomplished practitioner of PPB in DoD, and he reinforced his commitment to its success at NOAA by placing former DoD officials and other advocates of the system in key planning and budgeting positions.

It is important to emphasize at the outset that the effects of PPB (or any system of budgeting or management) do not lend themselves to precise measurement. As discussed below, obstacles to assessment include a lack of appropriate budgetary data and the difficulty of identifying causal relationships between decision-making processes and their outputs and outcomes. In addition, agency documents describing the role played by PPB in arriving at specific decisions are not available to the public.

Although this chapter presents various kinds of evidence, therefore, it relies heavily on confidential, loosely structured conversations with agency officials and other participants in NOAA's implementation of PPB. Among those interviewed were two current or former assistant administrators (who head NOAA's major components), the current or former leaders of three goal teams, and the leaders or members of eleven program teams (six of which were matrix programs). Most of these individuals are or were senior line managers with extensive agency experience, and most are scientists. I also interviewed seven headquarters officials, including at least two representatives from each of the NOAA headquarters units with a prominent role in implementing PPB (Office of Program Planning and Integration; Office of Program Analysis and Evaluation; and Office of the Chief Financial Officer). The latter were planning and management specialists rather than scientists, and some had relatively short tenure at the agency. Other interviewees included consultants that had helped NOAA design and implement PPB, current or former Office of Management and Budget (OMB) officials with a close knowledge of NOAA's budget, and congressional staff members from committees that deal with NOAA appropriations and authorization legislation. Most of the interviews lasted between thirty minutes and one hour, and I gathered additional information through follow-up e-mail questions in some cases.

Assessments of PPB by NOAA officials prove no exception to the axiom that where one stands depends on where one sits (Allison 1971). Not surprisingly, line and program managers were less positive about the agency's management reforms than were planning and budgeting staff. As one of the former put it, "The farther you get from headquarters, the less enthusiasm you will find for PPBES." Still, managers were aware of the broader organizational and political context in which they operated, including the expectations of external principals that NOAA improve its management practices. Most did not think that the old system was very good, and they generally endorsed the objectives if not necessarily the results of the process instituted by Admiral Lautenbacher.

Moreover, there was relatively little disagreement among those interviewed about the effects and limitations of PPB and matrix management. Varying assessments of the process instead were grounded in the subjective weights and valences that people attached to different factors. Although headquarters staff recognized that the additional work required by PPB could interfere with line officials' other duties, for example, this was naturally less of a concern for them than it was for the individuals directly affected. As another illustration, differing assessments of the need to demonstrate the practical benefits of programs largely reflected officials' conflicting beliefs about the importance of basic research and its relationship to NOAA's mission.[1]

Any conclusions about the "success" or "failure" of NOAA's management system are highly dependent on assumptions about what it was supposed to accomplish. It is easy enough for PPB to fall victim to the expectations that derive from its underlying logic and that are reinforced by the claims of its more zealous advocates. Yet to acknowledge that it falls short of the transformational rationality that it seems to promise on its face is not to conclude that it lacks merit. That practitioners of PPB often implicitly defend it on the basis of more modest criteria may suggest that its operational goals have become somewhat different than its theoretical goals over the years.

Subject to these caveats, it is fair to conclude that program budgeting and matrix management had mixed results at NOAA. They required the agency to identify and justify its goals with more clarity and precision, and they improved communications across organizational units. This reportedly facilitated several cooperative initiatives. NOAA's reforms required significant time and effort to execute, however, and they were perceived by some as having been inimical to the agency's scientific mission. They also had only a marginal effect on the allocation of resources and responsibilities. It is far from clear that budgeting became any less incremental at NOAA after the introduction of PPB.

The difficulties that confronted NOAA's implementation of PPB are the same as those that program budgeting encountered when it was introduced to the civilian bureaucracy more than four decades ago. They include the resistance that normally confronts efforts to change organizational processes and culture. They also include significant disjunctures between the assumptions of program budgeting and the managerial and political realities that define NOAA's operating environment. In light of these observations, it is not surprising that NOAA abandoned PPB in 2010 following an internal review of the process that had been initiated in anticipation of a new presidential administration.

Intended Effects

Some of the benefits of NOAA's management initiatives were self-evident. By almost all accounts, they helped to address the lack of interorganizational communication that had been the source of so much criticism before the appointment of Admiral Lautenbacher. In at least a few cases, they facilitated cooperative efforts across line components to propose solutions to important issues. Program budgeting also provided a framework for more rigorous planning and the clear articulation of linkages between NOAA's goals and its activities. There is little evidence that it led to a substantial redistribution of resources across agency line components, however, and its effects on NOAA's budget otherwise appear to have been modest, at best.

Communication and Coordination

Even many within NOAA who are critical of PPB on the whole feel that it improved communications across organizational units. It would be surprising to find otherwise given the extensive meetings and briefings required by the process. For instance, a goal team leader indicated that he held weekly meetings with his program managers and biweekly meetings with an advisory board that also included representatives from relevant laboratories, centers, and other line units. The preparation, circulation, and review of the various analytical and guidance documents that were generated throughout the process also naturally enhanced the sharing of information.

A senior career executive who had formerly served as a program team leader and then a goal team leader offered an anecdote from a recent meeting to illustrate the effect of PPBES in promoting shared organizational awareness. Shortly after taking office in the spring of 2009, the newly appointed NOAA administrator asked each of her assistant administrators (in charge of the agency's five major line organizations) to describe and justify an important program that was housed in another component. The fact that he and his colleagues could offer informed responses was evidence that NOAA had made significant strides in opening up dialogue across its components. As he noted, "We would not have been able to answer this question ten years ago. Now there is much more collaboration among assistant administrators. There had always been collegiality but not much fluidity and cross-pollination across stovepipes."

This same person added that communications had also improved at lower levels in the organization—both among and within its major line components. "Now people talk across boundaries. It is not just a matter of focusing on what my problems are." In a similar vein, a program manager from the Office of Oceanic and Atmospheric Research observed that, although there had always been informal communications among labs, the exchange of scientific information had become more frequent and less idiosyncratic as a result of their involvement in planning and programming.

Heightened communication across organizational boundaries that resulted from PPB and matrix management sometimes encouraged the exchange of ideas and cooperative problem solving. A manager from the National Weather Service (NWS) cited two examples of coordination across programs that he attributed to dialogue that had occurred within his goal team. In one having to do with a toxic pollutant, he indicated that "although the relevant bits were in many different PPBES programs, we were able to talk to . . . our colleagues and put together a top quality proposal." As another example, he observed that efforts to integrate homeland security programs across NOAA were "finally paying off."

Planning, Performance Assessment, and Accountability

PPB also led to a more explicit identification of the relationships between organizational objectives and activities. It would be misleading to imply that NOAA did not engage in goal-oriented planning and assessment before 2002. In fact, it was required to do so by virtue of its designation as one of the pilot agencies that would initially comply with the terms of the Government Performance and Results Act (GPRA). In its fiscal year (FY) 1998 budget, for example, the agency articulated a ten-year strategic plan that included an overarching vision supported by seven strategic goals. Each of these goals was a function that involved activities by two or more of NOAA's line components, and each was accompanied by its own vision and by a discussion of challenges, implementation strategy, benefits, accomplishments, key activities, and key performance measures. In each case, the total funding for that function was broken down according to each component's relative contribution. (The budget was also presented in a line-item format.) Of the $115,263,000 allocated for Seasonal to Interannual Climate Forecasts, for example, 58 percent was allocated for OAR; 32 percent for the National Environmental Satellite, Data, and Information Service (NESDIS); 4 percent for the NWS; and 2 percent for the National Ocean Service (in addition to 3 percent for program support and 1 percent for construction).

A veteran from NOAA headquarters characterized these earlier efforts as "an important intellectual step toward a program structure that could be used." As is often alleged of strategic planning, however, he felt that the "results were an ad hoc rationalization" by headquarters staff rather than the product of a decision-making process intended to arrive at a more efficient allocation of resources. Among the weaknesses he attributed to the system were its failures to tie the program structure directly to NOAA's strategic plan, on the one hand, and to the agency's budgetary process, on the other. The latter deficiency made "coordination and specific summing very difficult." His assessments are supported by the observation that internal and external reviews of NOAA's management practices conducted several years later (and discussed in the preceding chapter) concluded that the agency had not made substantial progress in integrating its operations (Lautenbacher 2002; Moore 2004).

The management system that was instituted by Admiral Lautenbacher clearly went beyond earlier efforts at planning and coordination. Its most salient changes included

- the introduction of a five-year budget;
- the formation of a clearly defined, hierarchically ordered program structure that incorporated matrix principles;
- the establishment of an analytical process and set of documents for assessing agency activities in terms of their contributions agency objectives, and for translating those assessments into budgetary decisions;
- the incorporation of systematic efforts to include all of NOAA's internal and external stakeholders in the planning process; and
- the creation of new headquarters offices for program planning and integration and for policy analysis and evaluation to provide guidance and support for the implementation of the foregoing changes.

Whether the elaborate planning process instituted by PPB involved a serious assessment and reformulation of organizational priorities is an open question. A skeptic might infer from the generality of its strategic objectives that they were ultimately intended to encompass everything that the agency had been doing (including its statutory mandates) and to satisfy the demands of all its stakeholders. In any case, there is little doubt that the reforms created a more systematic *process* for fiscal and policy planning. By the same token, they produced a more explicit articulation of means–ends relationships, as well as heightened efforts to hold people accountable for the effects of program implementation.

To its defenders and even some of its critics, the increased transparency and accountability that resulted from PPB were important benefits in and of themselves. One line manager and program leader observed that "there are people who would like to be left alone to do their work. That would be nice but it's not realistic [in NOAA's fiscal and political environment]." Characterizing the previous system as "Camp Run-a-Muck," another program manager who had recently come to NOAA from DoD noted that PPB had replaced "who you know" with objective criteria as a basis for budgeting and management decisions. In a similar vein, a member of the Office of the Chief Financial Officer who had previously worked in one of NOAA's component organizations argued that the program structure and the analysis required by PPB were valuable simply because they afforded the administrator and other executives a more comprehensive understanding of what the organization was doing and of how its parts fit together.

Competing for Resources

Ultimately, of course, changes in management processes are intended to yield substantive results. One possible effect of PPB is that it enabled NOAA to sell itself more effectively to its political principals in Congress and the executive branch. Some have alleged that program budgeting has served the military well in the competition for federal dollars (Jones and McCaffery 2005), and this perception was reportedly one of Admiral Lautenbacher's motives for bringing the system with him from the navy. Several PPI and PA&E officials noted that NOAA had, in fact, fared better in the budgetary process than other scientific agencies during the 2000s. Presumably this was because PPB provided a clearer picture of NOAA's objectives and more focused and compelling evidence of its success in achieving those goals.

The argument that PPB helped NOAA to secure more resources was not elaborated by its proponents, however, and it was disputed by several line officials. One noted that, although NOAA's overall budget had grown since 2002, the expansion was confined primarily to programs within NESDIS. Partly as a consequence, budgets for most of the agency's other activities remained relatively flat or declined. As quoted in an article on NOAA's FY 2009 budget, a close outside observer of the agency similarly observed that "by putting all its eggs in that basket [satellites], NOAA is not able to make progress in its operational and base programs." Another noted that "the real worry is the squeeze that the satellites are putting on everything [else]" (Showstack 2008, 74).

Interestingly, those who cited PPB as a source of budgetary success also observed that most NOAA programs were severely underfunded. Furthermore, no one suggested that budgetary growth for NESDIS had been a success or that it was attributable to PPB. In fact, it was driven by delay and by cost overruns that resulted in considerable criticism. As Senator Richard Shelby (2009) noted before an appropriations subcommittee in April 2009, for instance:

> I am also disappointed in the [Commerce] Department's lack of oversight of NOAA's satellite programs. . . . The N-POESS satellite system was supposed to cost $6.5 billion for six satellites. It is now estimated that taxpayers will be handed a bill for $13.6 billion for only four satellites that are less capable than originally planned. This program is a complete failure for NOAA and an even bigger failure for the taxpayer. . . . The second satellite program is also a grave failure. The GOES-R satellite procurement was a $6.2 billion program

for four satellites which has now ballooned to a $7.7 billion program for only two satellites with a delivery date six years behind schedule. The acquisition history of these two satellite systems . . . demonstrates that management and acquisition oversight does not exist at the Department of Commerce.

The year before, concerns about NOAA's satellite spending resulted in the Senate's unanimous passage of a measure to subject the agency to greater oversight by Congress, OMB, and the secretary of commerce.

Perhaps the most compelling reason to be skeptical of claims that PPB helped NOAA compete for resources is that use of the technique was confined within the agency. The Department of Commerce, OMB, and Congress made decisions based on NOAA's line budget. Although analyses conducted for planning and programming may have produced data that the chief financial officer or line officials disaggregated for the purpose of justifying activities within NOAA's components, any such arguments that might have been offered to the Department of Commerce, OMB, or Congress were divorced from the program structure that linked those activities to the organization's strategic goals.

Redistributive Effects

The ostensible purpose of program budgeting is not to help an agency compete for more resources. Rather, it is to conserve resources and allocate them more efficiently among competing alternatives. (In the early 1960s, for example, some advocates of PPB argued that the greater efficiencies it produced in defense would free up more money for domestic programs.) In this regard, improved communications and more systematic processes of planning and assessment at NOAA were arguably proximate objectives, the attainment of which would lead to more rational spending decisions.

Unfortunately, the redistributive effects of PPB are difficult to assess in terms of inputs and outputs. Among the reasons for this are that

- NOAA's budgets are not broken down for the public in a way that allows one to identify changes over time in funding for PPB programs and activities within programs.
- Even if such data were available, simply to correlate changes in spending with the institution of PPB would not demonstrate that those changes resulted from PPB. As with any agency, NOAA's budgets are influenced by a variety of factors both internal and external to the organization.
- Even if one could identify changes in NOAA's budget that resulted from PPB, this would not demonstrate that those changes produced a more efficient allocation of resources.

Nor are data available that might facilitate a systematic qualitative analysis of the effects of PPB. Although program assessments, strategic portfolio analyses, program plans, and program decision memoranda might yield considerable insight as to the nature, quality, and effects of analysis, these and other documents that informed agency decisions are (for legitimate reasons) reserved for internal use.

With these caveats, patterns of change in the allocation of resources among NOAA's line components may provide one indication of the substantive impact of PPB. Comprehensive planning and crosscutting analysis were instituted as a more rational alternative to "line-item" budgeting, in which the previous expenditures provided the starting point for "incremental" adjustments in spending. This is the sense in which an analyst who had come to NOAA from DoD endorsed PPB as a "significant improvement over base-plus initiative thinking that focuses tremendous attention on small changes in the budget and assumes existing programs are effective and the best way to attain future goals."[2] If PPB overcame precedent to produce (or at least substantially to further) "the best return on investment" (NOAA 2008, 1), therefore, one might expect its introduction to have resulted in greater fluctuations in the distribution of resources across line units from one year to the next.

With this hypothesis in mind, figure 5.1 graphs changes in the amount of funding recommended in the president's budget for each of NOAA's major line components as a percentage of the total amount recommended for all five components from FY 1998 to FY 2009. The smallest units for which consistent data are available, these components housed virtually all of NOAA's substantive programs throughout the period. Percentages are framed in this way (and not in terms of NOAA's total budget recommendation) in order to provide a more direct indication of the distribution of funds among programmatic activities that compete for resources (as opposed to spending for headquarters units and other support functions). Although the requests that NOAA submitted through the Department of Commerce to OMB and the White House are not available, the data here presumably reflect the input of NOAA's senior management.

Whether a change in spending is incremental can be subjective. Be this as it may, changes in the proportional allocation of funds among NOAA's line components did not become any less incremental following the introduction of PPB. This is further illustrated by a comparison of annual sums of percentage increments (ignoring whether they were positive or negative) across all five line-component requests in figure 5.2. Whereas the average yearly total from FY 1999 to FY 2002 was 12.18, it was 4.58 from FY 2003 to FY 2009.

This evidence is admittedly crude and inconclusive. One caveat is that the percentages in figure 5.1 do not reflect the allocation of fixed resources among a fixed set of activities. Annual proposals for NOAA's line components thus also include additions to or subtractions from their portfolios in response to new legislative requirements, new presidential and Department of Commerce priorities, and other inputs. For example, increased spending on NOAA's satellite programs, which again accounts for much of the agency's overall budgetary growth during the past decade, necessarily compromises efforts to identify the redistributive effect of PPB. Another caveat is that spending for line components may reflect organizational rather than programmatic changes. For instance, OAR's percentage decline after 2004 was attributable in part to the fact that one of its laboratories was transferred to the NWS. All this is to reiterate the ironic point that budgetary data are limited in what they can tell us about the effects of budgetary processes.

If they do not disconfirm it, however, the data offer little to support the hypothesis that PPB had a substantial redistributive impact on spending within NOAA. This is consistent with the observations of agency personnel and others familiar with NOAA's budgetary process. None of those interviewed could cite a specific instance in which PPB led to a dramatic reallocation of funds across programs or program elements. Although some retained hope that it might play a greater role in the future, both line and headquarters officials were unanimous in their assessment that its effects on the allocation of resources had been confined to the margins.

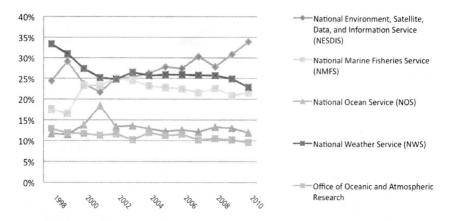

Figure 5.1. NOAA Agency Budget Trend by Percentage of Total 1998–2010

Source: NOAA Budget Office, "FY 2010 Blue Book."

The impact of comparative, performance-based analysis under PPB was reportedly circumscribed in two ways. One was its confinement to *particular areas.* As a member of PA&E observed, "We focus our efforts strategically [rather than comprehensively]." Another was its strong tendency to focus on competition for *additional resources* (as opposed to the optimal use of existing or diminishing resources). Theory and rhetoric to the contrary notwithstanding, PPB in practice did not replace "base-plus-initiative thinking" at NOAA. These limitations can be understood in terms that are familiar from assessments of PPB in the 1960s.

Obstacles to Change

There is much to be said for a management system that clarifies objectives and the means to achieve them, and that encourages the exchange of information and ideas across organizational units. There is also something to be said for a system that produces better-informed decisions, even if those decisions are confined to the margins. Yet a full assessment of NOAA's reforms must also consider their possible costs in terms of organizational efficiency and effectiveness. It should further consider why PPB fell short of the comprehensive rationality promised by its logic and the claims made by some of its advocates.

NOAA's implementation of PPB and matrix management encountered a number of obstacles. Although it is impossible to determine their relative importance, these included the tensions that normally accompany efforts at organizational change. The demands of PPB strained agency resources and introduced decision-making criteria that conflicted with established norms. As discussed in the following section, PPB also suffered from several interrelated weaknesses as a practical theory that went beyond the usual resistance to new routines. Among them were its simplistic assumptions about means–ends relationships and its incompatibility with the managerial and political realities of NOAA's operating environment.

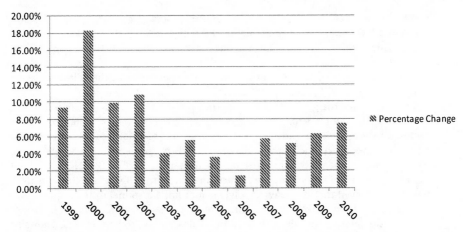

Figure 5.2. Total Percentage Change across Agencies, 1999–2010

Source: NOAA Budget Office, "FY 2010 Blue Book."

Resource Constraints

Altering the behavior of a large and complex organization is especially challenging if the demands imposed by new requirements are not accompanied by new resources. This was clearly the case with NOAA's implementation of PPB, which relied on line personnel to accomplish much of the initial work in planning and programming. Given that the leaders of goal and program teams were also full-time managers, the additional responsibilities imposed by NOAA's reforms were a source of concern and often resentment throughout the agency's line components. Not surprisingly, managers cite the analytical requirements of PPB as having been particularly burdensome. Meetings and other requirements for communication could also be time consuming, especially for matrix programs.

Although reactions vary in their intensity, some expressed considerable frustration over the demands imposed by PPB. One program manager estimated that it had consumed six to seven months of his time over the past two and a half years. Another team leader from Colorado indicated that he had been required to make fifteen trips to NOAA headquarters in Silver Spring, Maryland, during the preceding year. Another remarked that "all of your old duties are still there and now you're also a program manager." Still another observed that "PPB is an incredibly time-consuming and energy-sapping enterprise. Lab directors used to be scientists who were also science managers. Now they have to be full-time administrators."

The burden imposed by PPB can be attributed in part to NOAA's failure to provide additional personnel for its implementation. Although a position was created for each goal team to help coordinate planning and programming, the responsibilities of team leads remained sufficiently demanding that they were perceived as a second full-time job. Similar staff positions were not added at the program level. In addition, the relatively small size of PPI and PA&E (about fifteen and ten positions, respectively) limited the amount of assistance they could provide to goal and program teams in planning and programming. In the eyes of some line officials, this limitation was compounded by the fact that headquarters personnel lacked the scientific knowledge required to evaluate many programs. Several members of goal and program teams contrasted NOAA's limited resourcing of PPB with DoD, which dedicated hundreds of uniformed officers, civilian staff, and outside consultants solely to the implementation of its system.

Although a few of NOAA's line managers were perplexed by the failure to devote more resources to PPB, most speculated that it was attributable to a tight fiscal environment in which the great majority of agency programs were already underfunded. (One might be tempted to draw a parallel here between the budgetary demands imposed by Afghanistan and Iraq and the diversion of resources to Vietnam that allegedly undermined the implementation of PPB in the 1960s.) Yet whatever the role budgetary constraints might have played, the architects of PPB at NOAA did not want to adopt a DoD model that separated analytical from operational responsibilities. They believed that the heavy involvement of line personnel in the implementation of program budgeting would contribute to the system's effectiveness by bringing needed scientific expertise to bear in the evaluation of program effects. They also viewed such participation as a way to enhance the communication and coordination across organizational units that critics had found to be lacking at NOAA.[3]

Although they were aware that it would impose additional demands, moreover, the designers of NOAA's system of PPB did not fully anticipate the difficulties or the adverse reactions that it would encounter. A member of PA&E suggested that this could be explained in part by top leadership's overestimation of management capabilities within NOAA's line components: "Overestimated was the availability of the normal suite of management skills. Most of the program managers were highly skilled scientists who had little training or even the most basic skills needed to effectively manage a program. The lack of a skill set was a surprise to [top level] management and the need for training was resented by program managers."

PA&E officials contend that the burdens imposed by PPB often had less to do its actual requirements than with how those requirements were misinterpreted. One observed that, "The executives who instituted PPB were aware of the additional work required and considered it when adopting PPB for NOAA use. What they failed to understand was the corporate culture elements that caused a great deal more work [than was intended]."

NOAA's leadership may have assumed that highly intelligent people who were trained to approach problems in a systematic way would readily master the analytical requirements of PPB. According to headquarters officials, however, the agency's scientific orientation actually impeded the system's implementation. Given their emphasis on rigor, the members of program and goal teams allegedly produced more thorough and detailed analyses than were initially required. Noting that "a one-page summary is all we need in some cases" and that "we will ask for more information as we need it," a member of PA&E observed that scientists whose professional lives were structured around narrowly defined issues and whose frame of reference was peer-reviewed articles found it difficult to be succinct.

Another PA&E official felt that the tendency for scientists to view follow-up questions as criticisms of their work also generated unnecessary effort under PPB. Long and detailed analyses thus were allegedly motivated by a desire to preempt such queries. This in turn made the jobs of PA&E and other headquarters units more difficult:

> The NOAA culture viewed any question about a submission as an indicator
> that it was flawed or incomplete. So the initial Program Baseline Assessments

were very lengthy, attempting to address any foreseeable circumstance or question. This made the documents nearly unusable by the recipients. It is impossible for most of us to know every detail of every program in a large and diverse organization like NOAA. But these details were provided, making the job of especially PA&E analysts, but others as well, much more difficult because the key pieces of information needed to be separated from the hundreds of pages of complex information.

Headquarters staff occasionally resorted to word-count limits in an effort to force program teams to be more concise.

Not surprisingly, many of NOAA's line personnel take exception with these explanations for the length and detail of their analyses. Calling such assertions "incredibly disingenuous," an assistant administrator noted that PPI and PA&E set the tone for the implementation of PPB early on by repeatedly asking programs, "Where's your justification?" To him, this naturally created an expectation that initial analyses should be as thorough as possible. This expectation was reinforced by the perception (although apparently not the reality) that budgetary decision making was highly competitive under PPB and that insufficient justifications for programs would therefore be penalized by cuts in funding.

Inadequate Guidance

Whichever of these accounts is more accurate, the foregoing observations suggest that confusion about the requirements of PPB exacerbated the problems of implementing an unfamiliar system. The relationship between NOAA's program structure and its line structure was a source of confusion as well. Although the agency hired outside consultants to familiarize its personnel with the purposes and requirements of PPB early on, a member of the firm indicated that the training they provided was insufficient. This was due in part to the fact that it was only offered on a one-time basis, even though the sessions were designed to be repeated annually.

Several factors may explain the lack of guidance that inhibited the implementation of NOAA's reforms. One is simply the speed with which they were put in place. A consultant involved in the system's design and implementation also speculated that Admiral Lautenbacher was reluctant to spend more money on training in light of NOAA's tight fiscal environment and in symbolic recognition of the cost-cutting orientation of PPB.[4] The agency's leadership also undoubtedly recognized that NOAA was a very different organization than the military. Accordingly, they may have anticipated that the details of adapting DoD's system of program budgeting to NOAA's culture and task environment would have to be fleshed out through practice rather than be codified at the outset.

Inadequate guidance for the execution of PPB may also have been due to the fact that senior officials were not of a common mind about what it was supposed to accomplish. According to the consultant cited above, the three people who had been delegated primary responsibility for implementing the system had three distinct interpretations of its objectives that reflected their functional responsibilities in the agency. Thus, although she felt that her firm's training module presented clear and consistent guidance to program managers, subsequent presentations by NOAA's chief financial officer and the heads of PPI and PA&E allegedly did not present a coherent message to agency line personnel.

Insofar as they were based on a misunderstanding of its requirements, or insofar as those requirements, themselves, became clearer through experience, one might expect the burdens imposed by PPB to have subsided over time. In fact, two program team leaders noted that the system became less onerous after they accepted the admonitions of PPI and PA&E to provide less detailed analyses. Yet this in turn led one of them to question the value of a decision-making system "based on sound bytes." He noted that, although complying with PPB became easier as he gained familiarity with the process, he also took it less seriously because of its lack of rigor and its limited substantive effects.

Managerial Values versus Scientific Values

Aside from the tensions associated with resource constraints, the adoption of new routines can be especially difficult if those routines conflict with an organization's culture or sense of mission. In this regard, scientists' expectation that they define their own agendas was at odds with the top-down planning orientation of PPB. This expectation stemmed from the intellectual temperament that had led them to become scientists in the first place, as well as from the belief that they were the best judges of what research was important in their areas of specialization. Although such autonomy could obviously never be absolute in a government agency, it was furthered by the decentralization of operational authority within NOAA. It was also underwritten by a fragmented system of authorization, budgeting, and oversight in which programs were supported by influential constituents in institutes, universities, legislative committees, and elsewhere. PPB thus was resented because of its potential—indeed its intent—to impose more centralized control on the activities of units and individuals that had traditionally enjoyed considerable independence. This is the sense in which an OAR official commented that "the people in the labs have no use for it [PPB]. They want to be left alone."

If they were opposed to the idea of centralized control, per se, some within NOAA also felt that the specific means through which PPB sought to achieve centralization could be antithetical to one of the organization's core missions. Line managers responsible for research operations observed that the long-range projection of resource needs required by the process could be inconsistent with the fluid character of scientific inquiry, where agendas naturally evolved as the expansion of knowledge identified new problems and solved old ones. This was especially apt to be the case for environmental and ecological research, where the underlying subject, itself, was in constant flux. One scientist/manager observed that PPB was more conducive to thinking about weapons systems or building roads than about NOAA's research mission. Another noted that the system's "cumbersome" planning requirements could inhibit the agency's ability to respond to needs or targets of opportunity created by natural events.

Attempts at objective performance assessment were also a source of tension. Although managers felt that everything NOAA did should ultimately have practical benefits for society, a number of them emphasized that the most valuable research often did not have immediate and demonstrable results. Complaining about the inability or unwillingness of headquarters staff to appreciate the limitations of technocracy, a NOAA scientist noted that "they [NOAA executives and planning staff] don't understand that it may take a long time to realize scientific advances and benefits." Another observed that the professional planners at headquarters "wear [their lack of scientific sophistication] as a badge of honor." The reciprocal contribution of headquarters staff to the cultural conflict surrounding PPB is summed up in the assertion by a member of PPI that "scientists cannot plan." To professional planners, the idea that researchers should be able to pursue their own interests without regard to NOAA's strategic goals was pernicious and unrealistic.

The conflict between NOAA's culture and the substantive goals of PPB was reinforced in some cases by scientists' objections to the role they were required to play in the process. Given that much of the analysis was for the purpose of advocacy, some people were uncomfortable with the need to compromise the standards objectivity that were paramount in their careers as professional researchers. Some of them were also uncomfortable with the perceived need to "describe what we do on a sixth-grade level" for consumption by planners and agency executives who were not scientists.

NOAA's increased emphasis on applied research with measurable benefits began with GPRA in the 1990s. The introduction of PPB nevertheless amplified the importance of such criteria as a basis for accountability. It deserves to be mentioned that the NOAA administrator under Bill Clinton was himself a distinguished climate scientist. Whatever the personal orientation of Admiral Lautenbacher (who holds a PhD in applied mathematics and headed a nonprofit consortium for oceanographic research after leaving the navy), some within the agency viewed program budgeting as a reflection of the George W. Bush administration's lack of appreciation for science. One person went so far as to complain that the intent of the reforms was to "take the joy out of science." Several staff members were also apprehensive that the deemphasis on basic research would make it more difficult for NOAA to recruit and retain bright and creative people.

Some line personnel perceived in these regards that a mechanism designed to achieve organizational goals more efficiently was also part of an effort to *reshape* NOAA's goals and decision-making processes in ways that were at odds with important elements of its mission. Although it may not be supported by the budget data discussed above, a related concern in some quarters was that PPB was biased in favor of those entities within the agency whose performance could be measured with a relatively high degree of confidence. As one program manager noted:

> One of the issues is that part of NOAA (e.g., the [NWS]) has relatively clear and measurable objectives—lead time warnings, etc. The navigation services [also] have measurable values. Where the objectives break down is in the coastal and research or ecosystem management, and that provides an additional tension across NOAA. If the [chief financial officer] or OMB favor programs that have concrete measurements the perception or reality is that the "softer" portions of NOAA do not get funded.

As with complaints about the analytical burdens imposed by PPB, some members of PPI and PA&E contend that the tension between planning and performance assessment, on the one hand, and scientific values, on the other, was more perception than reality. In arguing that complex and detailed program baseline assessments were counterproductive, for example, a member of PA&E emphasized that "PPBES is not a tool for the evaluation of the scientific merit of individual research projects." Yet this contention is difficult to reconcile with the fact that PPB sought to promote accountability and efficiency precisely through a comparative *evaluation* of organizational activities. Perhaps his use of the term "merit" referred to sound methodology or to the value of research in some intrinsic sense (rather than in terms of its contribution to NOAA's strategic goals). In any case, a subsequent e-mail intended to clarify his point seems to underscore the tension between the managerial orientation of PPB and NOAA's scientific culture:

This issue is complicated by the differences in thinking between business decision makers and research scientists. Research scientists spend their entire lives devoted to very narrow and highly complex efforts. . . . Some members of the scientific community interpret business decisions as an evaluation of the merit of their work. Let me clearly state that I have never seen unimportant research efforts at NOAA. *But we must prioritize, and because of the different mindsets, there is a perception that we do not understand the importance of the efforts that are not funded.*" (emphasis added)

Limitations as a Practical Theory

Resistance to new ways of thinking and gaps between resources and new requirements often inhibit organizational change. Yet beyond these generic impediments, the implementation of PPB encountered several more fundamental obstacles related to its theoretical premises. These included difficulties associated with the measurement of performance and with the logic of NOAA's program structure. They also included managerial and political realities that limited the incentive to conduct and use objective analysis.

Obstacles to Performance Measurement

An extensive GAO (2004) report reinforces the assessments of many NOAA officials that the challenges of developing objective performance measures tend to be especially daunting for scientific agencies. The outputs of research programs often come in fits and starts, and their outcomes may take years to materialize. Even then, benefits may be difficult to translate into market values or other metrics. A NOAA manager expressed his frustration with performance assessment by noting that "skill scores" (i.e., metrics that originated in the 1990s as a response to the requirements of GPRA) might "bounce all over the place" as the result of factors that bore no relationship to the success of the program he was required to evaluate.

As noted just above, the limitations of performance assessment were more severe for some NOAA programs than for others under PPB. This was attributable in part to the varying talents and predispositions of the members of goal and program teams responsible for conducting analyses. An outside stakeholder who had followed NOAA's implementation of PPB was referring to this when she noted that "one manager would talk about a very specific tool or measurement versus another talking about very broad and ambiguous program goals." Variation in the quality of performance assessment was also attributable to the obvious fact that the effects of some activities were easier to measure than others. As a member of PA&E noted: "The reviews vary in their technical sophistication because of their widely varying subjects. Satellite procurement is carefully examined, but efforts like those to rebuild fish stocks are hard to measure and take decades to show any results. Because of the wide range of efforts NOAA engages in, we have found it difficult to use common measures across the entire organization."

One can argue that the objective assessment of NOAA programs can be a useful tool for management whenever and to the extent that it occurs. It is also important to note in this respect that PPI and PA&E did not take a Procrustean view of performance assessment. Although they wanted analysis to be as objective as possible, they encouraged the use of methods that were appropriate to the questions at hand. This included the use of qualitative techniques in some cases. As implied by the preceding quotation, however, the flexible application of performance assessment illustrates a broader limitation of NOAA's reforms: The inability to develop common measures and the unevenness of analysis more generally undermined the objective comparisons that were designed to take PPB beyond performance assessment per se. A consultant who had helped design NOAA's system was referring to this in noting that "to do it correctly, there needed to be consistency across programs and what they did, and this was missing at NOAA. Programs were apples and oranges."

The Difficulty of Hierarchical Integration

Any attempt to assess and compare performance objectively must begin with the definition of objectives. As an effort to promote planning and coordination, program budgeting assumes that it is possible at the outset to differentiate functions in terms of discrete and hierarchically ordered goals. A related but more basic obstacle to the implementation of PPB at NOAA was rooted in the limitations of this assumption.

That NOAA does not have a single bottom line is evident if one considers the four primary missions articulated in its 2005 strategic plan (NOAA 2004). For example, there is an obvious tension between *protecting coastal and marine ecosystems* and *promoting commercial activity*. In turn, the attempt to operationalize any of these individual goals can become complex and subjective in the context of actual policy choices. In addition to balancing the health of marine ecosystems against commercial interests in establishing regional take limits for different species of fish, for example, the National Fisheries Service must consider the often-competing needs of large commercial fishermen, small commercial fishermen, and those who cater to sport fishermen (charter boat operators) in promoting the latter objective.

Nor can NOAA's means and ends be neatly compartmentalized along hierarchical lines. The arrangement of different activities under the *same* program and different programs under the *same* goal sometimes ignores variation in the purposes that NOAA's operations have been established to achieve. Without discounting the redundancy that it sometimes produces, the creation of new programs and new organizational units is usually motivated by the desire to accomplish something different than is being accomplished by existing programs and organizational units. This helps to explain officials' misgivings about the validity of "common measures" that could be used as a basis for comparing the outputs and outcomes of different activities under PPB.

In addition, most of NOAA's activities contribute to multiple goals. As one of many possible illustrations, although research conducted under the Climate Forcing Program contributed to NOAA's climate goal (where it was placed in the agency's program structure), it also contributed to NOAA's weather and water goal. Similarly, many activities associated with particular programs contributed to other programs as well— even to the extent that their placement into one as opposed to another was sometimes arbitrary. This is the sense in which several of those interviewed suggested that PPB "replaced the old stovepipes with new stovepipes." It is also the sense in which an official from OMB observed that "a program is in the eye of the beholder."

This is not to deny that alternative stovepipes can provide useful new ways of looking at management issues, as one goal team member noted. Nor is it to deny that NOAA's program structure was somewhat more rational in a Weberian sense than its line structure. Unlike the latter, which had been built through ad hoc accumulation, the former was constructed through a comprehensive consideration of NOAA's activities and units at one point in time. It remains, however, that a discrete ordering of means and ends was impossible under any conceivable program structure.[5]

Competing Loyalties and Crosscutting Analysis

Many general critiques of program budgeting have noted the challenges that confront performance assessment and the obstacles that limit efforts to think about the allocation of resources in public organizations in terms of hierarchical means–ends relationships. Less attention has been devoted to the practical implications of the fact that—whatever its conceptual validity—a program structure is an abstraction superimposed on the operational structure that provides the basis for direction, accountability, and funding throughout the organization.

One factor that circumscribed the role of PPB at NOAA had to do with the motives of the line personnel who performed much of the planning and programming analysis. As in any organization, people at NOAA are loyal to the units that provide their jobs, evaluate their work, and perform the missions that have defined their careers in many cases. As a program manager from OAR put it, "We are all looking out for the labs we're in." This mentality was reinforced by the knowledge that funds were tight and the perception that interunit competition for those resources would be stiff. The same person added that the perception of institutional bias undermined his and other managers' legitimacy in cases where programs encompassed more than one organizational unit.

Loyalties that were grounded in NOAA's operational structure shaped the character of planning and programming in two ways that were antithetical to goals of PPB. One is that they militated against objective analysis. Self-assessment, which was central to NOAA's system, was not motivated by the desire to facilitate dispassionate comparisons of alternative uses of organizational resources. It was instead a vehicle for self-advocacy. Such advocacy was generally confined within the boundaries of plausibility and truthfulness, and central authorities (such as PA&E) could ask for more information in seeking to make objective assessments. Still, PA&E and PPI had a limited capacity for independent assessment, and much of the analysis in PPB involved the collection and comparison of best cases that were often presented in simplified form.

PPB at NOAA thus was a competitive system, and as in any such system, some players were better than others by virtue of their abilities and their attitudes. Although one program manager welcomed the opportunity to "tell his story," for example, others expressed discomfort at being cast into a competitive role. As one noted: "I'm a scientist, not a salesman." As in any competitive system, moreover, the rules of the game had the potential to shape outcomes. Again, whether or not it had an effect on spending, some perceive that the system's emphasis on performance assessment was biased in favor of programs with practical and measurable results.

A second important implication of competing loyalties is that they framed the boundaries of cooperation within program and goal teams. Although consensus building was important given that team leaders lacked formal executive power, it was also difficult to achieve given that team members were competing for limited funds. This is the sense in which the leader of a matrix team observed that you could not expect a member from the NWS to be enthusiastic about an OAR initiative and vice versa. He might have added that you would expect someone from the NWS to be decidedly opposed to any OAR initiative that came at the expense of her organization.

The dynamics of accommodation within program and goal teams help to explain some features of the PPB process discussed above. A program manager attributed the length and detail of program baseline assessments and other analyses to the fact that the discussion of every issue had to include everyone's perspective. More important, the need to build consensus explains why decision making at the team level focused on the allocation of additional resources as opposed to the redistribution of existing resources. As with the two examples of cooperation cited above, proposals that offered a piece of the action to multiple team members were the easiest to sell. Although such initiatives could be creative and worthwhile, they were not motivated by the considerations of efficiency that are central to the theory of program budgeting.

Given that teams lacked the motive to make zero-sum choices, PA&E was left as the primary source for objective, crosscutting analysis under PPB. Although it did this to some extent, it was constrained by its dependence on input from self-interested actors and by its small size and lack of scientific expertise in some cases. It focused its efforts selectively. One might speculate that the conflicting perceptions of PA&E's expectations for program evaluation discussed above reflect a tension that is at the core of the challenge it faced. On the one hand, PA&E needed to collect additional information as a basis for rigorous and objective decision making; on the other hand, it needed concise and simplified reports as a way of coping with the size and complexity of its workload.

PA&E also found it difficult to redistribute resources in a fiscal environment where most programs were perceived to be underfunded. A senior career executive thought that those who instituted program budgeting at NOAA had failed to recognize this constraint at the outset. As he put it, although the agency's political leadership assumed that "we could find lots of waste in NOAA's budget—programs that were not contributing to strategic objectives—that was just wrong." Of course, this observation still begs the question of why PA&E was reluctant to recommend cuts in underfunded programs if the purpose of PPB was to maximize the benefits derived from existing resources. The answer may have to do with its understanding of what was feasible. PA&E only provided advice to decision makers, and its perspectives competed with other, often-more-powerful influences that were grounded in NOAA's line structure and political environment.

Problems of Accountability and Authority: Planning and Programming vs. Budgeting and Execution

One manager attributed the limited substantive effects of PPB primarily to the fact that "no one has the guts to cut programs." Although this may be an accurate explanation, the crux of the problem might be better described in terms of authority as opposed to internal fortitude. Related to its implications for the motives of line officials in planning and programming, the disjuncture between NOAA's program structure and its operational structure also attenuated the linkage between those phases of the process and the budgeting and execution phases.

The fact that authority for execution was expressed in NOAA's line budget and exercised by the agency's line managers was an important constraint on PPB. Even the headquarters officials who were most sympathetic to NOAA's reforms stressed the problems associated with "two systems." One of them felt that the substantive impact of PPB would remain limited so long as these problems went unresolved. In much the same respect, a line manager and director of a matrix program indicated that, although

PPB had encouraged planning and thinking about NOAA's goals, its practical effects were circumscribed by the fact that there were "two separate budgets, two separate submissions, and two separate narratives."

That managerial and spending authority ultimately resided in NOAA's line structure obviously limited its program structure as a means of control. Interrelated with issues of accountability during the execution phase of PPB, several of those interviewed stressed the practical and cognitive difficulties of translating between the two budgets during the first three phases of the PPB process. A goal team leader was referring to these problems when he observed that "the financial system does not support the matrix system. It is impossible [because of this] to track spending across line offices. You can't tell where all the pieces fit together." Noting that there are so many cross-cutting relationships to be considered and "so many steps," another official emphasized the "slippage in the process whereby program goals have to be broken down and farmed out to their line components and communicated effectively. The story [compelling case for program goals] gets lost or becomes distorted."

Because of the close connection between spending authority and management, moreover, the heads of NOAA's line components had an independent voice in the budgetary process that they could use to appeal recommendations that emerged from planning and programming (or to discourage such recommendations from being made in the first place). Although they may not have "always won," as one line manager suggested, their advantage was underscored by their status within NOAA's hierarchy and by the corresponding need for the agency's political leaders to support its chain of command in the interest of managerial effectiveness. Line managers' advantage was also grounded in the related presumption that they were in the best position to know what levels of funding were needed to sustain their operations. Whether or not the heads of NOAA's major components "outranked" its goal team leaders under PPB, a senior official indicated that the former communicated with the administrator much more frequently than the latter.[6]

The disjuncture between planning and programming, on the one hand, and budgeting and execution, on the other, was reinforced by the fact that PPB was not used at higher levels in the budgetary process. The Department of Commerce relied on NOAA's line budget as the basis for its decision making. Because of this, assistant administrators in charge of NOAA's components often briefed their portions of the budget to Department of Commerce officials separately and without regard to how their units' activities related to other units' contributions to matrix programs. OMB officials similarly indicate that NOAA's program structure and the analysis that emerged from it had little direct bearing on their review of the agency's budget. Given their limited resources and the time constraints of the annual budget cycle, they preferred to focus on the organizational units and line appropriations that provided the framework for the budget that was submitted to the president and Congress. Nor did the legislature use NOAA's program budget. A staff member of the House Appropriations Committee noted that, although every agency had "some process" for preparing its recommendations, "we just look at the line budget."

It may be revealing that, although OMB emphasized performance assessment through the Program Assessment Rating Tool process, and although satisfying PART requirements was one of the stated justifications for the adoption of PPB, most of the NOAA programs listed by OMB under its completed PART reviews did not coincide with PPBES programs. The explanation for this illustrates the practical tension between NOAA's program and line structures: OMB preferred to define programs conterminously with organizational and spending authority to ensure that performance assessment could be used to improve accountability and managerial effectiveness. As its guidelines state (in part): "The identification of programs should relate to budget decisions because one goal of assessing programs is to develop information that will be useful to the budget process. This does not necessarily mean that the definition of programs should be restricted to accounts and activities in the budget (i.e., a single budget line), but rather that the programs are managed as a single unit" (OMB 2008, 6).

Internal and External Politics

A final impediment to PPB cited by all those interviewed for this study was simply that NOAA's activities were established and funded by Congress. Even where it might have had the will, legal mandates severely constrained the agency's discretion to redistribute resources among programs. Moreover, there was a widespread perception within NOAA that the legislature was motivated by policy goals and constituent demands that were apt to be at odds with any internal initiatives to rationalize its spending. Legislative constituents might include groups, such as environmentalists, or fishermen, or universities that benefited from or were otherwise affected by agency activities. Although NOAA attempted to accommodate such stakeholders during its planning process, to have thought that their efforts to influence its allocation of resources would be confined to the initial definition of goals would have been naive. As in the political process generally, those who are dissatisfied with decision-making outcomes in one forum naturally press their interests in other forums.

Legislative constituents also included entities within NOAA itself, and these often developed symbiotic ties with external stakeholders. For example, several officials mentioned that the relationships some of the agency's senior scientists had cultivated with Congress and with various universities, institutes, and consortiums reinforced the influence these individuals enjoyed within the organization by virtue of their expertise and professional reputations. A program manager (and himself a senior scientist) was referring to this when he noted that line offices won out when there is a difference in priorities between their goals and matrix goals. There was a "rigid do-not-touch mentality," as he said. This constraint on centralized management was illustrated when the head of the National Hurricane Center blocked a reduction in his satellite program with a direct appeal to Congress (and the media). This same official successfully challenged the agency's recent practice of referring to the Hurricane Center as a NOAA (as opposed to an NWS) program. When he was questioned about the director's actions, Admiral Lautenbacher responded that NOAA "valued his passion" (Lautenbacher 2007).

The problems that the legislature posed for PBB were exacerbated by the fact that Congress is not a hierarchical institution. Thus, a number of agency officials noted the difficulty posed by the fact that various committees, subcommittees, and individual legislators were involved in the authorization and funding of NOAA activities. This is borne out by the observation that eight House committees, four Senate committees, and two special or select joint committees held hearings on various NOAA responsibilities between 2005 and 2009.[7] These included hearings conducted by sixteen and seven different subcommittees in the House and Senate, respectively. As in other policy areas, fragmented legislative authority is antithetical to top-down planning and coordination based on a priori objectives. In part, this is because it provides multiple access points for the various interests that might take exception to recommendations produced by such efforts.

One should also emphasize the connection between external and internal politics. As the head of one of NOAA's major components noted, there is "nothing the administrator hates worse than to get a letter [from Congress or some other important constituent] complaining about a program cut." The context for this statement was the reversal by senior leadership of a goal team proposal to achieve "a better balance of resources" by cutting back on a program that the team judged to have become less beneficial. A program manager who had participated in the decision-making process cited this as an example of someone being "shot" for exercising "due diligence." To her, it was an exception that proved the general rule that substantial redistributive initiatives were politically infeasible and generally avoided. As she noted: "A mission goal lead proposed to discontinue [actually cut by 60 percent] a program and redistribute the funding to other programs within the goal. This idea was not endorsed by the senior leadership and the individual had to redo the program. It was a bold move that the individual should have been applauded for but instead it left the feeling that folks were not really interested in making the tough decisions."

Conclusion

The implementation of PPB at NOAA resulted in more systematic planning and a more explicit formulation of agency goals. As is normally the case with strategic planning, those goals were quite general. One suspects that they were more a synthesis of existing missions than the result of a serious examination and reformulation of priorities. Still, NOAA's program structure provided an overview of how its activities related to one another and to the agency's core objectives that was useful as a tool for managerial accountability. As supplemented by the matrix concept and with its heavy reliance on analysis by line officials, NOAA's system of PPB also promoted communication across organizational units that performed interrelated functions. Although its reforms did not immediately produce the "corporate culture" that the agency's critics had found missing, one would not expect such a transformation to occur over night. Whatever their long-term implications, PPB and matrix management yielded a higher level of shared awareness and encouraged cooperative efforts at problem solving in at least a few cases.

The effects of PPB on the allocation of resources were not as impressive. It is unlikely that the system helped NOAA obtain higher levels of funding. Claims to this effect are undermined by a consensus that most programs remained underfunded and that PPB played little role in external reviews of NOAA budget requests. More relevant to the present concerns is that any redistributive impact within the agency was modest at best. NOAA budgeting remained an incremental process in which previous years' expenditures were taken as a starting point and in which the competition for resources focused on the allocation of additional funds. The fact that additional appropriations were scarce further limited the role of PPB. It is instructive that neither of the cooperative program proposals cited earlier in this chapter was funded.

An assessment of institutional effects is always dependent on one's assumptions about institutional objectives. It may be easy enough in this sense for PPB to fall victim to its own hyperbole. The people who brought the system to NOAA were intelligent, and their criteria for success may have been more modest than the transformative objectives that are sometimes attributed to program budgeting. To them, improved communications, the introduction of multiyear planning, the advancement of objective performance criteria as at least one basis for accountability, and more rational decision making at the margins were probably important improvements over NOAA's old system. Practitioners' expectations for program budgeting may have become more realistic through decades of experience in DoD.

Nevertheless, it remains true that the substantive effects of PPB at NOAA fell short of the comprehensive planning and coordination that the logic of the technique seemed to promise. They were limited by the complexity of the task and by the conceptual and practical obstacles that confronted synoptic analysis. Among the obstacles were the difficulties of measuring and comparing program effects, the impossibility of categorizing activities according to discrete objectives, and the difficulty of translating between NOAA's program structure and its line structure for the purposes of analysis and control. PPB was limited in the latter regard by the fact that it sought to manage without the authority to do so. Nor did the decision-making process of PPB supplant the internal and external politics of budgeting. The influence of vested constituencies remained a critical limitation on the goals that program budgeting was designed to accomplish.

PPB was also a source of tension within NOAA. This is partly because its emphasis on planning, on the objective measurement of practical benefits, and on centralized accountability and control were at odds with the agency's scientific culture and sense of purpose in important respects. By relying on line officials for much of the work in planning and programming, moreover, NOAA's version of PPB demanded a good deal of time and effort from people who already had day jobs. The extensive emphasis on "process," as one official termed the problem, was the source of considerable frustration. It is necessarily a consideration in any overall assessment of NOAA's reforms.

Most of the obstacles that PPB confronted at NOAA are familiar from analyses of program budgeting in the 1960s. More generally, it appears as if some of the key assumptions behind NOAA's reforms were not well thought through. As a seasoned and accomplished public executive, for example, it is interesting that Admiral Lautenbacher may not have fully appreciated the managerial and political limitations of planning and programming as means of organizational control. Early in his tenure, he reportedly assumed that the leaders of goal teams would have the motive, the expertise, and the authority to overcome the agency's traditional fragmentation and rationalize activities within their areas of responsibility. He also reportedly assumed that these individuals would largely supersede the assistant administrators in charge of the agency's major components. These assumptions proved to be unrealistic as well as a source of confusion and resentment, and the admiral reportedly came to regret them.[8]

If it did not fully anticipate some of the problems that PPB would encounter, NOAA also seems exceptional for its willingness to engage in self-examination. In preparation for a new presidential administration, PPI conducted an extensive evaluation of PPB that was completed in the spring of 2009. Although the study was not made available to the public, it reportedly endorsed several initiatives to improve the system. These included training sessions intended to clarify and simplify the roles of line officials in planning and programming. They also included an effort to bring NOAA's program budget more closely into alignment with its line budget, thereby attempting to narrow some of the gaps between PP and BE discussed above.

One of the consultants who helped design the NOAA's system of PPB speculated that its survival would be contingent on the support of at least one high-level headquarters official. The same consultant noted that "all bets were off" if a scientist was appointed as the new head of NOAA. This latter condition was met by President Obama's selection of Jane Lubechenco, a distinguished marine biologist with an academic background. Noting that Admiral Lautenbacher had been unusual among political executives for his understanding of and appreciation for program budgeting, a DoD transplant added that "political types [at least those without a background in DoD budgeting] don't like PPB because of its complexity."

Anticipating that the new administration would take a year or so to determine the fate of PPB, the head of one of NOAA's major components noted that he and his fellow career executives had discussed this issue at length. Although he was critical of the process on the whole, he hoped that NOAA's leadership would retain the beneficial aspects of the system in the event that they decided to abandon program budgeting and matrix management. In particular, he hoped that the agency would find a way to maintain improved communications across organizational boundaries. Communication requires effort, however, and he was also adamant that the process costs of PPB must be reduced. Describing it as an interesting and unanticipated question, he added that Lubechenco had asked whether the additional communication required by PPB was even a good thing. Presumably, this was in recognition of its potential to distract people from their operational responsibilities. Although it flies in the face of management orthodoxy, this was at least a legitimate consideration if the substantive effects of PPB had been marginal. As another senior manager summarized the issue, "The good news is that NOAA had always been heavily stovepiped and PPBES did address some of that—but at a huge cost for many very expensive and busy people. The payoff was never there given the level of effort."

NOAA replaced PPB and matrix management with a new system in the summer of 2010. Although a thorough description of its features is beyond the present scope, Strategy Execution Evaluation (SEE) is intended to simplify planning and budgeting, and to align those processes more closely with the authority embodied in NOAA's management structure and legal mandates. SEE's departures from PPB include the following (Pitter 2010):

- The consolidation of the planning and programming functions to reduce the complexity of the process and allow time for its completion with the annual budget cycle.
- The accompanying elimination of PA&E as a separate headquarters unit and the merger of its analytical staff into PPI.
- The elimination of NOAA's forty-five programs (matrix and nonmatrix alike) in favor of Department of Commerce budget groupings and the line and staff organizations defined by the agency's legislation and operation structure. (This change was designed to eliminate the confusion associated with the crosscutting lines of accountability and control that had existed under PPB and matrix management.)
- The replacement of two budget documents (a program budget and a line budget) with one budget based on NOAA's operating structure.
- The elimination of "taskers flowing from all directions" and the replacement of ten "products" (analyses and planning documents) that had been required by PPB with three products.

PPI's 2009 evaluation of PPB incorporated feedback from throughout NOAA, and it candidly identified the resentment and many of the practical obstacles to implementation discussed in this chapter. Its report nevertheless concluded that the system should be tweaked and retained. This recommendation was based in part on PPI's assessment that, "considering the bipartisan support for legislation such as GPRA, it would be difficult for any agency to avoid linking its budget and its strategic planning and performance management." In fact, some management technique that incorporates the essential elements of program budgeting is arguably the way to pursue the objectives of GPRA and of enthusiastic advocates of performance management more generally.

The continued importance of planning and assessment at NOAA is evinced by the retention of PPI as a major line component headed by an assistant administrator (despite the fact that its budget and number of personnel are dwarfed by those of the other line components). Still, the changes reflected in SEE are much more fundamental than an adjustment of the management system introduced by Admiral Lautenbacher. It is likely that they did not occur without an internal struggle and serious reflection by the agency's new leadership. NOAA's abandonment of its program structure and program budget and its elimination of programming as a separate function arguably represent an abandonment of the essential foundations for PPB, and its efforts to simplify planning and budgeting signal a more constrained and selective use of performance-based analysis. Although it may not fully comport with GPRA's intent, SEE's more modest approach could well turn out to be more effective.

Notes

1. Not surprisingly, NOAA's scientists tended to be more positive on this issue than headquarters staff without scientific backgrounds.

2. This is also the sense in which scholars have advocated PPB as an antidote to budgetary inertia in other organizations. Most recently, Cindy Williams (2008) has advocated a viable system of PPB as an antidote to the lack of rational coordination she observes within the Department of Homeland Security. Among the manifestations of this alleged failure in her analysis is that the creation of DHS produced little change in the budgetary shares of its component organizations (Coast Guard, Secret Service, etc.).

3. DoD has also frequently been criticized for the fragmentation and parochialism that characterize its PPB process. It is unclear whether these assessments had any bearing on the design of NOAA's system of PPB.

4. One NOAA official took exception with this, noting that such an orientation would have been out of character for Admiral Lautenbacher.

5. This realization led some program-budgeting theorists in the 1960s to argue that the process should be modified by assigning percentage weights to the contributions that particular activities made to different goals. To continue with the illustration above, 60 percent of spending for the Climate Forcing Program might be assigned to the Climate Goal and 40 percent might be assigned to Weather and Water. These decisions were also inevitably arbitrary, however, and had the effect of further complicating an already-complex process. By the same token, they muddled the kinds of direct comparisons that made the idea of program budgeting appealing.

6. When asked this question, a senior careerist quipped that rank among members of the SES was like virtue among thieves.

7. In the House, these were the committees: Science and Technology, Natural Resources, Energy and Commerce, Foreign Affairs, Transportation and Infrastructure, Appropriations, Government Reform, and Armed Services. In the Senate they included Commerce, Science, and Transportation; Foreign Relations; Banking, Housing, and Urban Affairs; and Appropriations.

8. According to a senior career executive, Admiral Lautenbacher referred to the leaders of goal teams as "NOAA's royalty." In contrast, he allegedly observed that the primary function of the assistant administrators in charge of the agency's major components would be to "distribute paper clips and issue parking passes."

Chapter 6

PPB and the Holy Grail of Performance Management

The Department of Homeland Security (DHS) and the National Aeronautics and Space Administration have also recently adopted program budgeting in order to coordinate across organizational units. As is described in the appendix, its implementation in these agencies has been generally consistent with NOAA's experience. Still, the use of PPB remains limited. As one NOAA official asked, "Why should we be interested in an 'obscure' management technique?" The answer is that beyond its present application and historical significance, PPB is an extension of current trends that have much broader relevance for public administration. Much of its importance lies in what it says about the viability of performance management systems.

The goals of the performance movement are ambiguous in important respects. This is certainly true of its primary manifestations at the federal level in the United States: the Government Performance and Results Act of 1993 (GPRA) and the Performance Assessment Rating Tool (PART) reviews that were used in the Bush administration. If "managing for results" (MFR) is to make government more efficient, however, then its highest purpose is to rationalize what government does. It is here that experience with PPB is especially instructive, for something that incorporates the essential elements of that technique is necessary if planning and performance assessment are to coordinate the allocation of resources and responsibilities. The past and recent histories of PPB illustrate why this is not a realistic expectation.

The Performance Movement

What many refer to as MFR or performance-based management is a core element of a broader international movement with intellectual roots in public-choice economics and neoconservative political ideology (Terry 2005). Although its principles and prescriptions are not consistent (Hood and Peters 2004; Radin 2006), the New Public Management (NPM) is informed by the overarching assumption that public organizations are poorly run in comparison with their business counterparts. Some observers assert that the best executive talent is attracted to the private sector because of the higher compensation it offers. Whether this proposition is valid (Aberbach 2003), the performance of government agencies is allegedly impeded by civil service requirements and by other kinds of regulations that constrain (even capable) managers.[1] More fundamentally, it is allegedly limited by the fact that public organizations are not driven by customer demands, competition, and a measurable bottom line.

A practical extension of these assumptions has been the NPM's emphasis on outsourcing public functions to private firms. This has been fueled in part by (typically deductive) arguments that the lack of competition in the public sector gives bureaucratic "agents" the license to "shirk" and to engage in various other kinds of "rent-seeking" behavior (Tullock 1965; Niskanen 1968). Insofar as government functions must be performed by government, the NPM further prescribes that public bureaucracies should operate more like businesses. As Donald Moynihan (2006, 77) describes its premises: "The MFR doctrine argues that traditional forms of public organizations perform poorly because they lack explicit standards, managers are not held accountable for achievement of goals, and managers are too hamstrung by red tape to perform well in any case." Or as Robert Behn (2003, 586–87) bluntly asserts, "Business firms all measure their performance, and everyone knows that the private sector is managed better than the public sector."

Given these assumptions, one principle of MFR is that agencies should be attentive to the needs of their stakeholders or "customers." Another is that they should eliminate centralized, bureaucratic forms of control that prevent managers from acting as effective entrepreneurs. Yet another is that agencies should define hierarchical sets of objectives through strategic planning (that incorporates input from stakeholders) and then manage their operations by basing decisions on goal-related outputs and (preferably) outcomes.[2] In contrast to MFR's emphasis on decentralization, this last prescription is designed further to centralize accountability and control. As such, it arguably represents a more rational approach to management than traditional processes that focus decision makers' attention on inputs (such as salaries and capital outlays). Beryl Radin captures the logic of the performance movement in these regards:

> Although there is a wide range of examples of performance measurement . . . in various jurisdictional levels, most of the efforts have been constructed around a basic planning process. That process usually begins with the specification of long-term or mid-term goals and highlights the desired outcomes related to those goals. These goals can be defined at an organizational or at a programmatic level and often involve the translating of general, long-term strategic goals to more specific goals and objectives. Following this, the process involves the development of performance measures that give one a quantifiable set of expectations that are defined as reasonable levels of expected performance. These measures are usually annual or short term in duration. The third step involves collecting, verifying, and analyzing the data that allow one to assess the level of accomplishment of the stated goals (Radin 2006, 13–14).

Among the purposes of planning and performance assessment are to hold agencies accountable, to improve management, and to arrive at a more efficient allocation of resources.

Institutional Manifestations

The NPM and the performance movement originated in the United Kingdom, Australia, and New Zealand during the 1980s and are still applied to their fullest extent in those nations. They have provided a basis for institutional reform in many other countries, however, and at all levels of government in the United States (Moynihan 2006, 2008). Writing in 1998, for example, Julia Melkers and Katherine Willoughby (1998, 67) found that forty-seven states had made significant efforts to introduce performance-based budgeting through legislative requirements (thirty-one states) or administrative requirements (sixteen states). Most of these initiatives had occurred within the preceding five years. Although specific requirements varied from state to state, they generally stressed "themes of accountability, strategic planning, reinvention, and budget reform" that are common to the NPM. Melkers and Willoughby (1998, 68) describe the rationale for these developments:

> Performance planning takes place in state government in conjunction with the budget and management process. Performance planning is the catalyst for the strategic review by state departments and agencies of their current operations to identify trends which may impact their services. In addition, performance planning is the catalyst for the development of statewide and departmental goals, objectives, outcome measures, and strategies.

A popular book by David Osborne and Ted Gaebler (1992) was an important impetus for reforms in the United States. Based on the authors' informed judgment and on anecdotes from a handful of small and medium-sized municipalities, *Reinventing Government* prescribed virtually all the remedies for bureaucratic ineffectiveness that have come to be associated with the NPM. These include outsourcing, downsizing, fees for service, a customer orientation, accountability based on performance measurement, strategic planning and the development of multiyear budgets, performance-based budgeting, and (perhaps inconsistently with the latter three principles) the decentralization of organizational responsibility to allow for managerial initiative (and entrepreneurialism).

Osborne and Gaebler's book served as the inspiration for some state reforms as well as for the Clinton administration's National Performance Review. Supervised by Vice President Al Gore, the NPR was very much in tune with the market orientation popular among so-called New Democrats (and of course Republicans). Without being heavy-handed in its criticism, this orientation was also consistent with the electorate's general misgivings about the effectiveness of government. Among its elements were a continuation of the trend toward privatization that had begun in the Reagan administration, as well as attempts to streamline government organizations, simplify the language and processes associated with government requirements, and eliminate outdated or excessively burdensome regulations (Kettl and DiIulio 1995; Kettl 2002).

Especially germane to the present discussion have been efforts by the legislative and executive branches to institute performance-based management across the federal bureaucracy. The GPRA was heavily influenced by a Republican Senate staff member who had been praised extensively by Osborne and Gaebler for his earlier service as a councilman and mayor in Sunnyvale, California (Frederickson and Frederickson 2006).[3] Consistent with the premises of MFR, this legislation was based on Congress's "findings":

1. Waste and inefficiency in federal programs undermine the confidence of the American people in the government and reduce the federal government's ability to address adequately vital public needs.
2. Federal managers are seriously disadvantaged in their efforts to improve program efficiency and effectiveness, because of insufficient articulation of program goals and inadequate information on program performance.

3. Congressional policymaking, spending decisions, and program oversight are seriously handicapped by insufficient attention to program performance and results.

As an antidote to these perceived problems, GPRA requires agencies to engage in strategic planning for the purposes of articulating their missions and defining the subordinate goals, programs, activities, and resources that contribute to those missions. It also requires agencies to develop performance plans "covering each program activity set forth in the budget." The purposes of these plans are to

1. Establish performance goals to define the level of performance to be achieved by a program activity.
2. Express such goals in an objective, quantifiable, and measurable form unless authorized to be in an alternative form.
3. Briefly describe the operational processes, skills and technology, and the human, capital, information, or other resources required to meet the performance goals.
4. Establish performance indicators to be used in measuring and assessing the relevant outputs, service levels, and outcomes of each program activity.
5. Provide a basis for comparing actual program results with the established performance goals.
6. Describe the means to be used to verify and validate measured values.

The other generally applicable manifestation of MFR at the federal level was PART, which was instituted as the centerpiece of the President's Management Agenda in the George W. Bush administration. At least early in Bush's tenure, critics of bureaucratic excess and inefficiency were optimistic that the first president with an MBA would make government more businesslike and sensible in its operations (Moynihan and Roberts 2010). As designed and implemented by the Office of Management and Budget (OMB), a stated purpose of the PART process was to flesh out, standardize, and enforce GPRA (which clearly envisions that the Executive Office of the President play a leadership role in implementing its requirements).[4] OMB stated:

> The GPRA statute provides a framework under which agencies prepare strategic plans, performance plans, and performance reports that set goals and report on the extent to which they are achieved. The PART is a systematic method of assessing performance of program activities, focusing on their contribution to an agency's achievement of its strategic and program performance goals. The PART strengthens and reinforces performance measurement under GPRA by encouraging careful development of performance measures according to the outcome-oriented standards of the law.

PART reviews, which were done for a handful of each department's programs on a rotating, annual basis (and published on OMB's website), were based on an extensive questionnaire that focused on "overall program effectiveness, from how well a program is designed to how well it is implemented and what results it receives" (OMB 2008, 1). The instrument was divided into three sections dealing with strategic planning processes, program management, and program results and accountability. Although there were some who initially argued that PART reviews should be conducted by a separate unit within OMB, this was opposed by several prominent career officials as an arrangement that would usurp the evaluative function traditionally performed by the budgeting side of that organization. The predicted result would have been to undermine the linkage between performance assessment and spending decisions. Accordingly, the same program examiners with first-line responsibility for considering agencies' budget requests also initially graded PART reviews and played a consultative and oversight role in the completion of those documents.

The Goals of MFR: PPB by Any Other Name?

MFR has several objectives. For example, one of the fathers of the performance movement (who was also an advocate of PPB in the 1960s), identifies no fewer than ten complementary and overlapping benefits that can be derived from the measurement of program effects (Hatry 1999, 157–58):

- Respond to elected officials' and the public's demands for accountability.
- Make budget requests.
- Do internal budgeting.
- Trigger in-depth examinations of performance problems and possible corrections.
- Motivate.
- Contract.
- Evaluate.
- Support strategic planning.
- Communicate better with the public and build public trust.
- Improve.

In a broad sense, however, MFR seeks to promote effective management in two, interrelated ways. The more modest of its aims is to improve the implementation of programs on an individual basis by clarifying their objectives and identifying measures of effectiveness that can be used to diagnose problems and hold managers accountable. As an extension of this goal, a second purpose of performance management is to arrive at a more efficient allocation of resources. At a minimum, this entails the identification of programs that are underfunded and overfunded, and perhaps the elimination or deemphasis of ones that are not effective. A more ambitious manifestation of this second goal involves the systematic comparison of programs in order to identify conflicts and redundancies and to optimize the benefits of spending based on considerations of relative cost-effectiveness. If it is not always explicitly stated as an expectation, crosscutting analysis is nevertheless implied by MFR's emphasis on the integration of strategic planning, performance measurement, and budgeting.

If the last sentence sounds familiar, this is because it is the essence of program budgeting. The significance of PPB thus lies in its relationship to the coordinative goal of the performance movement. Although she does not elaborate on the comparison, this may be the sense in which Radin (2000a, 120) notes that "to some extent the current interest in performance measurement represents a return to the performance budgeting agenda of the early PPBS movement." Similarly, it may be the sense in which David Frederickson and George Frederickson (2006, 173) observe that in the United States, GPRA and PART are just the latest in a lineage of federal reform efforts: performance budgeting; planning, programming, budgeting systems; management by objectives; and zero-based budgeting. In addition, most of the fifty states have implemented performance measurement regimes, including unit costs application of the Government Accounting Standards Board's cost accounting requirements. The point is that the language of performance measurement may change, but the central concepts on which the performance measurement movement rests remain the same.

The labels attached to reform efforts do change, and program budgeting, per se, is seldom prescribed in the MFR literature. Although they fail to offer explicit comparisons, in fact, some current advocates of performance-based management distance themselves from PPB. Still, the performance movement assumes that planning and program assessment will result in coordination and greater efficiency in the allocation of resources, typically without specifying an alternative mechanism through which these goals are to be achieved. This lack of guidance is evident in the case of GPRA. As a GAO (1997a, 8) report on performance budgeting pursuant to the act's requirements notes, for example:

> The Senate committee report on GPRA emphasized that although "this Act contains no provisions authorizing or implementing a performance budget," it was imperative that the Congress develop a clear understanding of what is getting in the way of results from each dollar spent. Recognizing that "it is unclear how best to present [performance] information and what the results will be," GPRA requires pilot projects to develop alternative forms of performance budgets.

The same report characterizes PPB as one of several past management reforms whose defects may offer insights that are relevant to the implementation of performance budgeting under GPRA. In particular, it cautions against the excessively high expectations that accompanied program budgeting in the 1960s, adding the caveats that analysis can only provide advice to policymakers and that budgeting is inherently a political process. At the same time, however, the report does not suggest how either the goals of performance budgeting or the methodology for achieving those goals might differ from those of PPB. One can argue in this regard that the two critical elements of PPB are required if the bureaucracy is to comply with GPRA's intent as it has been interpreted in subsequent GAO documents. These are the combination of (1) a comprehensive program structure and budget with (2) the use of crosscutting analysis for the purpose of efficient resource allocation.

In the first instance, GPRA specifies that agencies develop strategic plans that present a hierarchical ordering of means and ends as a way of justifying their budget requests. This is the sense in which Nancy Roberts (2000, 299–300) observes that the act requires agencies to engage in *synoptic* planning:

> Under the GPRA, executives at the strategic apex (top of the agency) serve as the locus of decision making. Cognizant of their legal mandates, they are responsible for developing a comprehensive mission statement that covers all of the agency's major functions and operations. Armed with a mission statement, they then identify supporting goals for all major functions

and operations. Cascading down the hierarchy, goals move from the more general at the policy level to the more specific at the operational and functional levels. The point is to integrate all organizational activity into a comprehensive whole by having each level in the hierarchy develop more specific goals to support the more general ones above them in the hierarchy. To chart the agency's course of action and to ensure that it is moving toward its strategic goals, performance plans are submitted on a yearly basis and contain short-term goals and performance indicators. Performance indicators, linked directly to goals, are to specify agency results in a way that is objective, measurable, and focused on outcomes rather than on inputs or outputs.

This characterization of GPRA's objectives could just as well describe what PPB seeks to accomplish.

As discussed in chapter 5, NOAA had developed what amounted to a program structure and a rudimentary program budget in response to GPRA several years before Admiral Lautenbacher formally instituted PPB.[5] Similar efforts by other agencies (which can be accessed on their websites in most cases) usually proceed from a broad vision to a mission statement to subordinate goals to programs and activities that are arrayed beneath those goals. To offer a representative illustration, the Department of Transportation (DOT) articulated the following mission in its strategic plan for fiscal years 2006–11:

> The national objectives of general welfare, economic growth and stability, and the security of the United States require the development of transportation policies and programs that contribute to providing fast, safe, efficient, and convenient transportation at the lowest cost consistent with those and other national objectives, including the efficient use and conservation of the resources of the United States. (DOT 2010, 4)

Pursuant to this overarching statement of purpose, DOT describes six strategic goals: safety; reduced congestion; global connectivity; environmental stewardship; security, preparedness, and response; and organizational excellence. In turn, each strategic goal encompasses multiple subgoals (e.g., truck, transit, aviation, railroad, and pipeline in the case of safety).

In the second instance, GPRA contemplates that agencies analyze program outputs and outcomes "to reassess their missions and long-term goals as well as the strategies and resources they will need to achieve their goals" (GAO 2004, 5). In the case of railroad safety, for example, DOT uses "rail-related accidents and incidents per million train miles" as a measure of the effectiveness of various programs administered by the Federal Railroad Administration. Although GPRA does not explicitly require agencies to compare and rationalize activities in terms of their cost-effectiveness, this is arguably implicit in its expectations that they develop program structures and that they (and their legislative and executive principals) use performance data to inform the allocation of resources. (Otherwise, one might ask why agencies should have to perform these activities.)

In fact GAO has repeatedly emphasized the desired linkage between performance assessment and coordination in criticizing agencies and OMB for their failure to engage in comparative analysis. For example, this shortcoming is the most conspicuous theme in an extensive report occasioned by GPRA's tenth anniversary. Noting that the goal of the act is "to improve congressional decision making by providing more objective information on achieving objectives, and on the *relative effectiveness and efficiency of federal programs and spending*" (GAO 2004, 6; emphasis added), GAO goes on to observe that

> crosscutting issues continue to be a challenge to GPRA implementation. . . .
> We have previously reported and testified that GPRA could provide OMB, agencies, and Congress with a structured framework for addressing crosscutting policy initiatives and program efforts. OMB could use the provision of GPRA that calls for OMB to develop a government-wide performance plan to integrate expected agency-level performance. It could also be used to more clearly relate and address the contributions of alternative federal strategies. Unfortunately, this provision has not been fully implemented. (GAO 2004, 17)

To note GAO's dissatisfaction with coordinative efforts pursuant to GPRA naturally leads to the question of how agencies and OMB could more effectively integrate comprehensive planning, objective performance assessment, and budgeting. Although neither GPRA nor GAO prescribes a mechanism for accomplishing this, some management system that includes a programming function is *the* way to promote an efficient allocation of resources through crosscutting analysis. Again, the linkage that programming seeks to establish between planning and budgeting is the defining feature of program budgeting. It is instructive in this regard that NOAA took great pains to justify its resurrection of PPB as an effort to comply with the requirements of GPRA (and PART).

Limitations of MFR

If PPB is the full embodiment of MFR, then its history demonstrates the performance movement's inherent limitations. In fact ample evidence attests to the meager substantive effects of planning and performance measurement systems. Conceding that the obstacles to coordination would probably be even greater at the federal level, a congressional study of performance budgeting in the states observed that

> Despite long-standing efforts in states regarded as leaders in performance budgeting, performance measures have not attained sufficient credibility to influence resource allocation decisions. . . .
> Although panel members [state budgeting officials] generally agreed on the value of performance data within the budget process, they suggested that the tensions and obstacles that have frustrated state performance budgeting efforts, and the inherent difficulty of comparing performance across fundamentally different programs, would be at least as formidable at the federal level. . . .
> Generally, and despite inclusion of performance measures in some state budgets for many years, most state officials we visited reported little change in their budget process. Representatives from all the groups of officials we interviewed . . . said that there ought to be a stronger connection between performance and resource allocations. However, nearly all of the officials we interviewed were dissatisfied with the measures currently included in their budget documents. (GAO 1993, 1, 2, 5)

It bears emphasis that GAO's study focused on states that were regarded as leaders in the area of performance assessment.

More recent analyses by leading academics have done little to allay these misgivings. One is a study of five agencies within the Department of Health and Human Services, whose regulatory and service missions represent a cross section of federal administrative functions. In it, Frederickson and Frederickson (2006, 171) note that "federal performance budgeting is now rather well developed. The federal budget now includes agency performance measures with each agency's budget request. But performance budgeting is not the same thing as performance-based appropriations. Our findings show little evidence of an association among performance measurement, performance budgeting, and agency appropriation patterns."

Donald Moynihan (2008) arrives at similar conclusions based on extensive observations of performance management systems at the state and national levels. Like the Fredericksons, Moynihan feels that MFR can have some salutary effects: Planning can help to clarify organizational objectives, and performance assessment can be used by executives to protect programs that they favor or to justify organizational change. At the same time he finds that planning works best in those "agencies without competing demands from stakeholders and complex functions" (2008, 205) and that performance data are most useful in promoting change where agency managers have broad discretion under their legal mandates. Even under such favorable circumstances, Moynihan cautions that the substantive effects of MFR are confined to the margins and that performance information has little bearing on the allocation of resources. As he notes, "Efforts to create government-wide performance information systems certainly have not lived up to the standards of advocates and have done little to change how senior officials make decisions" (2008, 189).

Again, this is not to deny that comparisons across programs and activities can inform decision making on a selective basis. Crosscutting analysis (although frequently not of a sophisticated nature) provided a significant management tool in the Department of Defense under Robert McNamara, for example (Enthoven and Smith 2005). This said, the kind of systematic coordination that formal performance management requirements seek to achieve is unattainable for the same technical, conceptual, and political reasons that PPB cannot work as intended.

Organizational Incentives and Capacity

Policy analysis was foreign to most agencies in the 1960s. Allen Schick (1973) argues in this regard that a salutary result of the failed experiment with PPBS was the cadre of analysts it left behind (Schick 1973).[6] Subsequent developments have more than confirmed Schick's prediction that policy analysis would become institutionalized throughout the government. Elite universities had created graduate programs to train analysts by the early 1970s, and the field seemed to "be moving toward a professional identity" by the middle of that decade (Radin 2000a, 27).

Today, every federal agency of any consequence has at least one office that is devoted to policy analysis. The need for this function is underscored by statutes and executive orders that have required agencies to evaluate rules, public works projects, and other actions using cost/benefit analysis and related techniques (Baram 1980; West 2005). Whatever its pros and cons, however, the use of analysis to evaluate ouputs on a selective, case-by-case basis is different than its use for internal management. The systematic application of MFR requires more than a headquarters staff that advises agency decision makers concerning discrete decisions. If planning and performance assessment are to be employed as a comprehensive tool for allocating resources and for other internal management functions, then line officials and their staffs throughout an organization must play an ongoing role in evaluating the effects of the programs they administer. This is necessary if MFR is to promote accountability and efficiency in the implementation of individual programs. It also provides the data for centralized comparisons and coordination across organizational units. In 1993, the Office of Personnel Management estimated that GPRA would require the training of more than three hundred thousand federal managers (Roberts 2000).

The implementation of PPB illustrates the obstacles that impede the realization of these goals. One is the parochialism common to all organizations. Although a manager may seek objective feedback as a way of promoting accountability and efficiency within her area of responsibility, she does not have an incentive dispassionately to evaluate her own performance for the benefit of her superiors. As Frederickson and Frederickson (2006, 171) observe, "The point is simple based on an early lesson in public administration: Part of the job of agency executives is to look after and protect the interests of their agencies and to be dedicated to the purposes of their agencies." This generalization can obviously be extended to the heads of bureaus, divisions, offices, programs, and other organizational subdivisions. The fact that self-assessment is usually viewed as a means of self-advocacy necessarily limits its usefulness as a basis for centralized coordination. To the extent that it influences management decisions, it has the potential to reward those who can use the system most effectively to promote their own interests. An ability to game the PPB process has made more than a few careers within the military.

NOAA's implementation of PPB also illustrates the tension that can exist between the requirements of MFR and established organizational cultures and routines. NOAA's line personnel generally lacked the expertise needed for effective performance assessment, and many also viewed the analytical and reporting requirements of PPB as burdens that detracted from their responsibilities as managers and scientists. These observations mirror assessments of GPRA in some cases. Although it found that acceptance of the act's requirements had increased somewhat, GAO's 2004 report concluded that many agencies had yet to adopt a "culture of assessment." Fewer than half the officials surveyed for its study indicated that their agencies had provided training for the purpose of complying with GPRA.

Planning and performance assessment must also be supported by an organization's top management if it is to be viable. This accounts for the selective impact that systems analysis had at DoD under McNamara as well as for the more modest influence it has enjoyed more recently at the National Aeronautics and Space Administration. Conversely, the lack of leadership support in most agencies helped to ensure the failure of program budgeting when it was extended to the civilian bureaucracy in the 1960s, just as it has undermined recent efforts to implement PPB at DHS. Although DHS's enabling legislation requires it to use PPB, it has made relatively little progress in establishing a viable system. As discussed in the appendix, an immediate explanation for this failure is that DHS secretaries and other key political executives have neither understood PPB nor given it the emphasis needed for it to be taken seriously throughout the organization. This is illustrated by the fact that the directorship of PA&E at DHS went unfilled for a year and a half after the first occupant of that position stepped down in frustration.

Lack of leadership support has been an impediment to the implementation of GPRA as well. As GAO (2004, 7) notes in a somewhat contradictory assessment:

While a great deal of progress has been made in making federal agencies more results oriented, numerous challenges still exist. As we have noted before, top leadership commitment and sustained attention to achieving results, both within the agencies and at OMB, is essential to GPRA implementation. While one might expect an increase in agency leadership commitment since GPRA was implemented government-wide beginning in fiscal year 1997, federal managers reported that such commitment has not significantly increased.

Obstacles to Measurement

That planning and performance assessment have been slow to win acceptance in many agencies is undoubtedly attributable in part to resource constraints and to the congenital hostility of large organizations to new ways of doing things. To a considerable extent, however, the bureaucracy's lack of enthusiasm for MFR is attributable to the limitations of the movement's underlying premises. Perhaps the most obvious of these is the assumption that it is possible to measure the degree to which government programs achieve their objectives. In the most rigorous assessment of the effects of the PART process, John Gilmour and David Lewis (2005, 173) note that "the experience of OMB with PART reflects the difficulty of measuring results since barely more than half of programs assessed so far have been deemed to have adequate measures." This helps to explain the authors' finding that performance budgeting had little if any effect in "redirecting resources to programs that produce results" (p. 169).

It is an article of faith within some quarters of the performance movement that obstacles to measurement can be overcome through effort and imagination. As Radin (2006) argues, however, the fact that this is a much more realistic expectation with regard to some administrative functions than others is at odds with the one-size-fits-all mentality that informs comprehensive requirements for planning and assessment.[7] Consistent with the discussion of NOAA's experience, for example, GAO's 2004 assessment of GPRA concedes that the goals of many scientific programs have proven especially difficult to operationalize. As in the case of research, national defense, homeland security, educational programs, public health programs, and many other government activities, the greater the extent to which performance assessment aspires to measure outcomes as opposed to outputs (the desirability of which is a general tenet of MFR), the more problematic it becomes (Frederickson and Frederickson 2006). As also illustrated by NOAA, even individual agencies typically find it much more difficult to measure the effects of some activities than others.[8]

Inherent Limitations of Planning and Organizational Integration

Although the challenges that organizational resistance and measurement issues pose for the assessment of individual programs are well known, scholars have given less attention in recent decades to the practical and conceptual barriers that inhibit planning and coordination across organizational boundaries. The term "strategic planning" is used in various ways but generally refers to a formalized decision-making process that (1) seeks to anticipate future demands, opportunities, and constraints, and that accordingly (2) plots a course for the organization as an integrated whole (Mintzberg 1994). As in the case of PPB, and as at least implied by requirements such as GPRA, these two activities are supposed to be intertwined with performance assessment through an iterative process. The articulation of means–ends relationships through planning furnishes the criteria for evaluating organizational actions, just as the evaluation of organizational actions is intended to aid planning and the possible modification of goals.

The first of these functions is impeded by the difficulty of predicting the future in many contexts. Organizations can plan effectively to the extent that they deal with repetitive events (e.g., snowstorms in Minneapolis) or with trends that they can either manage or extrapolate accurately from past experience (e.g., urban growth patterns). In contrast, planning can be difficult and even counterproductive for organizations that must deal with one-time events (e.g., the development of new technologies or international crises) (Mintzberg 1994). Although formal systems of strategic planning (including PPB and its various analogs in the private sector) typically seek to incorporate performance assessment as a mechanism for the continual adjustment of organizational objectives and the means to achieve them, there is an obvious tension between the essential purpose of planning as a way of organizing and evaluating ongoing operations and the need to adapt to a changing and unpredictable task environment.

This tension is evident in recent attempts to implement PPB. In explaining why efforts to establish a program structure and budget were put on hold at DHS, for example, a headquarters staff member noted in an interview that "everyone's BlackBerry went off at the same time when Katrina hit." A number of managers at NOAA similarly complained that the need to justify their actions within the framework of a five-year budget made it more difficult for them to modify their agendas in response to new scientific discoveries or opportunities for research that were presented by unforeseen natural occurrences. The tension between planning and adaptation is also evident at DoD, where much of the budget is necessarily in the form of long-term investments but where armed conflicts are often impossible to anticipate and present unique needs for personnel, equipment, and logistical support. The difficulty of reconciling these competing realities is evident in both the adoption and the conceptual fuzziness of capabilities-based planning.

Even in a static or otherwise predictable environment, the fact that most government organizations do not have unified objectives poses a barrier to integration across units and programs. The absence of an a priori basis for efficiency often becomes evident as agencies attempt to satisfy two contradictory planning requirements that flow from core precepts of the performance movement: the inclusion of all relevant "customers" and statutory missions in decision making and the formulation of a hierarchically ordered set of ends and means. The following critique of GPRA in this regard might just as easily have been offered as an indictment of PPB in the 1960s:

> There is an implicit assumption in the GPRA that this synoptic model of strategic planning fits all situations and bureaus no matter what their context or situation. . . . [However,] the "one-size-fits-all" model of strategic planning is a poor fit for many public bureaus, particularly those in highly politicized contexts, with diverse missions, conflicting stakeholder interests, and cross-cutting programs that require collaboration among multiple bureaus and levels of government. . . . Many of the challenges and problems that agencies experience as they attempt to implement the GPRA can be directly linked to the strategic planning model that is being used. (Roberts 2000, 298)

A GAO (2004, 93) assessment of barriers to planning and coordination pursuant to GPRA similarly notes that "missions may not be mutually reinforcing or may even conflict, making reaching a consensus on strategies and priorities difficult." As in the case of NOAA, and as illustrated by DOT's mission statement quoted above, the product of such efforts is typically a general set of goals that encompasses everything the agency has been doing and that provides little guidance for prioritizing subordinate objectives.[9] To announce that DOT should promote "fast, safe, efficient, and convenient transportation at the lowest cost" consistent with "the general welfare, economic growth and stability, and the security of the United States" and with the "efficient use and conservation of the resources of the United States" is not particularly enlightening as a blueprint for action. This is the sense in which Henry Kissinger observes that "what passes for planning is frequently the projection of the familiar into the future" (quoted by Mintzberg 1994, 179).

And of course the conceptual problems, statutory constraints, and political realities that often make planning an exercise in post-hoc rationalization at the agency or departmental level are much greater in regards to the entire bureaucracy. As an OMB official described a government-wide performance plan developed by his organization in 1999, it was not a basis for coordination but "a derivative document, reflecting the budget and management decisions made throughout the process of formulating the President's budget submission" (GAO 2004, 94). This may explain why OMB declined to formulate government-wide plans in subsequent years, despite GAO's exhortations to do so.

A related obstacle to the goal of rational integration through planning is the difficulty of specifying hierarchical relationships between means and ends. Few government programs are fully redundant in terms of the purposes they serve. This is one of the reasons that practitioners of performance assessment have struggled to develop common measures for crosscutting analysis. This has even been true in agencies, such as DoD and DHS, where organizational goals are relatively homogeneous. In addition, it is seldom possible to arrange activities under *discrete* objectives. As illustrated by NOAA's implementation of PPB, the comparisons suggested by a program structure become arbitrary to the extent that the things agencies do have more than one purpose. Here as well, it may go without saying that the conceptual challenges to a hierarchical ordering of means and ends in even the most eclectic agency pale in comparison with those that confront the kind of government-wide performance plan that GAO contemplates as the ultimate extension of GPRA.

The Problem of Managerial Authority

Whatever its conceptual validity, moreover, a program structure remains an abstraction that is superimposed for analytical purposes on the actual organization that is the basis for spending, accountability, and control. Even for leaders who are intent on functional planning and coordination, the latter structure necessarily tends to supersede the former. In the case of NOAA, the heads of the agency's line components and of subordinate operational units proved to play a more important role in resource allocation than the heads of its goal teams and matrix teams (despite the initial assumption that the heads of NOAA's line components would be less influential than its goal team leaders). A similar dynamic helps to explain why the PPB process has evolved as it has at DoD. The decentralization of initiative to the individual services is a concession to managerial needs.

In a practical sense, therefore, MFR's application of strategic planning to coordinate across organizational boundaries is at odds with the use of performance assessment as a basis for accountability. This contradiction partly explains OMB's lack of emphasis on crosscutting analysis in its design and implementation of the PART process. Notwithstanding GPRA's expectation that MFR would be used for comparative purposes, OMB stated that a basic principle of performance assessment was that the definition of programs (and therefore the focus of performance assessment) should be coterminous with lines of managerial responsibility. As GAO (2004, 17) put it, OMB sacrificed "the integrated perspective of government performance envisioned by GPRA" in favor of an "agency-by-agency focus" that furnished "high-level information about agencies and certain program performance issues."

It is for this same reason that the structure of OMB itself parallels the structure of the federal bureaucracy. Program examiners thus are assigned to particular agencies and components thereof rather than to crosscutting oversight roles precisely in the interest of managerial accountability and control. To the limited extent that performance assessment results in comparisons of similar programs administered by different agencies, interviews with program examiners and their supervisors indicate that it occurs primarily through horizontal communications within OMB that are largely informal and idiosyncratic.

Political Obstacles to Planning, Assessment, and Integration

The lack of administrative rationality that the performance movement seeks to address reflects the institutional context in which the bureaucracy is embedded. The conceptual obstacles that confront planning based on a hierarchical integration of means and ends can similarly be framed in these terms. The piecemeal creation of organizations to serve redundant and sometimes contradictory purposes is an extension of a political system in which formal authority and influence are fragmented, and in which different actors have different interests and may agree on things for different reasons (Lindblom 1959, 1965). Although these dynamics are obviously not unique to politics in the United States, they are amplified by the Constitution's separation of powers, federalism, and other decentralizing features of American government (e.g., Long 1949; Truman 1951).

Related to the factors discussed above, the institutional and political environment of policy implementation may be the most formidable obstacle to MFR (Radin 2006). That most programs and organizations are established by law obviously limits the discretion of executive officials who would use planning and performance assessment to coordinate bureaucracy. Once created, moreover, administrative structures often acquire constituencies that reinforce fragmentation and inhibit change. These include external clientele, politicians, and bureaucrats with stakes in particular programs. Centrifugal forces both within and outside the department contributed to the decentralization of the PPB process at DoD in the post-McNamara years. As illustrated by NOAA's implementation of PPB, centrifugal political forces can also limit the ability of even committed leaders to secure cooperation for the purpose of planning and performance assessment. This helps to explain why agency headquarters staff and OMB officials have often struggled to obtain performance data that allow for crosscutting analysis.

GAO assessments of the implementation of GPRA reinforce these observations. It is clear from these reports that institutional structures and incentives within the broader political system have frustrated planning and the use of performance data. In the first instance, for example, interviews with bureaucrats and legislative staff indicate that efforts to include Congress in the articulation of agency goals have often merely underscored the absence of clear priorities. This is attributable in part to the fragmentation of authority and policy perspectives associated with bicameralism and the committee system. Even within particular committees, moreover, agency efforts to secure planning guidance have often yielded divergent recommendations that are grounded in partisan conflict or individual preferences. As one legislative staff member remarked, "When subcommittee staff met with the agency's officials, the discussion quickly became quite confrontational, and the session only served to reinforce tensions rather than resolve them" (GAO 1997a, 6). These problems are further exacerbated in some cases by differences between Congress and OMB about what agencies' strategic priorities should be (Roberts 2000).

GAO also expresses disappointment in the failure of Congress to use the performance data generated by GPRA. Citing a series of focus groups with agency managers conducted in 2000 and 2003, it reports officials' widespread perception that "appropriators have not bought into GPRA . . . and do not use performance data or tools to make decisions" (GAO 2004, 96). Donald Moynihan similarly observes that there is little evidence to suggest that politicians at any level of government in the United States have used performance information in more than an idiosyncratic way in allocating resources:

> We can say with some certainty that an extended period of creating performance reporting requirements has given rise to performance information systems and mounds of data. . . . We have weak and usually anecdotal data that the information is being used. The weakest evidence of use comes from the elected officials who asked for the information. In none of the three states studied, or at the federal level, do we see evidence that elected officials are frequent or systematic users of performance information. Their responses are sometimes characterized by indifference . . . and sometimes by hostility. (Moynihan 2008, 191)

Political indifference to performance data is not confined to legislators. Notwithstanding his stated managerial aspirations, and notwithstanding the more general view of the administrative presidency as a counterpoise to bureaucratic and congressional parochialism, accounts of PART's implementation indicate that the effects of performance measures on executive budget recommendations were at best highly selective under George W. Bush (Gilmour and Lewis 2005).[10] Career officials at OMB suggest that this had to do in large part with the fact that the administration's political goals took precedence over considerations of efficiency. Political leaders in OMB also showed relatively little interest in the use of systematic crosscutting analysis. Although low PART scores were sometimes used to justify budget cuts on an individual basis, this was usually confined to programs that were at odds with the president's agenda and had little effect on programs that were favored by the White House. As an illustration, one official noted that "there was no way that the Bush administration was going to cut funding for [education on sexual] abstinence"—despite the fact that a number of grant programs implemented in different departments sought to promote that goal with apparently varying levels of success.

Politicians' lack of support for performance-based management is reinforced by the fact that neither the presidency nor Congress is organized in a way that is conducive to the use of planning and program assessment for coordinative purposes. Again, OMB is differentiated to parallel the "stovepipes" that exist within the federal bureaucracy. Similarly, bicameralism and the committee system in Congress divide authority within and across the authorization, appropriation, and oversight processes with the predictable result that the capacity for legislative comparison and integration across programs and organizations is limited. NOAA officials cite Congress's fragmented structure as a key impediment to the coordinative goal of PPB.

As is discussed in the appendix, Cindy Williams (2007, 2010) emphasizes the organization of Congress and the presidency as among the obstacles to the establishment of a viable system of program budgeting at DHS as well. Accordingly, she argues that restructuring OMB and legislative committees along functional lines is a necessary condition for a planning system that can rationalize spending and other policy decisions in the area of homeland security. Whether this prescription is feasible at a conceptual level is an open question, especially given that organizational decisions in one area have implications that spread throughout government. It may ultimately be unrealistic for the same reason that no one has been able to devise a program structure for the federal bureaucracy in which activities can be arrayed discretely under hierarchically ordered purposes. In any case, the radicalism of this proposal speaks to the tension that exists between the coordinative goal of MFR and the political environment of public administration. Suffice it to say in the case of Congress, that the fragmentation of power in the committee system is closely aligned with the incentives and norms that define legislative behavior.

Limits on Comprehensiveness

The foregoing discussion should not be taken to imply that policy analysis is irrelevant as a management tool. As illustrated by its impact at DoD in the 1960s, it can provide important information for public executives with the will and political influence to use it effectively (Hitch 1965; Enthoven and Smith 2005). Yet even at the height of its effectiveness at DoD, systems analysis fell far short of the comprehensiveness that the logic of PPB seemed to promise and that its more zealous advocates claimed it could achieve. Moreover, it is doubtful that the annual requirements for assessment and planning throughout DoD played a critical role in identifying and analyzing many of the issues that were addressed by McNamara's staff. Some of the most important of these had been considered by civilian analysts at the RAND Corporation and elsewhere before PPB was instituted. Those in the best position to know further indicate that most of the studies produced by DoD's line components were of little value (Enthoven and Smith 1970). Crosscutting analysis arguably was effective to the extent that it was selective and dominated by a relatively small headquarters staff that was responsive solely to the interests of the secretary.

Herein lies an irony of MFR, at least as manifested in formal, synoptic models. The history of program budgeting at DoD suggests that cyclical and comprehensive efforts at planning, assessment, and resource allocation throughout a complex organization are at odds with the kind of useful analysis that can be done. The agility of the informal process that facilitated effective crosscutting analysis on a selective basis under Robert McNamara has been replaced by a process that is so convoluted and bureaucratized, and so resource intensive that it has become ineffectual.[11] Complying with its annual requirements has become a ritual that is an end in itself. The characteristics and limitations of the current system might be understood as an organizational manifestation of the obstacles that scholars have long associated with efforts to achieve comprehensive rationality in a complex decision-making environment (Dror 1968). Some have attributed the ineffectiveness of PPB at DoD precisely to the assumption that planning can be systematically integrated into the annual budgeting process.

So doing arguably ensures that too much analysis of too many nonstrategic issues will crowd out viable planning efforts (BENS 2000).

DoD's experience does not bode well for efforts at top-down coordination within other agencies, much less for the government-wide performance plan that GAO has interpreted the GPRA to require. That OMB has not attempted this is attributable to several factors, including the aforementioned conceptual barriers that confront a hierarchical ordering of means and ends, as well as the sheer amount of work such an effort would entail. Two senior career officials noted that even to attempt crosscutting analysis of a systematic nature would require such an augmentation of OMB's staff as to make the organization unwieldy and unresponsive to the president's needs. (Even at OMB's current size, presidents and their advisers often perceive that it is too large and bureaucratized to play an incisive role in shaping and executing White House policy priorities.)

As implemented during the George W. Bush administration, moreover, the annual PART process undermined OMB's ability to conduct coordinative analysis on a selective basis in much the same way that formal PPB requirements have inhibited targeted analysis at DoD. So-called spring reviews once provided a mechanism through which OMB staff could examine programmatic interrelationships in a few policy areas each year that were of particular interest to the administration. Although these had largely been abandoned before the George W. Bush administration, complying with PART requirements effectively precluded any chance that they might be reintroduced. Career executives at OMB observed that program examiners were too busy with the mechanics of performance assessment within particular organizations during the "off-budget" months of the year to reflect on crosscutting issues. The alternative to this would have been to divorce the PART process organizationally from those responsible for evaluating agencies' budget requests.

Conclusion

In brief, the broader significance of PPB lies in what it says about the performance movement that has had such an important impact on public administration during the past two decades. The linkage that MFR promises across the functions of strategic planning, program assessment, and resource allocation is highly appealing in the abstract, yet advocates of planning and performance assessment seldom offer specific prescriptions for accomplishing this integration. As argued above, some technique that incorporates the essential features of PPB is implied by requirements such as GPRA. If this is not the case, then the burden is on MFR proponents to suggest an alternative means of coordination.

Although performance assessment may be a useful diagnostic tool for managers of individual programs in some cases, an examination of the past and more recent histories of PPB as well as other evidence from the literature offer little reason to think that MFR can achieve its broader, integrative objectives. Aside from the resistance that normally confronts the adoption of new organizational routines, the obstacles include technical difficulties of measurement in some cases as well as more fundamental practical and conceptual barriers. The latter include the dominance of politics as a basis for resource allocation, the importance of formal organizational authority as a basis for managerial accountability, the impossibility of defining hierarchical means–ends relationships in most public organizations, and the sheer amount of effort and cognitive capacity that comprehensive analysis would require.

The fact that all of these explanations were offered for the failure of PPB in the 1960s begs the question of why so many continue to assume that public organizations can be managed to promote the kinds of businesslike efficiency to which MFR aspires. Given that this aspiration is unrealistic, it also begs the question of what values and standards of accountability we should expect from public administration. Although these questions may be impossible to answer in a conclusive way, they suggest issues that can best be explored through a consideration of competing doctrines prescribing the role of bureaucracy in American government. It is to these broader perspectives that the concluding chapter turns.

Notes

1. Empirical studies based on objective qualifications such as educational attainment consistently fail to confirm the superiority of private-sector managers over public-sector ones.
2. Advocates of MFR often gloss over the obvious tension between the accommodation of stakeholder interests and the formulation of coherent objectives.
3. John Mercer, who was a Republican counsel to the Senate Committee on Governmental Affairs in the early 1990s, drafted proposed legislation that evolved into GPRA (Frederickson and Frederickson 2006).
4. However, some (including Congress itself) have questioned how faithfully the PART process reflects the goals of GPRA (Radin 2006; GAO 2004).
5. NOAA was one of the pilot projects to which GAO alludes in the quotation above.
6. As Radin (2000a, 17) notes, "Most of the policy analysis offices that became part of the federal government landscape were created as a result of Johnson's PPBS directive."
7. Radin (2006) supports this point by citing James Wilson's (1989) categorization of public organizations based on the observability of their outputs and outcomes.
8. The timely dissemination of warnings and other kinds of information by the Weather Service has proven much easier to measure than the benefits of scientific research.
9. Readers are invited to verify this for themselves by examining the mission statements and goals that are available on agencies' websites. As an OMB official noted in this regard, "A strategic plan that achieved complete agreement among all interested parties was likely to be at such a high level of generality that its usefulness as a decision-making tool would be fairly limited (GAO 1997a, 44).
10. Although Gilmour and Lewis find a correlation between PART scores and executive budget recommendations, these are confined to PART's measurement of agencies' compliance with its requirements rather than to measures of program performance.
11. As Wildavsky (1969) and others have noted, DoD's formal PPB process was complex enough in the 1960s, and it certainly produced mounds of paperwork. The point is rather that this process, per se, had relatively little effect. Again, Enthoven and Smith (1970) note that the vast majority of analyses that emerged from the system were of little value.

Chapter 7

Administrative Doctrine and Administrative Reality

L ike other short-lived techniques that followed it, such as management by objectives and zero-based budgeting, program budgeting (PPB) has been portrayed as a fad that was superficially appealing but ultimately naive in its assumptions. The leading critic of the performance movement describes the Government Performance and Results Act (GPRA) in similar terms (Radin 2000b, 2006). Likening the relationship between the act's premises and the institutional environment of administration in American government to "square pegs in round holes," she notes that "GPRA—like a number of earlier federal management reform efforts—does not fit easily into the institutional structure, functions, and realities of the American system. Despite the array of management reform efforts over the years, couched in different guises and forms, few attempts to deal with management have resulted in any significant change" (Radin 2000b, 111).

Requirements for planning and performance assessment may have survived long enough by now to escape designation as fads. Yet this observation in turn raises important questions about the dynamics of administrative reform. Given its disappointing history and the compelling, theoretically grounded explanations that were offered for its failure, why did program budgeting live on at the Department of Defense (DoD), and why was it resurrected in some civilian agencies? More generally, what explains the persistence of formal planning and performance assessment in light of the process costs and the well-documented limitations of requirements such as GPRA and its counterparts in state and local jurisdictions?

There may be several answers to these questions. Those staff members who were responsible for implementing PPB at the National Oceanic and Atmospheric Administration (NOAA) and the Department of Homeland Security (DHS) are intelligent people, but most of them were only dimly aware of the extensive literature accounting for the demise of program budgeting in the 1960s. Without being prompted, for example, a staff member of the Office of Program Analysis and Evaluation at DHS expressed incredulity that anyone could defend an incremental approach to budgeting. An exception to this lack of familiarity with past criticisms of program budgeting was the person who had primary responsibility for implementing NASA's system. With a graduate degree in policy analysis from the RAND Corporation, his expectations for what program budgeting could accomplish were tempered by a familiarity with concepts such as bounded rationality. In general, however, the preceding chapters offer little reason to be optimistic about the practical influence of public administration scholarship.

Routines can also survive simply because they become embedded in an organization's culture. This probably helps to explain PPB's longevity at DoD. The sustained energy of a forceful leader was required to overcome the inertia of the old system, just as the new system may have acquired its own inertia during Robert McNamara's eight-year tenure. Complying with the annual requirements of PPB at DoD may have become an end unto itself during the intervening decades (even though DoD has arguably lost sight of the original goals of PPB). This same dynamic may be at work in the case of GPRA as agencies develop the institutional capacity to comply with its requirements (although they obviously have little choice in the matter so long as the act remains in effect).[1]

In much the same vein, management techniques can persist or spread through the influence of individuals who are accustomed to them or who otherwise have a stake in their survival. PPB was brought to NOAA by people who had used it in the military. By the same token, it was imposed on DHS at the initiative of staff from the Senate Armed Services Committee, and it was designed and implemented in that agency by people with DoD backgrounds in planning and financial management. More generally, the current performance movement is supported by government practitioners, academicians, and consultants who have built their careers around it in many cases.[2] Managing for results (MFR) has become a professional specialty, the legitimacy of which is underwritten by associations, conferences, journals, and university courses. Many of the GPRA staff that have grown up in the federal bureaucracy (as well as their counterparts in state and local government) identify with this profession and can be counted upon to defend it against those who question its precepts.

Like all of us, moreover, practitioners of planning and performance-based management develop psychological as well as material stakes in what they do that can compromise their objectivity. A member of the Congressional Research Service was referring to this when he characterized "performance types" at the Government Accountability Office (GAO) as "true believers" who have "drunk the Kool-Aid." It was in the same sense that Aaron Wildavsky referred to those who are committed to formal systems of strategic planning (including PPB) as "people of secular faith." As he noted, planners are "confirmed in their beliefs no matter what happens. Planning is good if it succeeds and society is bad if it fails. That is why planners often fail to learn from experience. To learn one must make mistakes and planning cannot be one of them" (Wildavsky 1973, 151).

Elaborating on Wildavsky's assessment, Henry Mintzberg argues that advocates of planning systems (in both the public and private sectors) may rely on several rationalizations (or "forms of flight," as he calls them) to cope with evidence that their techniques have had little effect:

> Instead of questioning planning, conventional planners retreated into a set of behaviors that psychologists might label various forms of "flight"—withdrawal, fantasy, projection. They denied the problem, falling back on faith; they acknowledged some superficial difficulties, but promoted the process anyway; they accepted the failures to date, but insisted that more planning would resolve them; and finally they projected the difficulties onto others, notably "unsupportive" managers and "uncongenial" climates, under the label of "pitfalls of planning." (Mintzberg 1994, 135)

As discussed in previous chapters, these responses to inconvenient evidence are familiar enough with regard to PPB and performance-based management. Advocates of MFR treat its value as axiomatic and assume that it can only fail because of people who are either unenlightened or who have perverse (usually selfish) motives. As with

Robert Behn's (2003) assertion about the superiority of management in the private sector, the advantages of planning and performance measurement are considered to be so self-evident that they require little support. Belief in their convictions leads advocates of MFR to contend that it is only a matter of time until their prescriptions will be widely accepted and yield important benefits.

To be fair, however, the performance movement would not be a movement if it were not based on appealing theoretical premises and if it did not resonate more broadly within America's political culture. Related to but beyond the influence of its professional advocates, the popularity of top-down planning and objective assessment can be described as the modification of a venerable perspective that views administration as an activity distinct from politics that should be governed by the value of efficiency. Accordingly, this perspective holds that public administration should conform to an idealized conception of private administration. PPB and the performance movement can similarly be evaluated in terms of an alternative model that stresses the complexity of administration and its inherent politicization within the American separation-of-powers system.

Competing Perspectives on Public Administration

As with other social structures, the extent to which procedural requirements, organizational arrangements, and other controls over the bureaucracy ultimately derive from ideas as opposed to "material forces" will not soon be resolved. Policymakers usually do not frame institutional choices in terms of abstract prescriptive theories. Because *how* policy is implemented has important implications for *what* policy becomes, moreover, the rules of the game that constrain public administration are often influenced by the same political forces that shape substantive policy (Seidman 1975; McCubbins, Noll, and Weingast 1987; Moe 1988). Still, bureaucratic institutions can be described and assessed in terms of the qualities that they are either explicitly or implicitly designed to promote. These assumptions about what constitutes "good government" reflect the interaction between normative and empirical premises. The "process values" that we expect administration to serve are informed by our beliefs about what is realistic to expect given the tasks that bureaucracy is called upon to perform.

With the caveat that administrative doctrines can be subdivided into finer categories (e.g., Light 1997; Kettl 2002), the tension between two perspectives offers a context for the preceding discussions of PPB and the performance movement. MFR is not identical to but has much in common with the "classical" or "traditional" model of public administration. Similarly, it can be critiqued in terms of what might be labeled the "pluralist" or "Madisonian" model. Although the competing values that underlie these two perspectives have had a practical influence on administrative institutions since the founding of the republic, the models themselves were not elaborated until American scholars began to write about public administration in the late nineteenth and early twentieth centuries.

The Traditional Model: Administration as a Science

The traditional model of public administration is commonly traced to the Progressive Era thinkers of the late 1800s and early 1900s. As Lawrence Lynn (2001) notes in a perceptive essay, there were important differences among leading scholars of that era. This is evident even in the most thorough and influential effort to describe traditional orthodoxy (Waldo 1948). Without presenting a caricature, however, the hallmark of the traditional school was its focus on efficiency as the primary goal of bureaucracy (Wilson 1887; Goodnow 1900; Willoughby 1919; Gulick 1937). As long as administration "had to do with getting things done" (Gulick 1937, 192), it consisted of objective functions whose performance could be refined through scientific analysis. Whether Woodrow Wilson's 1887 prescription to this latter end had much direct influence on subsequent writers (Waldo 1948; Van Riper 1984), it foreshadowed the direction that public administration scholarship would take during the next several decades. Although much of the early work in the traditional school focused on municipal administration (Mosher 1968), its values came to provide a basis for scholarship and institutional reform at all levels of government in the United States.

The view of administration as an instrumental process took two general forms in the early twentieth century. It was reflected in the work of Frederick Taylor (1911) and others who viewed the "one best way" to perform individual jobs as the key to organizational efficiency (e.g., Gilbreth and Gilbreth 1917). The "school of scientific management" typically focused on unskilled, repetitive tasks (e.g., hauling pig iron or working on an assembly line) that lent themselves to time-and-motion studies and similar techniques. More germane to the present discussion, the traditional view of administration also informed arguments that the performance of core management processes could be studied and rationalized. One of the most influential among the latter theorists, Luther Gulick (1937), categorized these functions as planning, organizing, staffing, directing, coordinating, reporting, and budgeting (POSDCORB for short).

The appeal of the traditional model lay in the intrinsic desirability of efficiency as a criterion for organizational accountability. As such, it reflected a faith that science could be enlisted for the betterment of humankind (although public administration scholars at the time may have employed a somewhat looser definition of science than we do today). Some have attributed this optimism to the intellectual influence of logical positivism, as well as to the efficiencies wrought by technological advances and by the rise of hierarchical, highly differentiated, machine-like organizations during the Industrial Revolution. Although Max Weber (1947) ultimately viewed the rationality afforded by such organizations as a mixed blessing, the prescriptions offered by traditional scholars in America were generally consistent with his description of bureaucracy. Frederick Mosher describes these prescriptions:

1. *Rationality*: the applicability of the rule of reason, based on research, to the organization, management, and activities of men.
2. *Planning*: the forward projection of needs and objectives as a basis for work programs.
3. *Specialization*: of materials, tools and machines, products, workers, and organizations.
4. *Quantitative measurement*: applied as far as possible to all elements of operations.
5. *"One best way"*: There is one single best method for doing a job.
6. *Standards and standardization*: the "one best," once discovered through systematic research, must be made the standard and thereafter systematically followed. (Mosher 1968, 72–73)

In these respects, many traditional theorists assumed that the principles of efficient administration were largely the same in the public and private sectors. It followed that the latter should serve as an exemplar for the former. To quote Dwight Waldo:

> The early reformers and the pioneers in public administration accepted business example enthusiastically and practically without reservation. "The field of administration is a field of business," wrote Woodrow Wilson in 1887, giving the cue to subsequent writers. . . . "By the first decades of this century, administration-is-business had become a creed, a shibboleth, and there was little serious criticism of the notion until the decade of the Great Depression." (Waldo 1948, 42, 43)

Noting that the idea of administration-as-science had its origins in the private sector, Mosher similarly observes that "the parallel movement in public administration . . . was seen, in part at least, as an effort to make government more business-like, meaning, literally, more like business" (Mosher 1968, 72). The assumption that public administration should emulate private administration was reinforced by the fact that a good deal of the early scholarship associated with the traditional school occurred under the auspices of the business community. This was particularly true of the so-called Bureau Movement, which focused primarily on administration at the municipal level and which preceded and influenced much of the literature on federal administration (Waldo 1948; Mosher 1968).

Traditional values were reinforced by the Progressives' allegations of bureaucratic corruption and incompetence under the spoils system. As such, the resulting prescriptions reflected both moral and instrumental objectives (Van Riper 1958; Mosher 1968). The appeal of traditional assumptions also lay in their attempt to reconcile a growing administrative state with constitutional precepts. Bureaucracy did not pose a problem for representative democracy and the separation of powers insofar as it merely served as an efficient "transmission belt" for accomplishing a priori goals that had been established by elected officials (especially legislators) through the political process (Appleby 1949; Stewart 1975). This was the sense in which Woodrow Wilson (1887) argued that America could borrow methods of sound administration from Europe's monarchical regimes (where scholars were already engaged in the study of the subject) without compromising its democratic values.[3] Traditional doctrine thus was based on the working premise that politics and administration were conceptually distinct and practically separable functions.

One should take care not to attribute either too much orthodoxy or too much simplicity and conceptual neatness to traditional scholars. As Lynn notes, they generally had a more complex view of administration than did the political elites of the time:

> The caricature [of the traditional model] better depicts the views of judges, legislators, the increasingly powerful business community, and urban professional elites who have shaped the emerging administrative state than of the profession's scholars, who have supplied broader, more thoughtful perspectives on practical issues of state building based on their grasp of Constitutional and democratic theory and values. (Lynn 2001, 145)

Although it tended to be presented in fairly rigid terms by students of municipal government (e.g., Cleveland 1913), sophisticated people such as Frank Goodnow

(1900), Leonard White (1926), and Luther Gulick (1937) recognized that a bright-line distinction between politics and administration was not possible in either a functional sense or with regard to institutional roles. Many individual writers were also inconsistent on this issue or changed their positions based on empirical observation. As Brian Cook (2007) observes, for example, Wilson's thinking about the role of bureaucracy in government became more nuanced over time.

At the least, however, although the leading traditional scholars recognized that politics would inevitably influence administration to some extent, this was not something that they emphasized. As the onetime dean of the Maxwell School at Syracuse University characterized their orientation, "For a half century or so while political science was developing as a distinct discipline, much of the literature tended to accept as substantially real a separation of powers which excluded from administration any—or at least any important—policymaking functions" (Appleby 1949, 3). If this statement may be a modest exaggeration, it is fair to say that most viewed the separation between politics and administration as an ideal that was sufficiently realistic to constitute a sound basis for practical theory. Its great appeal was its reconciliation of the growing need for an administrative state with the need for democratic accountability. The intrusion of politics into the administrative process was generally considered undesirable and something that should be minimized.

Whatever qualifications accompanied the scholarly literature, the view of administration as an instrumental process provided the rationale for institutional design at all levels of government during the Progressive Era. Merit systems of personnel administration sought to promote technical competence within the bureaucracy and to insulate civil servants from inappropriate political pressures that might compromise the objective performance of their duties. The city manager form of municipal government placed executive responsibility in the hands of professional administrators rather than politicians. Independent boards and commissions were created to ensure that the application of objective expertise to regulatory functions would not be undercut by pressures from elected officials.[4] Efforts to reorganize the bureaucracy according to functional criteria and under a strong chief executive were informed by the traditional assumption that the hierarchical integration of government would be a source of greater efficiency.[5]

Criticisms of the Traditional Model

Although the goal of instrumental rationality has never disappeared as a basis for administrative reform, the traditional model had sustained attacks from a number of quarters by the middle of the twentieth century. The Great Depression and the perceived need for government to act as an economic savior may have temporarily undermined people's faith that the private sector was worthy of uncritical emulation (Waldo 1948). In addition, some scholars noted that the traditional model had produced little in the way of concrete guidance. Despite their scientific pretensions, its "principles" were dismissed as contradictory proverbs (Simon 1946; Dahl 1947). Another criticism was that the model's hierarchical, mechanistic orientation neglected the human motives and informal relationships that were critical to organizational performance (Follett 1926; Barnard 1938). This criticism gave rise to an emphasis on management strategies that would nourish individual initiative and provide opportunities for achievement, both as keys to effectiveness and as humanistic ends in themselves (Maslow 1943; McGregor 1957).

Two other criticisms of traditional doctrine are especially relevant here. One was that its goal of comprehensive rationality was too ambitious to be realistic. Because of the complex and uncertain environments in which they operated, and because of the limited time, resources, and cognitive capacity of their members, it was not feasible for organizations to identify and thoroughly analyze the complete range of possible alternative solutions in many decision-making contexts. Consciously or unconsciously, they engaged in strategies of bounded rationality to arrive at decisions that were "good enough" but not necessarily optimal (Simon 1947). What Herbert Simon called "satisficing" was reflected in practices such as a reliance on past precedent and on menus of standard operating procedures in confronting organizational problems (Allison 1971).

Critics of the traditional model also argued that government bureaucracies typically lacked the hierarchical goals that were a prerequisite for any kind of instrumental rationality (either comprehensive or bounded). Scholars (some of whom are often associated with the traditional school) had begun to point out by the 1930s that the administrative process was often so thoroughly infused with policymaking and politics that it could not be confined to objective decisions (Gaus 1931). Rather, agencies had to balance competing demands or social values in carrying out broad grants of discretionary authority or in reconciling conflicting programmatic imperatives. As Pendleton Herring noted, because the "task of interpretation" was a "continuation of the legislative process," administrators were "subject to the same pressures that assailed the legislators" (Herring 1936, 218). The political dimensions of administration became increasingly important (and dominant in many cases) as one progressed to higher levels of authority within the bureaucracy (Appleby 1949).

Observations such as these were underscored by the unprecedented expansion of bureaucracy and of delegated authority at the federal level that began in the 1930s. The performance of municipal services, which provided the early focus for much of the traditional school, was often sufficiently simple and had sufficiently clear objectives that it lent itself relatively well to businesslike management approaches. In contrast, the federal bureaucracy's expanding portfolio tended to involve much more complex policy issues that could not be resolved on the basis of an objective bottom line (Mosher 1968). Referring to the open-ended mandates of recently established regulatory agencies such as the Federal Communications Commission and the Securities and Exchange Commission, for example, a prominent New Deal intellectual described the public interest that those organizations were charged to promote as "a texture of many strands" (Landis 1938, 23–24).

Ironically, the continued expansion of administrative authority that made traditional doctrine appealing as a way of legitimizing the role of bureaucracy in government also rendered its empirical assumptions increasingly untenable. By the 1950s, the most influential students of government and bureaucracy had decisively rejected the conception of administration as predominantly a technical process as a working premise for institutional theory (Gaus 1947; Waldo 1948; Appleby 1949; Sayre 1951). Public administration and business administration were therefore "fundamentally unalike" (Allison 1980). Paul Appleby's classic book *Policy and Administration* was representative of the new orthodoxy that was emerging among political scientists:

> The great distinction between government and other organized undertakings is to be found in the wholly political character of government. The great distinction between public administration and other administration is likewise to be found in the political character of public administration.

... Policymaking may take place with reasonable public safety at many levels in the executive government because the order of any decision is always
subject to political determination, and arrived at in a political environment.
(Appleby 1949, 12)

The Pluralist Alternative

One response to the breakdown of the so-called politics/administration dichotomy
was the advocacy of strong executive leadership (Kaufman 1956). The rational coordination afforded by hierarchical control had always been a key to efficiency according
to the traditional school (notwithstanding its inconsistency with the decentralization
implied by other prescriptions such as organizational specialization and the insulation
of experts from political influence through merit systems and independent commissions). At the same time, the assumption that a political system of separated and shared
powers would somehow yield cohesive objectives for the administrative system to
accomplish had always been problematic. The centralization of policymaking responsibility and administrative control in an elected chief executive together with the provision of resources needed to exercise those powers had the advantage of reconciling
the values of efficiency and democratic control. It furnished the a priori integration
of political purpose and institutional authority that was a prerequisite for administrative efficiency.[6] At the national level, these arguments were used to justify the creation
of an Executive Office of the President and other instruments of presidential control.

In important respects, then, although Herbert Kaufman (1956) and others treat it
as a separate doctrine, the prescriptive model of executive leadership can be viewed as
a modification of the traditional model that was designed to accommodate the delegation of authority to a large and powerful administrative state. This is consistent with
the fact that some of its first proponents were among the leaders of the traditional
school. Yet although it had—and continues to have—a good deal of theoretical and
practical influence (e.g., Kagan 2001), the centralization of administrative and political authority was difficult to reconcile with the particular kind of democratic control
established by the separation of powers in American government. If it might have been
disingenuous, this is why early advocates of strong presidential administration such as
Gulick and the other authors of the Brownlow Report divorced the president's role as
chief executive from his political roles as chief legislator and head of his party (Waldo
1948; Kaufman 1956).

As a practical matter, moreover, there was little evidence to suggest that most
elected chief executives had either the incentive or the capacity to manage the bureaucracy in the interest of economy and efficiency. None other than Louis Brownlow
(1958, 323–24) remarked that President Franklin D. Roosevelt's management practices "shocked every student of public administration to the marrow of his bones." The
obstacles to systematic, coordinative executive management could be framed in terms
of bounded rationality and the centrifugal forces of bureaucratic politics. As such, they
had become increasingly formidable (and discouraging of serious managerial effort,
one suspects) as government had become larger and more complex.

Whereas the doctrine of executive leadership retained the traditional goal of hierarchical coordination, another response to the observations recounted above was to
embrace the fragmentation of America's Madisonian system. Although they were
based on somewhat different premises, the breakdown of the politics/administration
dichotomy and the emphasis on bounded rationality complemented one another in

their emphasis on the complexity of agency decision making. Indeed, the political and technical complexity of administration were often difficult to disentangle in more than an abstract, theoretical sense. Together, these two challenges to traditional assumptions supported the rise of pluralism as the dominant empirical and normative theory of American government in the middle decades of the twentieth century.

Here, as well, there is a danger of attributing too much orthodoxy to the literature. With this caveat, many of the pluralists who concerned themselves with bureaucracy regarded its structure and behavior as extensions of a political system in which power was highly dispersed, different people (or groups) wanted different things, means and ends were tangled and ambiguous, and the direct and indirect effects of policy alternatives were so difficult to anticipate that they defied synoptic analysis. In response to these constraints, issues were often addressed on a piecemeal basis through compromise and logrolling among shifting coalitions of interests. The ad hoc and decentralized organization of authority within the administrative state both resulted from and reinforced the decentralization of political authority more generally. Some argued that this was consistent with the spirit if not the letter of the Constitution (Long 1952). Although it added to the messiness of the system, the fragmentation of bureaucracy was sometimes portrayed in positive terms as a feature of American government that afforded additional "access points" for the accommodation of group interests through "partisan mutual adjustment" (Long 1949; Appleby 1949; Truman 1951; Lindblom 1959, 1965). Politics was everywhere, and this was as it should be.

Like the traditional model and the model of executive leadership, the pluralist model of public administration has been associated with important institutional developments. Richard Stewart (1975) argues that key trends in the evolution of administrative law during the 1960s and 1970s grew from judges' realization that agency policymaking was a matter of reconciling competing interests. It followed that the administrative process could be perfected through measures ensuring that agencies considered all relevant views. These institutional reforms included the liberalization of standing and the imposition of more rigorous due process on agency policymaking. Much the same can be said for Congress's encouragement of negotiated rulemaking and for a wide array of statutory provisions guaranteeing legal rights for stakeholders to participate in administrative decisions. For example, requirements that agencies consult with advisory committees representing various groups have existed since the nineteenth century and have proliferated in recent decades. These and other mechanisms implicitly concede that there is no objective, a priori basis for many agency actions.

Alternatives to MFR and Businesslike Efficiency

One should take care not to exaggerate the practical effects of prescriptive administrative theory. Even among academics, moreover, doctrines of public administration do not improve upon and replace one another in the same way as theories in some of the natural sciences (Kuhn 1962). It is more accurate to say that the traditional and pluralist models describe alternative sets of empirical assumptions and institutional values that are in constant tension with one another as implicit bases for institutional choice. As such, they provide a useful framework for assessing efforts at administrative reform. Although neither has ever been completely dominant or completely dormant, some analyses have suggested that the relative influence of these values has ebbed and flowed as the emphasis of each in turn has exposed its limitations with respect to the other (e.g., Kaufman 1956; Shapiro 1988).

Be this dialectic as it may, the value of businesslike efficiency has clearly been ascendant over the past two decades in the form of strategic planning, performance assessment, and other elements of the New Public Management (NPM).[7] Although MFR and the NPM attempt to distinguish themselves from the traditional model in their emphasis on the elimination of bureaucratic procedures and the decentralization of managerial initiative, they are ultimately inconsistent in this regard given their simultaneous emphasis on comprehensive planning and coordination. In any event, they share the traditional model's assumption that public administration—like private administration—should be accountable to an objective bottom line. The popularity of this assumption is likely attributable to several factors, including disillusionment with the pluralist conception of public administration as a "science of muddling through" (Lindblom 1959) and concern about government spending. Still, the discussion in this and earlier chapters serves as a reminder of its limitations. The pluralist critique of the traditional model also serves as a reminder of alternative values that have been neglected in recent years.

The Persistence of Traditional Values

Traditional prescriptions have never gone out of style. As with the creation of NOAA and DHS, they are reflected in the popularity of attempts to reorganize all or parts of the bureaucracy along more rational, functional lines. And as in the case of Richard Nixon's Ash Council, Ronald Reagan's Grace Commission, and various other advisory bodies with narrower charges, business leaders have often played influential roles in these efforts. Traditional values are also reflected in attempts to ensure that the exercise of delegated authority is objective and well thought out (Diver 1981). For example, legislative and judicial requirements that agencies base their decisions on "evidence in a record" seek to ensure that rules and other policy actions are grounded in sound empirical evidence and accurate constructions of legislative intent. Requirements that decisions must be justified on the basis of cost/benefit analysis assume that the goal of economic efficiency should serve as an a priori basis for administrative rationality.

Formal systems of planning and assessment are especially significant as manifestations of traditional values (Mintzberg 1994). Indeed, the idea that a functional budget could be used for planning and coordination had its origin in the Progressive Era. The supplementation of this tool with the measurement of program effects and then with systematic, crosscutting comparisons of agency activities is arguably the ultimate extension of the idea that public administration can be structured in such a way as to promote businesslike efficiency.[8] These same techniques, which are explicit in PPB, are implicitly required if GPRA and other versions of MFR are to achieve their most important objective.

A useful comparison is never served by exaggeration. One significant difference between the traditional school and the performance movement of today is the Progressive Movement's faith in government as an instrument for social and economic progress (at least assuming that government was managed effectively in accordance with traditional precepts). In contrast, advocates of the NPM and MFR have often demonized bureaucracy. Another difference is the performance movement's lack of attention to constitutional and democratic values. If their arguments were flawed, the leading scholars of the traditional era struggled to reconcile bureaucracy with the broader political system in which it was embedded.

It is also important to recognize that other elements of the NPM are expressly at odds with what its advocates assume to be traditional precepts (Lynn 2001). This is particularly true of its emphasis on input from stakeholders (or "customers") and on outsourcing and the decentralization of managerial responsibility. These latter prescriptions are intended to address the rigidity and lack of responsiveness and entrepreneurial initiative that the NPM equates with the kind of rule-bound and hierarchical public bureaucracies that were allegedly spawned by traditional thinking. Contrasting it with the "bureau-pathology" of "public agencies unresponsive to the demands of citizens, led by bureaucrats with the power and incentives to expand their administrative empires and 'policy spaces,' Linda Kaboolian (1998, 190) characterizes the NPM as "an orientation to customer service [that] focuses managers and agencies on what users of the services define as important."

If the premises of the NPM are inconsistent, however, the similarities between the goals and assumptions of the performance movement and those that sustained the traditional school of the early twentieth century are notable in several respects. These similarities include the following, interrelated elements:

- an emphasis on efficiency as the primary goal of administration
- an emphasis on centralized planning and control, and on the hierarchical integration of organizational goals as keys to economy and efficiency (again, although this seems to be inconsistent with the NPM's emphasis on decentralization and its aversion to bureaucratization)
- faith that management decisions can be reduced to (or can at least be heavily informed by) objective techniques that utilize quantitative measures of inputs, outputs, and outcomes
- the corresponding view of politics (but somehow not the preferences of agencies' "customers") as an unwanted intrusion on efforts to achieve economy and efficiency in administration
- the assumption that public administration can and should be modeled after business administration, and
- the assumption that principles and techniques of sound administration can be transported from one political system, level of government, or agency to another

It is also revealing in this last instance that, although their ideas were extended to the federal bureaucracy, both the traditional school and the American versions of MFR and the NPM drew a good deal of their initial inspiration from local government. Just as traditional theory and institutional reforms built on the Bureau Movement, for example, the prescriptions of the book *Reinventing Government* were largely derived from experiences in a handful of small and medium-sized cities (Osborne and Gaebler 1992). Both the Clinton administration's National Performance Review and GPRA were influenced by management practices at the municipal level.

Several factors may explain the persistence of traditional values. Although a large and powerful administrative state is a practical necessity, it remains difficult to reconcile with representative democracy (Freedman 1978). Considerations of legitimacy may demand that we strive for objectivity, even though it is not fully attainable.

Moreover, public administration does have important objective elements. If it cannot be purely a technical process, neither are empirical analysis of means–ends relationships and considerations of effectiveness and organizational efficiency irrelevant for managers or for the politicians who authorize, fund, and oversee agencies and the programs they administer.

Why, then, should we not make government as objective and businesslike as it can be? Though it was never irrelevant, the appeal of efficiency has been reinforced since the 1980s by heightened fiscal concerns and by recent failures attributed to the lack of planning and coordination in areas such as the gathering and sharing of intelligence, disaster preparedness, and the regulation of financial institutions. Although we have often criticized government for its failure to do more, efforts to make agencies more efficient are also consistent with an antipathy toward public administration that is a hardy perennial among politicians and their constituents. Their rhetoric on the subject may vary as a matter of degree, but few elected officials from either party are willing to embrace bureaucracy as a positive force that should be trusted to do what is sensible and effective if left to its own devices. James Freedman (1978) and others have argued that these misgivings about public administration as the direct manifestation of government power may reflect several distinctive elements of American political culture.[9]

The appeal of planning and performance assessment is also reinforced by the absence of a compelling alternative. Although "letting things happen" may be attractive to some academic theorists, it has always been a hard sell as a "nonapproach" to management that fails to address apparent systemic defects. Few scholars are prepared to argue that the performance of government should not be improved. In this regard, pluralist values have always played a more latent role in administrative reform than traditional values. Since its apogee in the 1960s, moreover, enthusiasm for pluralism as a normative theory has atrophied substantially. Indeed, the term itself has largely fallen out of favor (even among scholars who continue to embrace its essential propositions).[10] Subsequent critics have portrayed the fragmentation of American government, not as something that facilitates the accommodation of relevant interests but as a source of irrationality and of inequity in the representation it provides (Schattschneider 1960; Lowi 1969).

The pathologies associated with bureaucracy and delegated authority are critical exhibits in support of the latter charges. Sufficiently powerful "special interests" are allegedly able to secure government programs and co-opt implementing agencies to serve their own ends at everyone else's expense. This dynamic, which is often linked to the legislative committee system and the politics of logrolling, is central to "regulatory capture," "iron triangles," and other unflattering metaphors that stress the parochialism of American government. Critics portray the fragmented system of bureaucratic politics as one that is not only unfair but inherently wasteful and incapable of coordinated effort (Lowi 1969). Again, its defects have arguably become increasingly intolerable in light of mounting budget deficits and ever more complex and pressing policy needs at the national level.

These indictments undoubtedly help to explain the current popularity of businesslike efficiency as a criterion for public administration. Some advocates of MFR acknowledge the constraints on planning, performance assessment, and rational coordination within a fragmented and politicized system, and they are usually quick to concede that the input furnished by these processes is just that. As Donald Moynihan (2008, 196) observes, "Careful proponents of performance budgeting argue that performance data is only one type of information that is relevant to decision makers and that the relationship between performance information and results should not be mechanical." Yet it is fair to say that many of these proponents view such competing influences as unfortunate realities that policymakers and managers should strive to overcome. If only Congress, the White House, and the bureaucracy would take MFR more seriously.

Empirical Constraints

After almost twenty years, however, there is little evidence to suggest that MFR has had a significant effect in promoting coordination and efficiency within the federal government (or other jurisdictions in the United States). The most important explanations for this are identical to the critiques of the traditional model discussed above. One is grounded in the theory of bounded rationality. Even to the extent that we might be able to formulate clear goals, comprehensive planning, analysis, and resource allocation are not feasible in a complex and unpredictable decision-making environment. This constraint helps to expose the hubris of arguments that government should operate more like business. The task environments of most public organizations are at least as polycentric as most of those in the private sector, yet the latter often fail dismally in their planning efforts. It is interesting to speculate whether the recent failures and documented waste and inefficiency in the financial, automobile, energy, and other industries will have an effect analogous to the Great Depression in tempering enthusiasm for business as an exemplar for government.

According to Henry Mintzberg (1994) and others (BENS 2000), in fact, formalized systems of strategic planning and assessment had largely fallen out of favor in the corporate world (if not necessarily among planning advocates in academia and consulting firms) by the time the GPRA sought to impose "sound business practices" on the federal bureaucracy. This was due to various factors, including the impossibility of anticipating future demands and constraints in many contexts and the inherent complexity of any effort at comprehensive analysis. As with PPB at DoD, formal planning systems instituted in the private sector often had so many interlocking stages and involved so much input from so many actors that they overwhelmed executive decision makers and stifled the creativity of their staffs. And as with DoD, the complexity of these systems was a direct manifestation of the ambitious goals they sought to achieve. Many business leaders came to realize that they were better served by small planning staffs that addressed issues on a selective basis. To quote a report comparing the size and complexity of the PPB enterprise at DoD with corporate practices as they have evolved:

> Such rich staffing is not seen in major private organizations. . . . One major private-sector corporation, having a strategic planning process that many in the business community consider to be very effective, reported that its staff devoted to planning and budgeting numbered about twenty including administrative support. Another major corporation with diverse international, holdings and activities also had a rather small staff that worked on both planning and budgeting. A representative of this second company stated that many budgeting functions had been abolished by the new CEO who felt that too much time was spent "filling out forms" and too little time was spent thinking about the major issues of where the company was going in the next five to ten years. A spokesman for the first company indicated that most contemporary CEOs take pride in "having eliminated more processes then they have initiated." (BENS 2000, 11)

Unlike the private sector, moreover, public management often lacks the prerequisite for rational coordination. Instead, multiple and conflicting objectives and fragmented authority ensure that decision making is often political and "arational." Although it is a challenging task in all democracies, the articulation of hierarchically ordered means–ends relationships is especially problematic in the United States. American bureaucracy "is not designed to be effective" (Moe 1989, 275) because other values trump efficiency and effectiveness in our constitutional system. This is why some scholars argue that planning and performance-based coordination may be more realistic in parliamentary regimes, where policymaking responsibility and lines of institutional accountability and control are relatively straightforward (Robinson and Brumby 2005). This is also why many Progressive Era thinkers struggled to reconcile the goal of administrative efficiency with the concept of the separation of powers (Waldo 1948).

Neglected Values

Although these are hardly new observations, they have not been emphasized in recent decades. Nor has skepticism about the viability of systematic planning and performance assessment been accompanied by a coherent alternative. This undoubtedly reflects the positive orientation of political science and public administration that has discouraged many scholars from venturing too far into normative territory. It also reflects the challenges that confront any effort at prescriptive theory. Popular approaches to management, such as the various prescriptions espoused in the NPM, are simplistic, to be sure; like the traditional school, they can be criticized as a list of contradictory proverbs. Yet these perspectives are easier to tear down than to replace. As just discussed, moreover, the relatively sanguine view of bureaucratic fragmentation as an extension of pluralist politics that was common in the middle decades of the twentieth century has come under attack and is seldom expressed today.

Still, the American system of politics and administration is what it is. And as an extension of broader constitutional principles, it may not be such a bad system in comparison with more centralized alternatives. Although this issue requires a much more extensive discussion than is possible here, the limitations of PPB and the performance movement may suggest a reconsideration of normative perspectives that have gone out of fashion. Whether or not these perspectives were built on a caricature of traditional theory, they emphasized realities of public administration in America that had not been given due consideration by previous scholars and policymakers. The same realities and their normative implications have received insufficient emphasis in the current literature.

The most basic point is that the institutional preconditions for comprehensive planning and coordination may not be desirable. A political system capable of defining the hierarchical objectives that can serve as a basis for top-down coordination is appealing in some respects, but any such system would necessarily aggregate interests in a different way than American government. Should we attempt to rationalize the jurisdictions of legislative committees in order to promote the viability of PPB at DHS (Williams 2007)? Should we further strengthen presidential powers (and correspondingly weaken those of Congress) in the hope that executive centralization will produce greater cohesiveness in policymaking and administration? (This, in fact, has been a persistent constitutional issue since the New Deal.) Although reasonable people have made these arguments, the assumption that a rational administrative system can be reconciled with our current political system ignores all that this implies. The conceptual and political obstacles that confront efforts at top-down integration, even within a relatively small "holding company" such as NOAA, are reflections of core institutional values.

An accompanying observation is that most agencies and programs represent legitimate interests and needs. It is in this sense that pluralist scholars such as Norton Long (1949) saw the fragmentation of bureaucracy as both an effect and a further extension of constitutional principles. Multiple and therefore ambiguous lines of institutional accountability rendered agencies independent actors that were left to fend for themselves. Much as business firms needed customers to succeed in the economic marketplace, bureaucracies had to maintain a favorable balance of support from constituents and their elected representatives in order to succeed in the political marketplace. This enhanced a certain kind of democratic representation by enriching the medium of "access points" at which groups could press their demands on government. Paul Appleby used the Bureau of Reclamation to illustrate this argument:

> The Bureau of Reclamation . . . is a special representative within the government of areas and interests concerned with reclamation. Its influence with Congress is not its own, but that of citizens concerned about reclamation programs. It is not merely representative, of course; within certain limits it is also the government of the United States in matters having to do with reclamation. In its operations it has to balance the interests of the Salt River Valley and the Imperial Valley, the Hood River district and Wenatchee, the different interests of Colorado and Idaho. Within certain limits, its balancing of these interests is a translation of special interests into more general public interest. The limits are the points where the bureau ceases to be "the" government of the United States and becomes only a small part of it. At those points the Bureau comes under the collateral influence of the Indian Service, the Division of Power, the Bureau of Land Utilization; at those points it comes in competition with these and other bureaus in the Interior Department for public funds, in Competition with the Corps of Engineers, the Department of Agriculture, and the rest of government. At those points it meets the Interior budget-making process, the Interior administrative leadership, the Bureau of the Budget, the President, the appropriations committees and the whole Congress. In the process, reclamation policy is more and more influenced by other agencies representative of other interests. (Appleby 1949, 82–83)

As this quotation indicates, Appleby also felt that the representation of constituencies and programmatic interests within the bureaucracy resulted in a kind of political coordination. This occurred both vertically (within agencies) and horizontally (across agencies), and it was motivated in large measure by the "learning" that "came from burning fingers." As Appleby (1949, 77) noted, "That which is likely to make trouble; trouble with associates, competing groups, or affected citizens, is that which is 'checked' both laterally and perpendicularly before action is taken." Building on his economic metaphor, Long similarly argued that this representative and coordinative dynamic within the bureaucracy was analogous to the invisible hand of the marketplace. As such, he felt it was superior to efforts at synoptic analysis. Just as centralized planning could not yield an efficient allocation of resources in the economic system, the political system was too complex and too unpredictable to allow for top-down rationalization.

These observations highlight one of the most fundamental inconsistencies in the NPM and the performance movement. Without articulating a theory of political coordination in the vein of Appleby and Long, the NPM does embrace customer service and the decentralization of administrative authority as ways in which government can promote competition and emulate the efficiency of the private sector. Yet although its advocates are presumably not in favor of a Soviet-style economy, the performance movement also prescribes top-down planning (and often five-year plans, no less) and objective program assessment as bases for achieving accountability and for coordinating the allocation of resources across agencies and programs. In addition to the barriers that render comprehensive analysis infeasible, a related irony of MFR is that the elaborate organizational processes that are required by efforts at top-down planning, assessment, and coordination are antithetical to the decentralization and de-bureaucratization that its advocates feel are prerequisites for competitive entrepreneurialism in the public sector. This was certainly the case at NOAA, where the administrative requirements of PPB consumed a good deal of time that managers might otherwise have devoted to more creative pursuits.

Whether in the private or public sector, of course, the idea of an invisible hand assumes the existence of healthy competition. Again, claims to the efficiency of the "political marketplace" became less fashionable with allegations that many important concerns were poorly represented and that policymaking and implementation were often dominated by "iron triangles" and the like. The delegation of power to a fragmented American bureaucracy was allegedly the root cause of such relationships. Given these observations, one might justify a technique such as PPB as an effort to address externalities in the political marketplace.

One needs to look no further than the agency formerly known as the Minerals Management Service to ascertain that these indictments retain some validity. Yet if the fragmented US system is far from perfect in terms of the representation and political coordination it provides, allegations of narrow clientelism are quite different from the charges of bureaucratic insularity and rigidity that animate MFR and the NPM. Again, the market-based logic of customer service and competition is difficult to reconcile with the logic of top-down planning, assessment, and control.

Moreover, influential accounts suggest that the environment of program implementation has generally become more competitive in recent decades. This has occurred partly as the result of institutional developments that have facilitated more balanced access to the administrative process and have broken up established subgovernments. Without using the term, for example, Hugh Heclo's (1978) influential description of policymaking within "issue networks" is similar to pluralist theory in terms of its emphasis on conflict, complexity, and the fluidity of relationships among bureaucratic actors and their constituents. A central element in Heclo's analysis is the proliferation of organized groups and of agencies and programs that have been created to represent those interests within policymaking environments that transcend the boundaries of single organizations and sets of legislative committees. Symbiotic relationships between bureaucrats and their clients may still exist under this model, but it has become less likely that such alliances will operate autonomously from other sets of agencies, constituents, and politicians with competing interests. Similar dynamics are central to Paul Sabatier's (1988) discussion of "advocacy coalitions" and to other leading models of policy change such as those offered by Kingdon (1995) and Baumgartner and Jones (1993).

A consideration of pluralist theory suggests other issues as well. One is that incremental decision making may be preferable to comprehensive planning and analysis under many circumstances. As a form of bounded rationality, it has the advantage of simplifying calculations and avoiding large mistakes. It is also more feasible than comprehensive approaches to resource allocation because of the sunk costs and the internal and external constituents that become attached to ongoing programs. An instructive observation is that, although practitioners of PPB disparage "base-plus budgeting," that is precisely what the process has yielded at DoD, NOAA, and the other agencies where it has been applied. By some accounts, its complex annual requirements institutionalize rather than combat incrementalism. To the extent that performance-based comparisons influence decisions, it is on a highly selective basis and it is usually confined to competition for additional funds (as opposed to the reallocation of existing or diminishing resources).

Another question that has received little attention in recent years is whether redundancy is always a bad thing. The traditional aversion to duplication and overlap as sources of inefficiency is usually presented as a self-evident truth by advocates of MFR. As Martin Landau (1969) argued in a classic essay, however, just as aircraft, nuclear power plants, and other engineering systems incorporate redundancy in order to minimize the risk of failure, so redundancy may be desirable as a way of ensuring that important interests and empirical considerations are not overlooked in the performance of many government functions. In fact, Landau framed this argument largely in the context of PPB, which was nearing the end of its first life in the civilian bureaucracy at the time. Characterizing its goal of comprehensive planning and rational restructuring as "a form of administrative *brinksmanship*" and as an "extraordinary gamble" (1969, 354) he noted that

> "streamlining an agency," "consolidating similar functions," "eliminating duplication," and "commonality" are powerful slogans which possess an obvious appeal. But it is just possible that their achievement would deprive an agency [or government] of the properties it needs most—those which allow rules to be broken and units to operate defectively without doing critical injury to the agency [or government] as a whole. Accordingly, it would be far more constructive, even under conditions of scarcity, to lay aside easy slogans and turn attention to a principle which lessens risks without foreclosing opportunity. (Landau 1969, 356)

Many present-day applications of Landau's arguments are possible. Would we want to consolidate all intelligence-gathering responsibility in one federal agency (or otherwise redistribute resources to the one agency deemed to be most effective)? Is it undesirable that several grant programs located in different departments are devoted to the prevention of teenage pregnancy? Is it bad that different research laboratories within NOAA or within the government more generally are investigating similar issues (e.g., global warming) more or less independently from one another?[11] (After all, replication is an important principle in the conduct of scientific inquiry.) Should legislative oversight of administration be "rationalized" so that agencies are not exposed to information requests or policy perspectives from more than one committee in each chamber?

The list could go on. To say that there are problems of communication and coordination associated with duplication and overlap at an operational level in some areas is not to say that the benefits of duplication and overlap do not often outweigh the costs at a programmatic level. As Long (1949) might have added, criticisms of governmental redundancy as a violation of "sound business practices" ignore the analogy to competition in the private sector and the "economic interest representation" it provides. Few would argue that consumers should be limited to one make of automobile or one television network. The logical inconsistency of the NPM bears reemphasis in this regard. Although the need for competition is one of its core precepts, the planning orientation of MFR also seeks to impose hierarchically integrated order on the performance of government functions.

Perhaps an obvious response to these observations is that duplication and overlap are simply no longer affordable in today's fiscal environment. Even if systematic efforts at performance-based management could yield significant efficiencies in spending, however, those savings would represent a very small part of the solution to the budget deficits currently faced by American government. And again, there is little evidence that such techniques can work in any case. This is illustrated most dramatically by the one organization where greater rationality in discretionary spending might have the most substantial effect in mitigating the deficit. Although it has had a formal and well-resourced system of planning and assessment in place for fifty years, few would commend DoD as a model of financial responsibility. Notwithstanding its original intent, in fact, the informational demands of PPB may contribute to wasteful defense spending by precluding strategically focused analysis.

Management as an Art

Of course, these are complex issues. To raise them is not to argue that incremental policymaking strategies or redundancy in the structure of government is always desirable. Nor is it to argue that public organizations should not seek to anticipate future needs or be concerned with the effects of the programs they administer. Rather, the point is that—much as the traditional school a century ago—formal systems of planning and performance assessment stress a one-dimensional view of public administration that is unrealistically ambitious in its aims, that is based on simplistic empirical premises, and that minimizes or neglects important values. Whether or not such systems work in the private sector or even in the provision of some municipal services, those who advocate their wholesale extension to the federal bureaucracy ignore the political context that makes government administration fundamentally different from business administration. Efficiency and effectiveness, themselves, can become elusive concepts when one considers all of the criteria that are relevant to management in the public sector.

What is the alternative to the managerialism prescribed by PPB and requirements such as GPRA and PART? As implied by the pejorative meaning of this term, there is not a mamagement system that can solve the complex issues that bureaucracy must confront. Public management is instead more art than science. It should be informed by experience and knowledge of cause-and-effect relationships, to be sure, and it should plan and adapt to changing needs. But although it should be concerned with objective results, it occurs in a complex political and technical environment requiring judgment that cannot be reduced to a generally applicable formula or set of procedures. This is the view of public administration expressed by "posttraditional" scholars of the mid–twentieth century such as Appleby (1949), John Gaus (1947), and Wallace Sayre (1951). For example,

> Importance in the administrative organization turns in some part on expert valuations; in some degree on novelty; in some part on prerogatives and other institutional valuations; in some part on dimensions and scope of the

action—the weight of impact it will have or has had on citizens, and the number of citizens affected; in some part on ideal values, such as are involved, for example, in questions of the *kind* of impact on even a single citizen. In very considerable part all this is reaction to diverse political forces. . . . It is a process, then, in which many unlike things are weighed on the same scales, and simultaneously. (Appleby 1949, 13)

Appleby's description of public management at high levels is essentially the same as those offered by a few current students of public management. Describing the role of the secretary of health and human services as an "accountable juggler," for example, Beryl Radin notes that

I have tried to convey a sense of the fluidity and turbulence that make the task of managing the Department of Health and Human Services challenging, at the least. The secretary of the department has been described as an accountable juggler—someone who has to balance multiple actors and pressures. Dropping one of those elements not only has political consequences but it also has substantive consequences for those individuals who are affected by DHS programs as well as for those thousands of career public servants and others who make those programs come alive.

Radin adds that "the ability to respond to these attributes calls for leaders who are highly skilled, able to listen to the cacophony of voices around them, and capable of adapting to constantly changing circumstances" (Radin 2002, 136).

The goal, then, is to recruit and rely on competent public managers rather than on mechanical constraints. The ability to weigh "many unlike things" on the "same scales" naturally becomes more important as one progresses to higher levels within the bureaucracy. On the basis of this observation, some early advocates of executive leadership sought to preserve the traditional model by making the boundary between political and (objective) administrative functions coterminous with the boundary between political and career officials. As a practical matter, however, senior careerists typically act as brokers who are counted upon to identify and facilitate mediation among the various political interests and technical and legal criteria that are relevant to administrative policy decisions. This is because their resources for navigating within the environment of bureaucratic policymaking—their substantive expertise and personal connections within government—are often superior to those of the transient masters they serve (Heclo 1977).

Some in the performance movement would undoubtedly argue that this prescription is at odds only with a distortion of their position. It remains, however, that the logic of efforts to make public administration more efficient in pursuit of a bottom line contradicts the view of administration as a matter of balancing competing values and political influences. In addition, whatever benefits formal systems of planning and performance assessment confer at the margins must be weighed against the burdens they impose. These include the potential for organizational goal displacement in many areas where straightforward measures of outcomes are not available. They also include the time and effort that are needed to comply with such requirements. As discussed in earlier chapters, in fact, the bureaucratization and time constraints associated with management systems such as PPB ironically can reinforce the pathologies they are designed to confront by crowding out opportunities for creative planning and analysis in selected areas. This has arguably been the effect of program budgeting as it has evolved at DoD. It was also true of the PART process at the Office of Management and Budget.

It is in recognition of such costs that some feel the adoption and design of performance management is best left to the discretion of individual agencies. This may help to avoid the inflexibility and excessive costs associated with government-wide performance-information systems such as some states have adopted and that GPRA represents at the federal level. In many cases, however, this recommendation begs the question of where in the organizational hierarchy such discretion should reside. As illustrated by NOAA and DHS, even relatively homogeneous agencies can encompass functions that are sufficiently diverse as to frustrate uniform performance management systems or meaningful comparisons across programs.

Conclusion

The immediate explanations for the resurrection of PPB are straightforward. People gravitate toward the familiar, and most of those responsible for bringing program budgeting to NOAA and DHS had used it at DoD. Yet the logic of program budgeting is also eminently appealing on its face; it is difficult to argue with the proposition that government organizations should plan and should be more accountable and more efficient. PPB can be characterized in this regard as both a precursor to and an extension of the performance movement that has had such an important effect on the theory and practice of public administration in recent years. Again, a technique that incorporates its essential elements is required if agencies are to achieve what is arguably the movement's most ambitious and most important objective: the integration of planning and the objective assessment of program effects in order to allocate government resources in a more efficient way.

Unfortunately, PPB has never lived up to this expectation. Moreover, the challenges that confronted its recent implementation at NOAA might have been predicted from accounts of its demise in the 1960s. Those who imposed program budgeting on DHS might easily have anticipated its problems there as well. Although some of the people responsible for the resurrection of PPB in these organizations had been vaguely aware of its history, agency documents and conversations with agency officials and consultants indicate that earlier studies of its implementation were not given serious consideration. Again, this observation offers little cause for optimism that past experience—much less academic research—will guide efforts at institutional reform.

The same can be said for many who assume that planning and performance assessment can be used to rationalize what government does. Given the similarities between program budgeting and the synoptic planning and coordination that GPRA seeks to achieve, and given the well-documented failures of the former technique, it is especially discouraging that the National Academy of Public Administration was among the organizations that supported the act (Roberts 2000). (As Lynn [2001] notes, the academy also gave its uncritical endorsement to the list of proverbs that informed *Reinventing Government* and the Clinton administration's National Performance Review.) Even those MFR advocates who acknowledge the past failures of PPB do not offer a distinction between its objectives and the coordinative goals that GPRA seeks to promote. If PPB cannot apply comprehensive planning and performance assessment to achieve coordination across organizational boundaries, then what can? Alternatively, if the coordinative goals of PPB are too ambitious, then what return can we expect from the investment of time and effort required by formal planning and performance management systems?

Thoughtful answers to these questions would no doubt detract from the appeal of MFR. Although formal systems of planning and performance measurement may be useful in some contexts as tools that allow managers to clarify objectives and identify problems or best practices, their value is considerably attenuated to the extent that they do not influence the allocation of resources in a substantial way. It is tempting to speculate in this regard that the GPRA's longevity owes in part to the fact that—much like MFR generally—it has not defined its goals in terms of clear operational requirements. Abstract aspirations are often more appealing than concrete prescriptions. The longevity of the performance movement is also undoubtedly attributable to the negative stereotypes of government and the positive stereotypes of the private sector that are staple elements of America's political culture. Conceding that GPRA had had "little effect on anything," for example, a former GAO official who had studied its implementation added that it was important "as a way to cover yourself." What politician would take exception with the proposition that government should plan, coordinate, and be accountable for program results?

Less jaded advocates of performance-based management systems typically confront inconvenient evidence by arguing for patience. They assert that old ways die hard in the bureaucracy and that it will take time to develop better performance measures and to replace established routines and constituent ties with a "culture of assessment" (GAO 2004). Their faith may be evidenced by the fact that their evaluations of MFR requirements often focus more on the processes that agencies have instituted than on the substantive effects of those processes. In any case, the analysis here suggests that the most important obstacles to comprehensive planning and performance assessment cannot be overcome through experience and enlightenment (Roberts 2000; Radin 2006). They reflect more fundamental tensions between the assumptions of MFR and the environment of public administration in the United States.

Notes

1. It bears repeating that assessments of GPRA, PART, and other planning and performance assessment requirements have often focused more on the processes that agencies put in place than on the effects of those systems.

2. After all, professors and consultants have an obvious incentive to advocate practical theories for consumption by their academic peers, students, and clients.

3. The perceived effectiveness of the German state during World War I may have amplified concerns about the inferiority of administrative methods in America during the 1920s (Waldo 1948).

4. However, some argue that the true motive for the creation of such bodies has been to strengthen the influence of Congress as opposed to the president.

5. These initiatives were obviously at odds with the creation of independent boards and commissions.

6. Also, as Waldo (1948) notes, most members of the traditional school had little use for the separation of powers.

7. Although the emphasis that the New Public Management places on stakeholder involvement implies that different "customers" are likely to have different interests or analytical perspectives, its primary emphasis on top-down planning and the objective assessment of outcomes implies that administration is an instrumental

function. Implicitly, it assumes that all stakeholders can be accommodated in building a consensus around a cohesive set of organizational objectives.

8. It bears mention that program budgeting was developed and first implemented in the 1950s and 1960s, even as pluralist theory was at the height of its influence among academics.

9. These include the importance of laissez faire ideology, a belief in individual self-reliance sometimes associated with the frontier experience, anti-intellectualism and a distrust of experts, and the fact that democratic institutions preceded the development of an administrate state in America (but not in Europe).

10. Much as today's liberals call themselves "progressives" to avoid the negative connotations that have come to be associated with the former term, many pluralists prefer to call the system they favor "Madisonian democracy."

11. Such an indictment would obviously call for a drastic restructuring of American research universities.

Appendix

As is mentioned in chapter 6, program budgeting has been adopted not only by NOAA but by the Department of Homeland Security (DHS) and the National Aeronautics and Space Administration (NASA). Like NOAA, DHS and NASA are composed of units that perform related functions. Although their planning, programming, budgeting (PPB) systems may not be sufficiently well established to warrant a thorough assessment at this point, their initiatives bear a brief description as a complement to the discussion of NOAA in chapters 4 and 5. The frustrations encountered by DHS may be particularly relevant in this regard.

PPB at the Department of Homeland Security

In consolidating twenty-two agencies from throughout the government, the creation of DHS in the wake of the September 11, 2001, terrorist attacks was the most ambitious reorganization of the federal bureaucracy since the establishment of Department of Defense (DoD) after World War II. As with NOAA, the creation of DHS was based on the venerable assumption that the centralization of authority was the key to organizational integration. Most of those involved realized at the time that the rationalization of homeland security functions would not be easy, however, and this has certainly proven to be the case. The brief history of DHS has been marked by a lack of integration and other management problems that have received considerable attention from academics as well as from the agency's legislative and executive principals. Although some view PPB as a tool for addressing these challenges, the agency has struggled to put an operational system in place.

Origin and Structure

The introduction of PPB at DHS dates to the agency's inception in 2002. Reportedly at the initiative of Senator Joseph Lieberman and several staff on the Senate Homeland Security Committee, Section 874 of the Homeland Security Act required DHS to develop a Future Years Homeland Security Program to accompany its budget submissions. This document was to be modeled after DoD's Future Years Defense Program. As the act states: "Each budget request submitted to Congress for the Department . . . shall . . . be accompanied by a Future Years Homeland Security Program. . . . The Future Years Homeland Security Program . . . shall be structured, and include the same type of information and level of detail, as the Future Years Defense Program submitted to Congress by the Department of Defense" (6 U.S.C. 342, sec. 874). One might speculate that this provision stemmed from Senator Lieberman's long experience as a member of the Armed Services Committee.

Although the Homeland Security Act almost certainly contemplated that there be a programming process, and although DHS had an Office of Program Analysis and Evaluation (PA&E) early on, these provisions were explicitly mandated in 2005. Amendments to the departments enabling legislation thus stipulated that the secretary of homeland security "establish an Office of Program Analysis and Evaluation," the director of which would report to an official "no lower than the Chief Financial Officer." The amendments further prescribed a list of PA&E functions that included the analysis and evaluation of "plans, programs, and budgets of the Department in relation to United States Homeland Security objectives," the development and analysis of "alternative plans, programs, personnel levels, and budget submissions" based on the same criteria, and the establishment of policies for the integration of PPB within DHS. PA&E was also given the responsibility of helping DHS to comply with government-wide planning and performance assessment requirements contained in GPRA and the President's Management Agenda (particularly Office of Management and Budget, OMB, Program Assessment Rating Tool, reviews) (6 U.S.C. 342, sec. 702).

The first chief financial officer appointed at DHS was well prepared to oversee the implementation of PPB. Although he had served most recently at the Department of Energy, he had worked before that for many years in DoD. The career Senior Executive Service official whom he recruited to organize and direct an Office of PA&E had also come from Energy and had previously worked in planning and budgeting for the Department of the Navy. Several other staff with DoD backgrounds were brought in to implement PPB as well. Common to all these individuals was the view that PPB (or something that embodied its key elements) was the only sensible way to plan and allocate resources.

The program structure developed by DHS is built around seven strategic goals that cut across its components: awareness, prevention, protection, response, recovery, service, and organizational excellence. Each goal encompasses a number of more specific performance objectives, and these subsume (often multiple) performance measures associated with particular activities performed by particular organizational units. In the case of prevention, for example, the agency's *FY 2006 Performance and Accountability Report* lists thirty-seven performance goals together with sixty-one specific performance measures. Included in this array are prevention programs administered by eight different units within DHS: Customs and Border Protection, the Domestic Nuclear Protection Office, the Science and Technology Directorate, the Coast Guard, the Federal Law Enforcement Training Center, the Transportation Security Administration, the Citizenship and Immigration Services, and Immigration and Customs Enforcement.

PPB at DHS is defined by the same distinct but interrelated stages that characterize the processes at DoD and NOAA. Planning, which relies heavily on the Office of Planning, Policy, and International Affairs, produces an Integrated Strategic Assessment Report that is intended as a key resource to be used in the preparation of the secretary's Integrated Planning Guidance. This IPG in turn provides the basis for the preparation of Resource Allocation Plans (RAPs) during the programming phase. RAPs are prepared by the individual operating elements (component agencies) of DHS, and they are to be accompanied by objective analyses of program performance. The RAPs are consolidated and evaluated by PA&E at departmental headquarters. PA&E and the DHS Budget Office analyze and compare the RAPs in conjunction with performance measures and other considerations to prepare draft Resource

Allocation Decisions for consideration by senior DHS leadership (as embodied in the several boards and councils that ultimately advise the secretary).

Implementation

The functional orientation of PPB is obviously consistent with the objectives that informed the creation of DHS. To date, however, the system has had little substantive impact. As Cindy Williams (2007) notes, for example, it has failed to address significant redundancies in the efforts of DHS components, such as the separate air forces maintained by Customs and Border Protection, Immigration and Customs Enforcement, and the Coast Guard. Williams also points out that although DHS's total budget has grown substantially since its inception, the percentage shares allocated to its components have remained quite stable.

Williams (2007, 4) further rejects the possibility that "budget shares were about right to begin with" as an explanation for this latter observation. As she notes: "Given the haste with which the department was assembled and Secretary [Tom] Ridge's own 2002 forecast of significant reallocations, . . . that hardly seems likely. Glaring examples of persistent overlaps, such as the DHS's three air forces, also require another explanation." Accordingly, Williams equates the stability of DHS component budget shares with the failure of PPB to perform its intended role of comparing the effectiveness of programs as a basis for rationalizing the allocation of resources.

One might argue that program budgeting has not received a fair test at DHS. Thus, although it has existed on paper since 2003, the agency has struggled to put in place a working system that incorporates adequate participation from relevant organizational actors. This failure has been both a cause and an effect of turnover among the officials responsible for its implementation. The first chief financial officer left to take a position with a consulting firm after serving only six months in the new agency. His departure was reportedly motivated by a combination of pecuniary incentives and frustration with the lack of progress in establishing PPB. Although the first director of PA&E was responsible for securing the 2005 legislative amendments that codified that office's existence, this in itself resulted from concern that his position would be abolished. He subsequently concluded that he was in an untenable situation, and he left PA&E for another DHS position in 2007. Thereafter, the directorship of PA&E was vacant for eighteen months until it was filled by someone recruited from DoD.

The challenges that have impeded the implementation of program budgeting at DHS are familiar. Component agencies have often struggled to develop meaningful performance indicators, especially of the kind that allow for comparisons across activities and organizations. Although mitigating risk is arguably the ultimate purpose of all DHS programs that can theoretically provide a basis for top-down coordination across the department, all but the most devoted advocates of cost/benefit analysis might find it difficult to weigh the marginal benefits of hurricane preparedness against efforts to improve airport security. In any case, the effort to measure outputs and outcomes in terms of risk remains in its infancy in most areas. Official rhetoric to the contrary notwithstanding, moreover, planners and analysts at both the component and departmental levels at DHS have found the performance measures required by GPRA and PART to be counterproductive for the purpose of implementing PPB.

DHS's components have also resisted PPB as being foreign and difficult to master. Only the Coast Guard had a system that was remotely similar before DHS's creation. Noting that a "true performance-based system" that might serve as a basis for rational resource allocation was a long way off, a staff member of the US Federal Emergency Management Agency (FEMA) with a DoD budgeting background felt that the implementation of PPB had been impeded by the "tyranny of the present." This included FEMA's (and other agencies') adherence to established ways of thinking and doing things along with the practical demands of ongoing operations. The same individual also cited limited resources as a factor that prevented PPB from being applied in a systematic way. FEMA thus did not require its line managers to do programming because they were "too busy with their missions." With a staff of only five individuals, however, the agency's Office of PA&E could only perform analyses on a very selective basis.

The implementation of PPB has also been limited by a lack of standardization. Individual agencies have had the latitude to design their own systems, and these comply with the general requirements outlined above in various ways and to varying degrees. This lack of uniformity is attributable to legitimate needs for managerial discretion as well as to the political realities that limit centralized control by DHS headquarters. Whereas the coast guard and FEMA have established small PA&E offices, for example, most DHS components have not. Structural variation in PPB in turn naturally produces variation in the type and quality of information that the components produce. One problem DHS's Office of PA&E has faced has been its inability to persuade components to adopt comparable performance measures.

Especially given the other obstacles it has faced, a lack of strong leadership commitment has ultimately been a critical impediment to the establishment of program budgeting at DHS. Secretaries Tom Ridge and Michael Chertoff reportedly had little understanding of or appreciation for the technique, and some other key executives have been indifferent at best. Particularly notable was the lack of support for PPB by the undersecretary for management to whom the chief financial officer and the director of PA&E reported between 2003 and 2007. This individual was an experienced budgeting official who had previously worked as a political executive at OMB and in the civilian line bureaucracy (she had come to DHS from the Department of Health and Human Services), and she felt that the goals of PPB were unrealistic given the fluidity and hectic pace of policymaking at DHS. She and others cited Hurricane Katrina as an (extreme) example of the kind of event that necessarily disrupted efforts at long-range planning. (Several individuals also noted that Katrina had the practical effect of displacing any priority senior management might have otherwise given to the establishment of an effective PPB system.)

The lack of leadership support for rational planning and resource allocation within DHS has been intertwined with fragmented lines of external accountability and constituency influence that have been antithetical to coherent planning. OMB's review of component budgets is divided among program examiners who report to different superiors. In addition, legislative responsibility for DHS authorization, appropriation, and oversight is fragmented among various committees and subcommittees. According to Williams (2010, 22), one result of congressional fragmentation is that the "back door is always open for legacy agencies and concentrated interests."

At least during the George W. Bush administration, the White House was allegedly unwilling to act as a counterweight to such forces by underwriting centralized managerial control at DHS in budgeting and other areas. Speculating on why the department has not been successful in implementing PPB, Williams (2007, 4) observes that

> one [reason] is that the White House never wanted the new secretary to take
> central control of the budget, and made that known through early budget

iterations. Another is that Secretary Ridge and Secretary Chertoff did not engage early enough or forcefully enough in the annual PPBES [cycle] to bring the components to heel. A third is that the secretaries were simply no match for the component fiefdoms, which still have their own powerful allies in the White House and Congress.

This is not to imply that stronger leadership within DHS would be sufficient to achieve the broader objectives of PPB. Just as the sharing of most government functions among departments contributed to the defeat of PPB during the 1960s, the location of many homeland security activities in organizations outside DHS also militates against the comprehensive planning and coordination that PPB is designed to achieve. Although such determinations are subjective to a degree, Williams (2010) estimates that DHS only controls about half the federal spending that contributes to homeland security. (By the same token, Williams estimates that about 40 percent of the DHS budget goes for functions other than homeland security.)

PPB at NASA

The National Aeronautics and Space Administration is also beset by centrifugal tendencies. Unlike DoD, DHS, and NOAA, however, these are grounded in a highly decentralized and matrix-like project structure rather than in separate bureaucratic components with their own identities and routines. NASA's missions (of which there are currently sixty) are executed by teams that are divided for operational purposes among the four mission directorates for aeronautics research, exploration systems, science, and space operations. Missions are housed within and draw personnel and physical resources from ten centers that are located in different parts of the United States (e.g., the Johnson Space Center in Houston and the Jet Propulsion Laboratory in Pasadena). Many projects also rely heavily on contractual relationships with outside entities such as aerospace companies and universities.

Although NASA's projects or missions are temporary in theory, they may last for years or even decades. They can become closely identified with people's careers, therefore, with the predictable consequence that they may become the primary source of organizational loyalty for team members. The ability of NASA headquarters to manage in the face of such fragmentation is impeded by the agency's need to cede a measure of autonomy to its teams in the pursuit of their scientific and engineering missions. It is further impeded by the ambiguous lines of accountability and control that are inherent in the agency's matrix structure. Thus the assistant administrators in charge of the directorates that oversee missions in an operational sense and the heads of centers that provide the necessary resources for those missions are coequal within the agency's hierarchy and report separately to the NASA administrator.

Origin and Structure

The impetus for PPB at NASA can be traced back at least as far as the early 1990s. As reflected most notably in the *Report of the Advisory Committee on the Future of the U.S. Space Program*, known as the Augustine Report (Augustine 1990), the agency's critics in the post-Apollo era cited a lack of planning, cost overruns and poor accounting practices, excessive decentralization, organizational redundancy, and a culture of complacency as among the management challenges it faced (Levine 1992). These concerns were amplified by well-publicized mission failures that occurred both before and after the Augustine Report, as well as by more general expectations for performance-based accountability that were imposed by requirements such as GPRA, PART, and the Chief Financial Officers Act of 1990.

Although NASA had already implemented a number of reforms that anticipated the introduction of PPB, the formal establishment of program budgeting in 2005 came at the initiative of Administrator Michael Griffin. This might be viewed as ironic given that the new agency head was a scientist and that his predecessor was a professional technocrat with a DoD budgeting background. In any case, Griffin wanted to institutionalize a system of "governance" within NASA that would transcend individual personalities. Although some of its key elements were already in place, PPB was appealing in this regard as a mechanism that allowed for greater predictability and transparency in planning and performance assessment. It was viewed as a means of top-down control, but it was also as a framework of internal checks and balances to ensure that all relevant perspectives would be brought to bear in decision making (including the often-competing considerations of risk and the timely accomplishment of mission objectives). Griffin chose an experienced space policy analyst to design a PPB system and head the newly created Office of PA&E. Although this individual did not have an extensive budgeting background, he was familiar with PPB from his time at the RAND Corporation as a PhD student and later a researcher.

Like other systems of program budgeting, PPB at NASA is structured around a hierarchically ordered set of ends and means. At the top are six *strategic goals*, one of which (science, exploration, and aeronautics) encompasses six *subgoals* (that seem to have roughly the same status as goals). With the caveat that the agency does not always use consistent terminology in describing subordinate elements, next come *themes* and then the *programs* that contribute to these themes. Finally, programs provide the organizing framework for specific *missions* that represent ongoing or planned activities (e.g., the Kepler probe and the Hubble telescope).

Like other PPB systems, PPB at NASA consists of a planning process that establishes priorities and a programming process that links those priorities to resource requirements for specific programs and missions. Each of these involves several stages that generate a number of documents. The planning phase consists of sequential steps—for example, internal/external studies and analysis, the NASA strategic plan, annual performance goals, implementation planning, and strategic planning guidance. With the last of these documents as a starting point, the programming phase moves from program and resource guidance to program analysis and alignment to institutional infrastructure analyses to a program review/issues book to a program decision memorandum. All these decision-making steps and documents rely on data describing the costs and effectiveness of NASA programs.

Planning and programming are orchestrated by NASA's Office of PA&E but involve actors from throughout the agency. Especially important in these processes are the four mission directorates, which are supposed to play an integrative role similar to the role that goal teams were intended to perform under NOAA's system of PPBES. Primary staff responsibility for implementing PPB at the directorate level resides with control account managers. These individuals are accountable to the assistant administrators that run the directorates but communicate extensively with PA&E. Planning and programming also bring to bear the perspectives of the centers and NASA's various headquarters offices (e.g., safety and mission assurance, and program and institutional integration), as appropriate.

Implementation

NASA's efforts to implement PPB have not been without problems. As reported to its Advisory Council, for example, it has been unable to develop a satisfactory, agency-wide data system for "performance monitoring and decision making due to data entry labor [demands] . . . and unclear data definitions and standardization" (NASA Advisory Council 2006, 3). There has also been "creative tension" between PA&E and those responsible for directing NASA's missions. This has been primarily attributable to managers' perceptions that questions about mission execution and outputs are meddling, and to their occasional disagreements with recommendations that emerge from planning and programming.

As a matter of degree, however, PPB has not encountered the same resistance at NASA as it has at DHS (and as it did at NOAA). This may be attributable to several factors. One is simply that it has had the support of the agency's leadership. Although NASA has always been geographically and functionally dispersed, moreover, efforts at centralized management are facilitated by its relatively small size and by the fact that it is not made up of components with distinct organizational cultures and identities. In addition, the introduction of PPB did not represent a precipitous change at NASA but rather the "evolution of a process . . . that had been under way for some time" before 2005 (NASA Advisory Council 2006, 3). The agency's program structure had been in place for several years, for example, and other elements of the planning and programming processes had accumulated since the 1990s. As an individual who helped design PPB noted, "The same work happens at NASA under PPBE as did earlier, but it [the PPB process] is more integrated, consistent, and traceable. To some extent, we just gave new labels to things." In a related vein, the fact that NASA has traditionally relied on a team or matrix approach in accomplishing its missions has made the crosscutting orientation of PPB less of a departure from past practice than in a traditional bureaucracy where functions coincide with discrete organizational units.

Changes in planning and budgeting have introduced more transparency and predictability on the input side of NASA management. As a leading academic authority on the agency noted in an interview: "NASA has always considered itself a program agency. . . . Until fairly recently, however, budgets were not revealing enough to be very useful for the purposes of management and accountability. That is, it was very difficult to tell how much programs actually cost. . . . Although things are not perfect, now it is much easier to discern total program costs than it was ten years ago."

PPB has also led to a stronger expectation within NASA that programs should be justified on the basis of reasoned argument, and it has provided a framework for selected analyses by the Office of PA&E and the Office of Program and Institutional Integration. These analyses, prepared at the direction of NASA's leadership, have helped to inform budget recommendations in several areas. One might speculate that the former PA&E director's previous service in the White House Office of Science and Technology Policy during the Bush administration helped to align these recommendations with political priorities.

Yet PPB has not been used in an attempt to rationalize spending in any systematic way. This is the sense in which a close observer of the agency noted that "NASA has not adopted the systems analysis of a meaningful program budget." Interestingly, in fact, optimizing the use of available resources is only implied at best in agency documents describing and justifying PPB. Attributing the emphasis that other agencies place on this goal to a combination of hubris and insecurity, one PA&E official noted that "there are so many real-world constraints on allocating funds to diverse mission areas that truly 'rationalizing the distribution of funds among organizational components' is not something that can really be done in practice." He added that budgetary decision making at NASA "may not usually rise to the level of satisficing."

Among the obstacles that confront top-down coordination are legal mandates and internal and external political pressures to fund particular projects. In a related vein, planning is inhibited by the "lack of consensus as to what should be the goals of the space program and how they should . . . be accomplished" (Augustine 1990, 1). Even in a world dominated by hierarchical goals, comprehensive rational planning and analysis would be thwarted by limited staff resources and (more fundamentally) by the incomparability of outputs. Assuming that both programs are successful, for example, how does one compare the marginal benefits of spending for the International Space Station versus those for the MAVEN project designed to address scientific questions about the evolution of Mars?

References

Aberbach, Joel D. 2003. "The U.S. Federal Executive in an Era of Change." *Governance: An International Journal of Policy, Administration, and Institutions* 16, no. 3:373–99.

Allison, Graham. 1971. *Essence of Decision.* Boston: Little, Brown.

———. 1980. "Public and Private Management: Are They Fundamentally Alike in All Unimportant Respects?" In *Proceedings for the Public Management Research Conference.* OPM Document 127-53-1. Washington, DC: US Office of Personnel Management.

Appleby, Paul H. 1949. *Policy and Administration.* Tuscaloosa: University of Alabama Press.

Arnold, Perry E. 1980. *Making the Managerial Presidency: Comprehensive Reorganization Planning 1905–1980.* Princeton, NJ: Princeton University Press.

Art, Robert J. 1985. "Congress and the Defense Budget: Enhancing Policy Oversight." *Political Science Quarterly* 100, no. 2:227–48.

Augustine, Norman R. 1990. *Report of the Advisory Committee on the Future of the U.S. Space Program.* www.freemars.org/history/augustine/index.html.

Baker, D. James. 2004. "Ocean Commission." Testimony before the Senate Committee on Commerce, Science, and Transportation, September 21.

Ban, Ray. 2004. "Comments on the NOAA Research Review Team Draft Report by the Weather Coalition."

Baram, Michael S. 1980. "Cost-Benefit Analysis: An Inadequate Basis for Health, Safety, and Environmental Regulatory Decision Making." *Ecology Law Quarterly* 8:473–531.

Barnard, Chester I. 1938. *The Functions of the Executive.* Cambridge, MA: Harvard University Press.

Baumgartner, Frank R., and Bryan D. Jones. 1993. *Agendas and Instability in American Politics.* Chicago: University of Chicago Press.

Behn, Robert D. 2003. "Why Measure Performance? Different Purposes Require Different Measures." *Public Administrative Review* 63 (September–October): 586–606.

BENS (Business Executives for National Security Tail-to-Tooth Commission). 2000. "Special Report on the Department of Defense's Planing, Programming, and Budgeting System." Unpublished.

Bowsher, Charles A. 1983. *The Defense Budget: A Look at Budgetary Resources, Accomplishments, and Problems.* Report GAO/PLRD 83-62 to the Congress of the United States. Washington, DC: US Government Printing Office.

Brownlow, Louis. 1958. *A Passion for Anonymity.* Chicago: University of Chicago Press.

Bureau of the Budget. 1970. *Bulletin,* no. 66-3.

Cleveland, Frederick A. 1913. *Organized Democracy: An Introduction to the Study of American Politics.* New York: Longmans, Green.

Commission on Roles and Missions of the Armed Forces. 1995. *Directions for Defense.* Washington, DC: US Government Printing Office.

Cook, Brian J. 2007. *Democracy and Administration: Woodrow Wilson's Ideas and the Challenges of Public Management*. Baltimore: Johns Hopkins University Press.

Dahl, Robert A. 1947. "The Science of Administration: Three Problems." *Public Administration Review* 7, no. 1:1–11.

Davis, Paul K. 2002. "Analytic Architecture for Capabilities-Based Planning, Mission-System Analysis, and Transformation." Washington, DC: RAND National Defense Institute.

Diver, Colin. 1981. "Policymaking Paradigms in Administrative Law." *Harvard law Review* 95:393–434.

DOT (US Department of Transportation). 2010. *Strategic Plan: New Ideas for a Nation on the Move*. www.dot.gov/stratplan2011.

Downs, Anthony. 1967. *Inside Bureaucracy*. Boston: Little, Brown.

Downs, George W., and Patrick D. Larkey. 1986. *The Search for Government Efficiency*. New York: Random House.

Dror, Yehezkel. 1968. *Public Policymaking Reexamined*. Scranton, PA: Chandler Publishing.

Enthoven, Alain C. 1963. "Memorandum for Mr. Hitch: The Programming-Budgeting Process Reconsidered." November 26.

Enthoven, Alain C., and K. Wayne Smith. 1970. "The Planning, Programming, and Budgeting System in the Department of Defense: An Overview from Experience." In *Public Expenditures and Policy Analysis*, edited by Robert H. Haveman and Julius Margolis. Chicago: Markham.

———. 2005. *How Much Is Enough? Shaping the Defense Program 1961–1969*. Santa Monica, CA: RAND Corporation.

Follett, Mary Parker. 1926. "The Giving of Orders." In *Scientific Foundations of Business Administration*, edited by H. C. Metcalf. New York: Williams & Wilkins.

Ford, Robert C., and W. Alan Randolph. 1992. "Cross-Functional Structures: A Review and Integration of Matrix Organization and Project Management." *Journal of Management* 18 (2): 267–94.

Frederickson, David G., and H. George Frederickson. 2006. *Measuring the Performance of the Hollow State*. Washington, DC: Georgetown University Press.

Freedman, James O. 1978. *Crisis and Legitimacy: The Administrative Process and American Government*. Cambridge: Cambridge University Press.

Freeman, Myric A. 1970. "Project Design and Evaluation with Multiple Objectives." In *Public Expenditures and Policy Analysis*, edited by Robert H. Haveman and Julius Margolis. Chicago: Markham.

GAO (US Government Accountability Office; before 2004, US General Accounting Office). 1993. *Performance Budgeting: State Experiences and Implications for the Federal Government*. Report GAO/AFMD-93-41. Washington, DC: GAO.

———. 1996. *Federal Personnel: Issues on the Need for NOAA's Commissioned Corps*. Report GAO/GGD-97-10. Washington, DC: GAO.

———. 1997a. *Managing for Results: Prospects for Effective Implementation of the Government Performance and Results Act*. Report GAO/T-GGD-97-113. Washington, DC: GAO.

———. 1997b. *Performance Budgeting: Past Initiatives Offer Insights for GPRA Implementation*. Report GAO/AIMD-97-46. Washington, DC: GAO.

———. 2004. *Results-Oriented Government: GPRA Has Established a Solid Foundation for Achieving Greater Results*. Report GAO-04-38. Washington, DC: GAO.

Gaus, John M. 1931. "Notes on Administration." *American Political Science Review* 25, no. 1:123–34.

——. 1947. *Reflections on Public Administration.* Tuscaloosa: University of Alabama Press.

Gilbreth, Frank, and Lillian Gilbreth. 1917. *Applied Motion Study.* New York: Sturgis and Walton.

Gilmour, John B., and David E. Lewis. 2005. "Assessing Performance Budgeting at OMB: The Influence of Politics, Performance, and Program Size." *Journal of Public Administration Research and Theory* 16:169–86.

Goodnow, Frank J. 1900. *Politics and Administration.* New York: Macmillan.

Gordon, Vance C. n.d. Untitled brief on the difficulties confronting capabilities-based planning in the context of PPB. Unpublished.

Gordon, Vance C., David L. McNicol, and Bryan C. Jack. 2008. "Revolution, Counter-Revolution, and Evolution: A Brief History of the PPBS." Unpublished manuscript.

Gulick, Luther. 1937. "Science, Values, and Administration." In *Papers in the Science of Administration,* edited by L. Gulick and L. Urwick. New York: Institute of Public Administration.

Hatry, Harry P. 1999. *Performance Measurement: Getting Results.* Washington, DC: Urban Institute Press.

Haveman, Robert H., and Julius Margolis, eds. 1970. *Public Expenditures and Policy Analysis.* Chicago: Markham.

Heclo, Hugh. 1977. *A Government of Strangers.* Washington, DC: Brookings Institution Press.

——. 1978. "Issue Networks and the Executive Establishment." In *The New American Political System,* edited by Anthony King. Washington, DC: American Enterprise Institute.

Henry, Ryan. 2005-6. "Defense Transformation and the 2005 Quadrennial Defense Review." *Parameters* 35, no. 4.

Herring, Pendleton. 1936. *Public Administration and the Public Interest.* New York: McGraw-Hill.

Hitch, Charles J. 1965. *Decision-Making for Defense.* Berkeley: University of California Press.

——. 1996. "Management Problems of Large Organizations." *Operations Research* 44 (March–April): 257–64. Reprinted from the Phi Beta Kappa lecture delivered by Hitch at Trinity College, Hartford, April 22, 1978.

——. 1968. "The Systems Approach to Decision Making in the Department of Defense and the University of California." *Operations Research* 19:37–45.

Hitch, Charles J., and Ronald N. McKean. 1960. *The Economics of Defense in the Nuclear Age.* Cambridge, MA: Harvard University Press.

Hoffman, Fred S. 1970. "Public Expenditure Analysis and the Institutions of the Executive Branch." In *Public Expenditures and Policy Analysis,* edited by Robert H. Haveman and Julius Margolis. Chicago: Markham.

Hood, Christopher, and Guy Peters. 2004. "The Middle Aging of New Public Management: Into the Age of Paradox." *Journal of Public Administration Research and Theory* 14, no. 3:267–82.

JDCST (Joint Defense Capabilities Study Team). 2004. *Joint Defense Capabilities Study: Final Report.* Washington, DC: US Department of Defense.

Johnson, Cathy Marie. 1990. "New Wine in New Bottles: The Case of the Consumer Product Safety Commission." *Public Administration Review* 50, no. 1:74–81.

Jones, L. R., and Jerry L. McCaffery. 2005. "Reform of the Planning, Programming, Budgeting System and Management Control in the U.S. Department of Defense: Insights from Budget Theory." *Public Budgeting and Finance* 25 (Fall): 1–19.

———. 2008. *Budgeting, Financial Management, and Acquisition Reform in the U.S. Department of Defense*. Charlotte: Information Age Publishing.

Kaboolian, Linda. 1998. "The New Public Management: Challenging the Boundaries of the Management vs. Administration Debate." *Public Administration Review* 58, no. 3:189–93.

Kagan, Elena. 2001. "Presidential Administration." *Harvard Law Review* 114, no. 8:2245–385.

Kaufman, Herbert A. 1956. "Emerging Conflicts in the Doctrines of Public Administration." *American Political Science Review* 50:1057–73.

———. 1976. *Are Government Organizations Immortal?* Washington, DC: Brookings Institution Press.

Kettl, Donald F. 2002. *The Transformation of Governance: Public Administration for Twenty-First Century America*. Baltimore: Johns Hopkins University Press.

Kettl, Donald F., and John J. DiIulio Jr., eds. 1995. *Inside the Reinvention Machine: Appraising Governmental Reform*. Washington, DC: Brookings Institution Press.

Kingdon, John W. 1995. *Issues, Agendas, and Public Policies*. New York: HarperCollins.

Kuhn, Thomas S. 1962. *The Structure of Scientific Revolutions*. Chicago: University of Chicago Press.

Kutz, George D., and Keith A. Rhodes. 2004. "Long-Standing Problems Continue to Impede Financial and Business Transformation." Testimony before the Congressional Subcommittees, Report GAO-04-907T, US General Accounting Office, Washington, DC.

Kutz, George D., and David R. Warren. 2002. "DOD Management: Examples of Inefficient and Ineffective Business Practices." Testimony before the National Security, Veterans Affairs, and International Relations Subcommittees, Committee on Government Reform, House of Representatives, Report GAO-02-873T, US General Accounting Office, Washington, DC.

Landau, Martin. 1969. "Redundancy, Rationality, and the Problem of Duplication and Overlap." *Public Administration Review* 29, no. 4:346–58.

Landis, James. 1938. *The Administrative Process*. New Haven, CT: Yale University Press.

Lautenbacher, Conrad C. 2002. "NOAA Program Review Results: Memorandum for All NOAA Employees." *Access NOAA*. www.accessnoaa.noaa.gov/laut__letter.html.

———. 2005. *NOAA Annual Guidance Memorandum for FY 2008–2012*. Washington, DC: National Oceanic and Atmospheric Administration, US Department of Commerce.

———. 2007. Interview with Greg Allen. *Morning Edition*, National Public Radio, May 23.

Levine, Arthur L. 1992. "The Future of the U.S. Space Program: A Public Administration Critique." *Public Administration Review* 52 (March–April): 183–203.

Light, Paul C. 1997. *The Tides of Reform: Making Government Work*. New Haven, CT: Yale University Press.

Lindblom, Charles E. 1959. "The Science of 'Muddling Through.'" *Public Administration Review* 19 (Spring): 79–88.

———. 1965. *The Intelligence of Democracy: Decision Making through Mutual Adjustment*. New York: Free Press.

Long, Norton E. 1949. "Power and Administration." *Public Administration Review* 9 (Autumn): 257–64.

———. 1952. "Bureaucracy and Constitutionalism." *American Political Science Review* 46 (September): 808–18.

Lowi, Theodore. 1969. *The End of Liberalism*. New York: W. W. Norton.

Lyden, Fremont J., and Ernest G. Miller, eds. 1972. *Planning Programming Budgeting: A Systems Approach to Management*, 2nd. ed. Chicago: Rand McNally College Publishing.

Lynn, Lawrence E., Jr. 2001. "The Myth of the Bureaucratic Paradigm: What Traditional Public Administration Really Stood For." *Public Administration Review* 61, no. 2:144–60.

Margolis, Julius. 1970. "Shadow Prices for Incorrect or Nonexistent Market Values." In *Public Expenditures and Policy Analysis*, edited by Robert H. Haveman and Julius Margolis. Chicago: Markham.

Marvin, Keith E., and Andrew M. Rouse. 1970. "The Status of PPB in Federal Agencies: A Comparative Perspective." In *Public Expenditures and Policy Analysis*, edited by Robert H. Haveman and Julius Margolis. Chicago: Markham.

Maslow, Abraham H. 1943. "A Theory of Human Motivation." *Psychological Review* 50:370–96.

McCubbins, Mathew, Roger Noll, and Barry Weingast. 1987. "Administrative Procedures as Instruments of Political Control." *Journal of Law, Economics, and Organization* 3:243–77.

McGarity, Thomas O. 1991. *Reinventing Rationality: The Role of Regulatory Analysts in the Federal Bureaucracy*. Cambridge: Cambridge University Press.

McGregor, Douglas M. 1957. "The Human Side of Enterprise." *Management Review* 46:22–28.

McNamara, Robert S. 1968. *Essence of Security: Reflections in Office*. New York: Harper Row.

Melkers, Julia, and Katherine Willoughby. 1998. "The State of the States: Performance Budgeting Requirements in 47 out of 50." *Public Administration Review* 58 (January–February): 66–73.

Meltsner, Arnold J. 1976. *Policy Analysts in the Bureaucracy*. Berkeley: University of California Press.

Meyer, John R. 1969. "Transportation in the Program Budget." In *Program Budgeting: Program Analysis and the Federal Budget*, 2nd ed., edited by David Novick. New York: Holt, Reinhart & Winston.

Mintzberg, Henry. 1994. *The Rise and Fall of Strategic Planning: Reconceiving Roles for Planning, Plans, Planners*. New York: Free Press.

Moe, Terry. 1989. "The Politics of Bureaucratic Structure." In *Can the Government Govern*, edited by John Chubb and Paul Peterson. Washington, DC.: Brookings Institution Press.

Moore, Berrien. 2004. *Review of the Organization and Management of Research in NOAA: A Report to the NOAA Science Advisory Board by the Research Review Team*. Silver Spring, MD: National Oceanic and Atmospheric Administration Science Advisory Board, US Department of Commerce.

Mosher, Frederick C. 1968. *Democracy and the Public Service*. New York: Oxford University Press.

Moynihan, Donald P. 2006. "Managing for Results in State Government: Evaluating a Decade of Reform." *Public Administration Review* 66 (January–February): 77–88.

———. 2008. *The Dynamics of Performance Management: Constructing Information and Reform*. Washington, DC: Georgetown University Press.

Moynihan, Donald P., and Alasdair S. Roberts. 2010. "The Triumph of Loyalty over Competence: The Bush Administration and the Exhaustion of the Administrative Presidency." *Public Administration Review* 70, no. 4:572–81.

NASA Advisory Council. 2006. "Meeting Minutes," National Aeronautics and Space Administration, Washington, DC, February 8–9.

National Commission on the Public Service. 2003. *Urgent Business for America: Revitalizing the Federal Government for the 21st Century*. Washington, DC: Brookings Institution Center for Public Service.

Niskanen, William A. 1968. "The Peculiar Economics of Bureaucracy." *American Political Science Review* 58, no. 2:293–305.

NOAA (National Oceanic and Atmospheric Administration, US Department of Commerce). 2002. *Bureau Restructuring Plan Based on Instructions Provided by the Office of Management and Budget, Bulletin 01-07*. Washington, DC: NOAA.

———. 2004. *New Priorities for the 21st Century: NOAA's Strategic Plan*. Washington, DC: NOAA.

———. 2005. "NOAA History." www.history.noaa.gov/noaa.html.

———. 2008. *Business Operations Manual*. Washington, DC: NOAA.

NOS (National Ocean Service). 2009. "About the National Ocean Service." http://oceanservice.noaa.gove/about/.

Novick, David. 1954. *Which Program Do We Mean in "Program Budgeting?"* Santa Monica, CA: RAND Corporation.

———. 1969. "The Department of Defense." In *Program Budgeting: Program Analysis and the Federal Budget*, 2nd ed., edited by David Novick. New York: Holt, Reinhart & Winston.

OAR (Office of Oceanic and Atmospheric Research). 2005. "NOAA Research." www.oar.noaa.gove/climate/climate_arl.htm.

OMB (Office of Management and Budget). 2001. *Workforce Planning and Restructuring*. Bulletin 01-07, Washington, DC: Executive Office of the President.

———. 2008. *Guide to the Program Assessment Rating Tool (PART)*. Guidance 2008-01. Washington, DC: Executive Office of the President.

Osborne, David, and Ted Gaebler. 1992. *Reinventing Government*. Reading, MA: Addison Wesley.

Pietrafesa, Leonard J. 2004. "Cover Letter Accompanying the Review of Organization and Management of Research in NOAA by the Research Review Team." NOAA, Washington, DC.

Pitter, Shanna. 2010. "From PBES to SEE: Strategy Execution Evaluation at NOAA." www.start.nesdis.noaa.gove/star/documents/meetings/GPM2010/dayOne/Pitter.pdf.

President's Advisory Council on Executive Reorganization. 1971. *A New Framework: Report on Selected Independent Regulatory Agencies*. Washington, DC: US Government Printing Office.

President's Committee on Administrative Management. 1937. *Report with Special Studies*. Washington, D.C.: US Government Printing Office. (Commonly referred to as the Brownlow Committee Report.)

Proxmire, William. 1970. "PPB, the Agencies, and the Congress." In *Public Expenditures and Policy Analysis*, edited by Robert H. Haveman and Julius Margolis. Chicago: Markham.

Radin, Beryl A. 2000a. *Beyond Machiavelli: Policy Analysis Comes of Age*. Washington, DC: Georgetown University Press.

———. 2000b. "The Government Performance and Results Act and the Tradition of Management Reform: Square Pegs in Round Holes." *Journal of Public Administration Research and Theory* 10 (1): 111-35.

———. 2002. *The Accountable Juggler*. Washington, DC: Congressional Quarterly Press.

———. 2006. *Challenging the Performance Movement: Accountability, Complexity, and Democratic Values*. Washington, DC: Georgetown University Press.

Rivlin, Alice M. 1970. "The Planning, Programming, and Budgeting System in the Department of Health, Education, and Welfare: Some Lessons from Experience." In *Public Expenditures and Policy Analysis*, edited by Robert H. Haveman and Julius Margolis. Chicago: Markham.

Robb, Charles S. 1996–97. "Rebuilding a Consensus on Defense." *Parameters* 26, no. 4.

Roberts, Nancy. 2000. "The Synoptic Model of Strategic Planning and the GPRA." *Public Productivity and Management Review* 23, no. 3:297–311.

Robinson, Marc, and Jim Brumby. 2005. *Does Performance Budgeting Work? An Analytical Review of the Empirical Literature*. Working Paper WP/05/210. Washington, DC: International Monetary Fund.

Rubin, Irene S. 2003. *Balancing the Federal Budget: Eating the Seed Corn or Trimming the Herds?* New York: Chatham House.

Sabatier, Paul A. 1988. "An Advocacy Coalition Framework of Policy Change and the Role of Policy-Oriented Learning Therein." *Policy Sciences* 21:129–68.

Sayre, Wallace S. 1951. "Trends of a Decade in Administrative Values." *Public Administration Review* 11, no. 1:1–9.

Schattschneider, E. E. 1960. *The Semisovereign People*. New York: Holt, Rinehart & Winston.

Schick, Allen. 1966. "The Road to PPB: The Stages of Budget Reform." *Public Administration Review* 26: 243–58. As cited here, reprinted in *Planning, Programming, Budgeting: A Systems Approach to Management*, 2nd ed., edited by Fremont J. Lyden and Ernest G. Miller. Chicago: Rand McNally College Publishing, 1970.

———. 1973. "A Death in the Bureaucracy: The Demise of Federal PPB." *Public Administration Review* 33:146–56.

Schilling, Thomas C. 1968. "PPBS and Foreign Affairs." *The Public Interest*, Spring, 26–36.

Schlesinger, James R. 1997. "The Office of the Secretary of Defense." In *American Defense Policy, Seventh Edition*, edited by Peter L. Hays, Brenda J. Vallance, and Alan R. Van Tassel. Baltimore: Johns Hopkins University Press.

Seidman, David R. 1970. "PPB in HEW: Some Management Issues." In *Planning, Programming, Budgeting: A Systems Approach to Management*, 2nd ed., edited by Fremont J. Lyden and Ernest G. Miller. Chicago: Rand McNally College Publishing.

Seidman, Harold. 1975. *Politics, Position, and Power*. New York: Oxford University Press.

Seidman, Harold, and Robert Gilmour. 1986. *Politics, Position, and Power*, 4th ed. New York: Oxford University Press.

Shapiro, Martin. 1988. *Who Guards the Guardians?* Athens: University of Georgia Press.

Shelby, Richard. 2009. "Opening Statement of Ranking Member Richard Shelby, Hearing of the Subcommittee on Commerce, Justice, Science, and Related

Agencies Appropriations Subcommittee to Examine the Proposed Department of Commerce Budget for Fiscal Year 2010." US Senate Appropriations Committee, Washington, DC, April 23.

Simon, Herbert A. 1946. "The Proverbs of Administration." *Public Administration Review* 6:53–67.

———. 1947. *Administrative Behavior: A Study of Decision-Making Processes in Administrative Organizations*. New York: Macmillan.

Simon, Mary Ellen. 1983. "Matrix Management at the U.S. Consumer Product Safety Commission." *Public Administration Review* 43, no. 4:357–61.

Showstack, Randy. 2008. "NOAA Budget Increases to $4.1 Billion, But Some Key Items Are Reduced." *EOS* 89, no. 8:74–75.

Smithies, Arthur. 1969. "Conceptual Framework for the Program Budget." In *Program Budgeting: Program Analysis and the Federal Budget*, 2nd ed., edited by David Novick. New York: Holt, Reinhart & Winston.

Stewart, Richard B. 1975. "The Reformation of American Administrative Law." *Harvard Law Review* 88 (June): 1667–1814.

Taylor, Frederick W. 1911. *Principles of Scientific Management*. New York: Harper and Brothers.

Taylor, Maxwell D. 1959. *The Uncertain Trumpet*. New York: Harper and Brothers.

Terry, Larry D. 2005. "The Thinning of Administrative Institutions in the Hollow State." *Administration and Society* 37:426–44.

Truman, David B. 1951. *The Governmental Process*. New York: Alfred A. Knopf.

Tullock, Gordon. 1965. *The Politics of Bureaucracy*. Washington, DC: PublicAffairs.

US Army War College. 1999. *How the Army Runs: A Senior Leader's Handbook*. Carlisle, PA: US Army War College.

US Commission on Marine Science, Engineering, and Resources. 1969. *Our Nation and the Sea: A Plan for Action*. Washington, DC: US Government Printing Office.

US Commission on Ocean Policy. 2004. *An Ocean Blueprint for the 21st Century*. http://oceancommission.gov.

Van Riper, Paul P. 1958. *History of the United States Civil Service*. Evanston, IL: Rowe, Peterson.

———. 1984. "The Politics-Administration Dichotomy: Concept or Reality?" In *Politics and Administration: Woodrow Wilson and American Public Administration*, edited by Jack Rabin and James S. Bowman. New York: Marcel Dekker.

Waldo, Dwight. 1948. *The Administrative State: A Study of the Political Theory of American Public Administration*. New York: Ronald Press.

Walker, David. 2003. Major Management Challenges and Program Risks: Department of Defense. GAO-03-98. DoD Challenges. Washington, DC: US General Accounting Office.

Weber, Max. 1947. *The Theory of Social and Economic Organization*, translated by A. M. Henderson and Talcott Parsons. Glencoe, IL: Free Press.

West, William F. 2005. "The Institutionalization of Regulatory Review: Organizational Stability and Responsive Competence at OIRA." *Presidential Studies Quarterly* 35 (March): 76–93.

West, William F., and Joseph Cooper. 1989. "Legislative Influence v. Presidential Dominance: Competing Models of Bureaucratic Control." *Political Science Quarterly* 104 (Winter): 581–606.

White, Leonard D. 1926. *Introduction to the Study of Public Administration*. New York: Macmillan.

Wildavsky, Aaron. 1969. "Rescuing Policy Analysis from PPBS." *Public Administration Review* 29 (March): 189–202.

———. 1973. "If Planning Is Everything Maybe it's Nothing." *Policy Sciences* 4:127–53.

———. 1974. *The Politics of the Budgetary Process*. Boston: Little, Brown.

———. 1988. *The New Politics of the Budgetary Process*. Glenview, IL: Scott, Foresman.

Williams, Cindy. 2007. *Paying for Homeland Security: Show Me the Money*. Cambridge, MA: MIT Center for Security Studies.

———. 2008. *Strengthening Homeland Security: Reforming Planning and Resource Allocation*. Washington, DC: IBM Center for the Business of Government.

———. 2010. "Getting Inside the Budget Process for Homeland Security." Security Studies Program at MIT 1129707. http://web.mit.edu/ssp/seminars/Williams520Presentation.ppt.

Willoughby, William F. 1919. *An Introduction to the Study of the Government of Modern States*. New York: The Century Co.

Wilson, James Q. 1989. *Bureaucracy*. New York: Basic Books.

———. 1975. "The Rise of the Bureaucratic State." *The Public Interest* 41 (Fall): 77–103.

Wilson, Woodrow. 1887. "The Study of Administration." *Political Science Quarterly* 2 (June): 197–222.

Index